HOW TO INTERVIEW

HOW TO
INTERVIEW

by
Walter Van Dyke Bingham
and
Bruce Victor Moore

FOURTH REVISED EDITION
Prepared with the collaboration of
John W. Gustad

HARPER & BROTHERS, NEW YORK

Contents

To

MILLICENT TODD BINGHAM

ELSIE KOHLER MOORE

RUTH FICKEN GUSTAD

Preface to the Fourth Edition

SINCE the publication of the third edition of *How to Interview* in 1941, many developments have had an impact on the theory and practice of interviewing. A book on interviewing is no longer complete without considering these developments. This revision emphasizes the results of research and other objective findings related to the interview. Thus, it rests on what has been learned by the study of recorded interviews, what was gained from personnel assessment studies for the armed forces and industry, and from results of research in the rapidly expanding specialties of counseling and clinical psychology. New developments in self-concept, personality, and information theory have not been neglected. Psychodynamic and psychoanalytic conceptions have been taken into account as widely accepted approaches to understanding the behavior of persons alone and in interaction. The very different contribution to interviewing by Carl Rogers is also included as a development since the previous edition. It should be stressed that Dr. Bingham might not have agreed with our evaluation of some of these recent approaches which have assumed added importance since his death in 1952.

The developments in several aspects of interviewing have been so rapid and great that they have become specialties in themselves. Each in itself deserves one or more volumes. Market research and public opinion polling, counseling and clinical psychology, as well as certain industrial applications are good examples. We have dealt with each of these in this edition, but no claim is made for comprehensive treatment. In order to avoid enlarging this volume unduly, only a relatively small number of selected references are included at the end of each chapter.

In revising *How to Interview* we have attempted to preserve what we believe is its most useful and distinctive characteristic: a critical

vii

but elementary presentation of the major known facts about interviewing. It is intended not for the expert in psychology, social work, psychiatry, or personnel work, but for the beginner, the person who wishes to acquire some substantial picture of the variety of applications of the interview.

We have received invaluable assistance from a number of individuals in the preparation of this edition. Among these we would like to mention Drs. Lester Guest, Joseph Matarazzo, Harold B. Pepinsky and Victor C. Raimy who kindly consented to read selected chapters and give us the benefit of their criticism. They were most helpful, and their efforts are deeply appreciated. We are also grateful to Mrs. Walter V. Bingham who has read the manuscript in its entirety and brought to bear on it her literary experience and editorial skill.

In addition, we are indebted to the many workers whose publications have served as the basis for this revision.

BRUCE V. MOORE
JOHN W. GUSTAD

Washington, D.C.
July 8, 1958

Part I

General Principles of the Interview

1. First Principles

AN INTERVIEW is a conversation directed to a definite purpose other than satisfaction in the conversation itself. This will serve as a working definition, but the word "conversation" is used in a broad sense. There is give-and-take between the interviewer and interviewee, and much of the interaction between these two is carried on by gestures, postures, facial expressions, and other communicative behavior. Even the words acquire varieties of meanings and values as they are spoken with different inflections or in different contexts. All of these means of communication—the spoken words, the gestures, the expressions, the inflections—contribute to the *purposeful exchange of meanings*, which is the interview.

The interview, the conversation with a purpose, is relied upon in a variety of situations. Almost everyone makes use of it at some time, but few are really proficient in its use. Some whose profession demands expertness in interviewing—social workers, psychiatrists, psychologists, employment managers, salesmen, market analysts, and opinion pollers, to name a few—have developed, consciously or unconsciously, considerable skill in applying a variety of techniques designed to help them do their jobs effectively. The legal profession has long been concerned with methods of interrogating witnesses. Anthropologists have studied the problems involved in using the interview to collect their data about cultures and have listed numerous precautions to be observed. Knowledge of the procedures developed and the problems encountered by these experts is a help to less experienced interviewers and especially to novices who will ordinarily not be aware of the pitfalls which experienced interviewers have learned to avoid.

Many questions about interviewing are continually asked by newcomers to the field as well as by those who have been in it for some

3

time. What are the pitfalls of interviewing? Can they be adequately described? Under what conditions is it safe to rely on information secured by the interview? How can the reliability of such information be measured? How can this reliability be increased? Are there either general rules or specific guides which can be used to improve the interview? How can such an enormously complex and subtle process as the interview really be studied?

Interviewer Bias

The variables affecting the interview, its conduct and outcomes, are many and complicated. One of the most troublesome is the tendency for supposedly factual statements to be substantially affected by the personality characteristics, the attitudes of the participants. This is most noticeable in those interviews which are conducted for the purpose of discovering facts about the person being interviewed. These tendencies must be faced, studied, and understood if interview practice is to be improved.

The problem and its complexity may be illustrated by several investigations. One of the classical research studies in the field was reported by Rice (46)* under the title "Contagious Bias in the Interview." In 1914, the New York commissioner of public charities ordered a study of the physical, mental, and social characteristics of 2,000 destitute men, consecutive applicants for a night's rest at the Municipal Lodging House. Twelve men, trained in social work, did the interviewing. The applicants were assigned to the interviewers in random order so that each interviewer dealt with an unselected sample of the total group. Each interview took from twenty to thirty minutes and was guided by a four-page folder of questions having to do with the economic and social history of the man being interviewed. Upon reviewing the results obtained, it was noted that certain kinds of answers to the questions tended to show up frequently in the case of men interviewed by certain of the investigators.

One of the questions, for example, required each man to give an explanation of his destitution; it also provided that each interviewer should give *his* explanation of the man's destitution. One of the interviewers happened to be an ardent prohibitionist. He reported that the destitution of 62 per cent of the applicants was due chiefly to liquor; only 7 per cent of the cases were attributed to economic conditions.

* Numbers in the parentheses refer to items in the references at the end of the chapter.

Another interviewer, a Socialist, reported that, while only 22 per cent of the cases were due chiefly to liquor, 39 per cent could be attributed to such economic conditions as hard times, layoffs and other industrial conditions. These were the interviewers' judgments. The explanations given by the destitute men themselves were even more intriguing. The prohibitionist reported that 34 per cent of the applicants reported liquor as the cause of their difficulties while 42.5 per cent cited industrial conditions. The Socialist, on the other hand, said that only 11 per cent of the men blamed liquor while 60 per cent laid their troubles to industrial conditions. Each of these interviewers was well trained, conscientious, and probably was unaware of how his own attitudes were biasing the results of his work. The point of interest is that, by ways which are still not well understood and are subtle but nevertheless effective, each interviewer had conveyed his own bias to the man being interviewed. Thus, not only were the judgments of the interviewers colored by their own attitudes, but the actual statements of the men being interviewed reflected these same predispositions or biases.

More recent work has served both to cast doubt on the Rice study and to suggest other explanations for the effects noted. Speaking of the interpretation of Rice's study, Hyman (30) says:

The findings reported are perfectly compatible with the notion that the interviewer simply distorted the recording of given answers in accordance with his own prejudice, or that he interpreted ambiguous answers in autistic ways. (p. 35)

In other words, the explanation provided by Rice, that the interviewer's bias was "contagious" and transmitted to the person being interviewed, is only one of at least two possible interpretations. Wyatt and Campbell (63), repeating Rice's earlier study, found no consistent or statistically significant bias. Their interviewers were students, and it is possible that the experiment lacked sufficient realism to motivate either the interviewers or the respondents.

Back, Hill, and Stycos (4), on the other hand, using Guttman (28) scales, found that interviewers produced significant effects on scales dealing with communications with the spouse, communications with friends, and with feelings about modesty. Interestingly, they found *no* effects on the scale dealing with prohibition.

Two other studies are relevant here. Stanton and Baker (52) conducted a study in 1942 which purported to demonstrate interviewer bias. Two hundred students were shown some meaningless geometric figures. Later on, five professionally trained interviewers asked each student to select these figures from other figures. The other, or wrong, figures were simply mirror images of the correct, previously seen, ones. The interviewers were given code sheets which supposedly gave the correct answers. Actually these code sheets were so arranged that half of the answers were right and half of them were wrong. The experimenters found that when the key gave as the correct answer the one really shown in class, the frequency of correct responses from those interviewed was significantly higher than when the reverse was true. Stanton and Baker concluded that this demonstrated the presence of a biasing effect of the interviewer.

The Stanton and Baker study has been repeated twice, once by Friedman (21) and once by Lindzey (35). Neither one supported the conclusions of the earlier study. Lindzey in particular took great care to duplicate the conditions of the Stanton and Baker study as exactly as possible but still failed to get the same results.

From the foregoing discussion of the question of bias, it may be seen that simple generalizations about the interview process cannot be made. The issues are complex, research is lacking on many important points, and it is contradictory on others. Bias, contagious or not, is but one of the central problems of the interview.

Discrepancies due to a personal bias of the interviewer, a bias of which he may be unaware or at least unaware of the ways it affects his interviewing, can be matched by inaccuracies due to the unwillingness, prejudice, ignorance, or inarticulateness of the interviewee. Another source of error lies in the interviewee's misunderstanding of the interviewer's questions. This problem has been extensively studied by workers dealing with public opinion polling and market research; it will be discussed in detail in a later chapter.

A good example of this problem, however, showed itself in a setting of industrial conflict. Interviewing some textile workers who were on strike, one of the writers found that the word "arbitration" had come to mean in the workers' vocabulary the same as "surrender." By some of these strikers, the question, "Are you in favor of arbitration?" was interpreted as, "Are you in favor of giving in completely to the employers?" This is what the term signified to them before its meaning, as the interviewer intended it, had been made clear.

Uses of the Interview

Experiences such as these are likely to arouse a lively suspicion, even an unfavorable opinion, of the results obtained through the interview. They encourage some to question the dependability of public opinion surveys, census findings, or research in any of the social sciences which uses data obtained by means of so allegedly undependable an instrument as the interview. Equally questionable is the reliability of medical (including psychiatric) diagnosis, legal findings, journalistic statements, and judgments about employees made by personnel managers and vocational counselors when interview data are ordinarily at the bottom of these conclusions. This poses a difficult dilemma. In studying human beings and their relationships, many of the necessary data can be obtained only through the use of the interview, a technique whose reliability is often open to serious question. Since knowledge of human relationships is so badly needed and since we cannot abandon attempts to obtain it, we appear to have little choice other than to try by every means at our disposal to improve the interview as a data-gathering technique.

We ask, in a preliminary way, for what uses the interview is feasible; to define our own position with respect to the point of view which an interviewer should take toward his task; and to indicate certain perils, certain pitfalls, of which he should be forewarned.

The interview may have any one or all of three main functions. It may be used in securing information from people, in giving information to them, and in influencing their behavior in certain ways. Included in this last, although differing somewhat in intent and strategy, is psychotherapeutic interviewing.

The kinds of information sought in the interview cover not only observable, objective facts as to conditions or events but also subjective facts such as opinions, interpretations, and attitudes of the person being interviewed. A congressman may be interviewed about the way he voted on, for example, a child labor bill. The way he voted is sometimes recorded in the *Congressional Record*; if it is not so recorded, there are ordinarily others who observed his behavior and can report it. In either of these cases, his behavior is objective and can be ascertained by means other than interviewing the congressman. The facts of his early life as a breaker boy in a coal mine, although equally objective, may not be matters of record or readily obtainable from sources other than the man himself. His *opinion* as to whether the

business sentiment of the country favors or is opposed to the legis-
lation and his own *attitude* toward the desirability of it are *subjective
facts*. To learn objective facts of common knowledge recourse is often
had to the interview, but its more appropriate uses are to ascertain
facts, whether of personal history, opinion, or attitude, which only
the individual himself can supply. Even where the facts are readily
available from other sources, perhaps more accurately than they could
be determined from an interview, it is frequently important to find out
how the individual *feels* about the facts, how they seem to affect his
opinions, attitudes, and behavior.

The interview is often the only means available to obtain these subjective facts of attitude, preference, and opinion as well as objective
facts known only to the individual being interviewed. Its use in gathering information known to many reliable observers and available in
public documents, records, or other dependable sources is ordinarily
wasteful and subject to serious error. A court of law, for example,
gives little credence to the sworn testimony of witnesses affirming the
authenticity of a signature if the watermark of the paper on which the
signature appears shows that the paper was manufactured a year subsequent to the death of the person who allegedly signed the paper. It is
when such strictly objective facts are unobtainable that courts, physicians, social scientists, and industrial executives need to turn to admittedly less reliable sources of information such as the oral interview.
It should be noted, however, that many court cases hinge not upon
purely objective facts but upon opinions of people involved. For such
purposes, the interview, so conducted that error and distortion are at
a minimum, is practically the only choice.

It must be recognized at the same time that the interview may
serve a useful function in finding, securing access to, and verifying
dependable sources of objective data. Other similar uses of the interview are in winning co-operation and establishing sound working relations with those in the situation under study and in getting advice and
opinions helpful in defining the problem, formulating hypotheses, and
planning methods of attack. Here, the interview is a useful although
somewhat incidental tool, not the main instrument of research. When,
however, the interviewee is a source of essential information or when
he becomes himself the principal object of study, the interview
acquires major significance. The interviewer must then be concerned
with making his interviewing as reliable as possible for securing dependable, valid data.

Sources of unreliability inhere in the interviewer, in the person interviewed, and in the relationship between the two. Paradoxically, it is precisely these same elements which make the interview a valuable instrument. The difference lies in the conduct of the interview and the quality of the relationship. These will be discussed in detail in the following chapter.

Processes of Communication

The interview is basically a communication system. Recent developments in communication theory (42) (15) and in psychology (47) (37) provide analytic models which help to make the basic processes clearer than they have been heretofore.

There are several aspects of the communication system to which we must pay attention.

1. There are *situations, problems, states of feeling,* or *desires* to be discussed. These are the subjects of the interview. The interviewee may have a problem which is troubling him; he wishes to discuss it. The interviewer, at the same time, wishes to convey his willingness to help, his interest, his intention to keep matters confidential, his refusal to be critical of the interviewee. Later, he will wish to convey his understanding of the interviewee's problem.

2. There are, next, *encoding devices.* In sending a telegram, it is necessary to translate the message from words to Morse code, a system of electrical impulses. In an interview, a message about the situation or feeling must also be translated, this time into words which describe the situation. Thus, an interviewee in a depressive state must describe it, must be able to say, "I am terribly unhappy." An interviewer, feeling a desire to be of assistance, must put this feeling into words such as, "I am here to help you."

3. Next, there is the *transmission system.* The telephone, telegraph, and radio are examples of means for sending messages from one point to another. In the interview, there are two such systems: spoken words and gestures. Much less attention has been paid to the latter than to the former although there is little doubt about the power of gestures in conveying meaning and feelings. The spoken word, however, is by all odds the commonest transmission device.

4. There is also the *decoding device.* The same message will not mean the same thing to two different people. Each interprets what he hears in terms of his own unique history. Even such a simple statement as "It is hot today" may be interpreted in one way by an Eskimo, in another by a native of the tropics. People attach different values to

words as signals. This is one of the reasons why scientists often resort to the use of mathematics and other symbolic systems in communicating with one another. Fundamentally, a decoding device is used to analyze a message for its meaning. In conversations between people, such as in the interview, decoding is perhaps the critical point, the place where most troubles occur. The reader will recall the case cited earlier where a group of striking workers were asked whether they wished to arbitrate. They interpreted—decoded—this as an invitation to surrender and therefore refused.

These four elements, the message, the encoding device, the transmission channel, and the decoding device all have obvious counterparts in the interview situation. Problems can arise at any or all of several points. For example, the individual may be unable to see clearly the situation which troubles him. This often occurs, and clients frequently describe problems which are quite removed from the "real" one. An interviewer, uncertain about his professional role, may be unable to see precisely what he should be doing in the interview.

Or, there may be difficulties in the encoding. Most adults have vocabularies amounting to several thousand words, but most of us are occasionally, or often, at a loss for the correct word to describe what we see or feel. For example, few men have as many words at their disposal as do women to describe shades of colors. A man might describe several objects as "red" where a woman might apply such words as "burgundy," "rose," "magenta," or "scarlet." Similar situations are often encountered in the interview where a client, anxious and tense, may be unable to say anything more definitive or helpful than, "I just don't feel very well." In part, the interviewer must help the client to find and apply words which actually describe the situation.

This difficulty is not limited to the interviewee. Many interviewers find it difficult to encode their messages, to select the words which convey what they want to. The overworked "Uh-huh" is probably, in many cases, a noncommittal substitute for the interviewer unable to select words to convey his understanding of a statement. It must be emphasized that the encoding applies not only to the intellectual content of what is to be said, but also to the feeling tones which are to be conveyed. The old saying, "When you say that, smile" is an example of this.

The transmission system is also a source of problems. We mentioned above that, in the interview, both words and gestures are transmission devices. Little has been done to study gestures and their meaning. One recent work (44) has been devoted to the language of signs and gestures, but this is only a small start. Most attention has been paid to words. It is well known that the same words, spoken in different tones of voice, can carry quite different messages. Communication engineers often refer to "noise" in a system as something which distorts the signal. Static on a radio is an example. A noisy interview room may have such interference, making voices hard to hear. Or, the interviewer may have a very soft voice; he may pronounce or enunciate his words badly. There are many things which can disrupt the transmission system.

The decoding system is perhaps the single most likely place for trouble in the communication system. We mentioned some of these problems earlier. An analogy is the situation where a message is encoded by means of one code system and decoded by means of another. Either the message comes out garbled and meaningless or at best not meaning what was intended. Errors in decoding can often be very informative if detected, but, for most kinds of interviews, every attempt should be made to encode messages so simply and clearly that the possibility of such errors is kept to a minimum.

The communication system model can be used to develop many more illustrations of difficulties in the interview. The examples just described will suffice for our present purposes. The major point is that the interview, involving as it does two persons who must communicate their feelings and ideas to one another, is enormously complicated, subject to difficulties at several points. If interviewing is to be improved, it is essential that attention be paid to all similar points at which trouble occurs.

Attitudes Toward Interviewing

Before passing on to consider sources of unreliability in the interview, something must be said about the attitude which the interviewer takes, particularly toward the person being interviewed. There are those who hold that the interviewer must be shrewd, politic, able and willing to outguess the person being interviewed and to extract from him the information desired through the use of clever tactics. There are others who insist that such an attitude creates more difficulties than it overcomes, that the only sound basis for interviewing, whether for fact finding or for helping, is an attitude of forthright honesty and frankness.

Whereas the clever detective attitude may sometimes produce results, contrast it with the straightforward approach which attempts to establish a sound, co-operative relationship with the interviewee as a person who is as interested in providing the facts as the interviewer is in obtaining them. Here, the interviewer not only tells the other person what he wants to know and why he wants to know it; in doing so, he also tries to arouse in the interviewee a high degree of motivation to co-operate actively. This process tends to minimize errors due to misunderstanding or defensiveness. The clever or "tricky" approach is often difficult to conceal; when the interviewee detects it, his defenses may be aroused. Getting the facts is difficult enough without introducing any unnecessary handicaps to mutual understanding.

As we shall see in the next chapter, the personality characteristics of the participants in the interview are central to our understanding of the process itself. Several alternative theories of personality are available, but the one which has been most widely accepted was first developed by Freud and modified by later theorists. Of special interest to us are the so-called "dynamics" of personality. These include repression, sublimation, projection, identification, rationalization, and suppression. Several excellent discussions of these dynamics are available (5) (8) (38) (55). Repression, suppression, and rationalization are directly relevant to the present discussion.

Suppression refers to the "burying" of facts, ideas, and memories. Obviously, if an interviewee does this, it is necessary to break through this defense, to get him to discuss the suppressed material. It might be accomplished by the clever, detecting process, but there is the real danger that this will in turn create anxiety, a desire to suppress other and perhaps more important facts. The other major possibility is to create in the interviewee the motivation to discuss these things, willingly and in his own way.

Rationalization is the process of excusing one's behavior, of finding socially acceptable reasons for having done certain things. Essentially unrealistic and defensive, it is resorted to in order to protect self esteem and social position. Everyone is acquainted with individuals who, according to their own lights, are never wrong and always have a good reason for doing whatever they have done or may wish to do.

Since no one is perfect, it must be assumed that these people are not being frank or realistic about themselves. Simply to argue with such a person does no good; he creates new and more elaborate rationalizations as quickly as the old ones are stripped away. He usually becomes angry and may counterattack the questioner. Obviously, this does not create a good interview relationship.

Repression is the most troublesome of the mechanisms. The reason is that the individual himself is literally unaware of the "answers" to certain questions. It is not quite the same as forgetting, because, when one forgets something, he can be reminded of it; whereas, in the case of repression, he is motivated to keep certain facts, ideas, and feelings hidden, not only from the interviewer *but from himself*. The repressed material is buried in the unconscious. Direct probing or clever subterfuges more often than not merely increase the motivation to keep the repressed material hidden. Psychotherapists deal with repression routinely; less attention has been paid to it in the fact-finding interview.

The difference between these two different attitudes toward the interview and the interviewee—the subtle and the frank, the strategic and the co-operative—is analogous to the difference between the old conception of salesmanship and the new one. Strong (53) has well described these differences. Traditional salesmanship started with the salesman, interested in selling his goods and thus making a good living. Sales strategy was concerned largely with manipulating the potential buyer. It has come to be recognized, however, that the buyer is not basically interested in the problems of the seller, his wants and needs. The buyer becomes interested only in the sense that he sees in the situation something of value to him. The newer salesmanship, then, starts with the buyer's wants and tries to discover how the product may be related to these. Honest service to a buyer, so that his needs are satisfied, means that his wants, not the seller's, are paramount in the sales campaign. Obviously, the seller's wants are satisfied if there is a sale, but the strategy is centered about the customer. Translated to the interview situation, this new conception points toward centering attention on the interviewee, on his needs and defenses, rather than on the interviewer whose purposes will best be served if the full co-operation of the interviewee is secured. To put it another way, the problem of the interview is the utilization of motivation which already exists.

This change is illustrated by the experience of an investigator co-operating with the senior authors in one of their studies. This investigator was an Englishwoman who was gathering information from American workers in the metal trades with respect to their extra-trade training and experience. She first tried direct questioning. After about two months of using this method with poor results, she adopted the indirect method of casual conversation, inducing a man to talk about himself and so picking up what information she could regarding his occupational history. This free conversational method, though it led to better results, was expensive in time and subject to error. For instance, at the close of one such informal conversation, the worker said, "I worked three years in the cotton mills, but of course you're not interested in that." This was precisely what she wanted to know! After still more experience, she again found herself using direct questioning but with better success. The essential difference was that she had learned how to approach the worker from the point of view of his own interests, telling him frankly that she was studying the training of workers in the field of the metal trades, and the value, if any, of experience in other lines of work; that she wanted to know what he had worked at and how he had reached his present position in order that boys coming in on their apprenticeships might have the benefit of his experience. After tying in the problem of her investigation with his interests in this way, she could go directly to the point and get the desired facts systematically and promptly.

In most situations, as for example in industrial disputes, people speak freely and frankly when they feel that they will not be misunderstood and that no unfair advantage will be taken of what they have said. The principle, as it applies to the interview, is that the interviewee is as frank as he can be (within the limits imposed by the defense mechanisms discussed earlier) when he feels that his point of view is appreciated and respected, that the interviewer has some right to the information, and that the questions are relevant and not impertinent.

For a long time, there was considerable discussion about technique in interviewing, particularly in psychotherapeutic and counseling work. It was felt that there were right and wrong strategies, right and wrong ways to meet certain kinds of situations, that there were, in short, formulas for the interview. Recent work, particularly that of Fiedler (19), has shown that this is not necessarily so. As we shall see in the following chapter, *experienced* interviewers, whatever their theoretical position, tend to describe the interview relationship in essentially similar ways. They are more like each other in this respect than they are like novices of their own "schools."

Rogers (48) has, perhaps more than anyone else, worked to dispel the notion that technique and strategy were the major concerns of the interviewer. His thesis is that the relationship is all important, that, unless the interviewer really accepts and respects the interviewee, little can be accomplished.

An example will illustrate how one interviewer may use a technique successfully while another fails with the same technique because of an essential difference in the method. Two young women were engaged on a government investigation of the effect of industrial employment of mothers on the welfare of their children. Although they were interviewing in the same community and for exactly the same purpose, one of them decided after trying it that she had better not show her schedule of questions or her record blank to the interviewee, while the other always showed the schedule and even allowed the interviewee to look over her shoulder as she recorded the answers. The essential difference, however, was not technique but something more basic. The first interviewer did not win the cooperation of her interviewees but depended on subtlety in drawing out the facts she wanted. The other interviewer approached her interviewees by feeling her way into the attitudes they presented and convincing them of the value of the investigation. After that, it did not matter much whether the questionnaire was shown or not.

Many other such differences in technique are unimportant, their effect on the interview being more apparent than real. One of the writers, along with one of his doctoral students (27), studied the effects of a variety of methods of handling tests in vocational counseling. Methods of introducing tests into counseling and of interpreting them were examined. The net result showed that these differences in technique contributed nothing to the outcomes of counseling; but a subsequent investigation (59) showed that the relationship between the participants was important.

This is not to say that there are not several techniques and that they should not be applied when appropriate. It is to say, however, that skill in the use of various techniques is no substitute for a proper attitude toward the interview and especially toward the person being interviewed.

The techniques employed in interviewing must be adapted as much as possible to the problem at hand; but there are limits to this adaptability. Several writers (11) (22) (50) have reported that the behavior of the interviewer tends, from one interviewee to another, to be relatively consistent. That is, even highly skilled interviewers who are presumably aware of a variety of techniques follow generally consistent patterns of behavior. Within this consistency, which probably is a reflection of the personality structure of the interviewer, there is still considerable room for shifting methods to conform to the needs of the interviewee and the situation; encouraging the interviewee to talk; working to establish a sound relationship of frankness and confidence; linking the topic of inquiry to the interests of the person being interviewed; focusing his attention on the issues in question; making certain that he understands what is wanted and that the interviewer in turn understands what is said; bringing the interview back to the point if it wanders too far away; changing the interviewee's natural self-concern from a liability to an asset; minimizing tendencies to exaggeration, loose statement, or deliberate deceit; checking on statements of fact; verifying indications of preference or attitude; accomplishing, in short, the long- and short-term goals of the interview.

Wording of Questions

The wording of questions may profoundly affect the answers given. Elmo Roper, preparing to make a poll for *Fortune* magazine on attitudes toward governmental attempts to keep peace, pretested the following question: "Should the United States do all in its power to promote world peace?" Ninety-seven per cent of the answers were in the affirmative. With a similar sample of respondents, the question, "Should the United States become involved in plans to promote world peace?" was responded to in the affirmative by only 60 per cent of those questioned.

One of the classic studies in the field of the interview is the one by Professor Muscio (39), a British psychologist. This study was designed to measure the fullness, assurance, and accuracy of statements made in reply to questions worded in different ways. To 21 women and 35 men, he showed five motion-picture films, each of which consisted of 450 photographs. The time required for each film was 25 to 28 seconds. Each person was repeatedly shown each film until he had a certain grasp of it as judged from his narrative description of it. Then, each subject was asked approximately 100 questions. Not all questions were asked of each subject, for some anticipated certain questions in their narrations. The questions were of eight types as shown in Table 1. *Caution* was measured by the number of times the subject said, "I don't know." *Suggestiveness* was measured by the number of times the lead contained in the question was followed. *Reliability* was assessed by the percentage of correct answers. Muscio concluded that the unsafest or poorest question form was the implicative as illustrated in the question, "Was the hair of B very dark?" The

TABLE 1

INFLUENCE OF THE FORM OF A QUESTION

Type	Example	Rank orders for		
		Cau-tion	Sugges-tiveness	Relia-bility
Subjective Direction				
A. Indefinite article	Did you see a......?	2	2	1
B. Definite article	Did you see the....?	4	5	4
C. Negative and indefinite article	Didn't you see a....?	3	1	6
D. Negative and definite article	Didn't you see the..?	1	3	3
Objective Direction				
W. Indefinite article	Was there a ....?	5	7	2
X. Negative and indefinite article	Wasn't there a ....?	6	6	5
Y. Incomplete disjunction	Was the K, m or n..?	7	4	8
Z. Implicative	Was the K, m......?	8	8	7

most reliable was the subject-direction form which uses neither negative nor definite article as in the question, "Did you see an umbrella?" Muscio points out, however, that when the subject denies seeing an umbrella, he is not necessarily denying that there *was* an umbrella. Conversely, a commonly noted unwillingness to deny that it was present does not imply its presence. Other of his conclusions were:

Changing the indefinite into the definite article in a question form decreases suggestiveness, caution, and reliability.

Introducing a negative into a question form increases suggestiveness, decreases caution and reliability.

Changing a subjective-direction into an objective-direction form decreases suggestiveness, caution, and reliability.

The incomplete disjunction form of question, Y, possesses a relatively high degree of suggestiveness, relatively low caution and reliability.

The interviewer interested in improving the accuracy of the results he obtains will study Muscio's results carefully. Similar findings have been reported elsewhere, particularly in connection with public opinion polling (30).

Estimates of Personality

In order to adjust the interview technique to the needs of the individual being interviewed, it is essential that estimates about his personality be made continuously. These judgments may involve intelligence and abilities as well as many other aspects of personality. The interviewer must, if he is to operate effectively, make judgments about the quality of the relationship, how the interviewee feels about certain topics, how he reacts to a variety of questions, and whether he is being frank or defensive. The interviewee ordinarily makes his own judgments at the same time, for the interview is a give-and-take process in which the interviewee also learns a good deal about the interviewer.

More and more tests are being developed which provide reliable and valid measures of a variety of personality traits. Particularly in the counseling interview, these are used extensively and to advantage. There are many situations in which it is either undesirable or impossible to obtain test scores. In these cases, the interviewer has no choice but to rely on his own judgments based on what he observes in the interview.

There is still controversy about the reliability of such judgments. Some are inclined to feel that these "clinical" estimates possess a special, superior kind of validity, are better than any test score or combination of scores. Others insist that the interviewer is a seriously fallible measuring instrument, that his limited observations and his own human weaknesses combine to make sound and complete judgments difficult if not impossible. There recently appeared an excellent discussion of this controversy, a book by Meehl (36) entitled *Clinical versus Statistical Prediction*. Having surveyed the literature for studies comparing predictions made on the basis of statistical formulae and predictions made by experienced clinicians, Meehl concludes that the former, the statistical predictions, are generally superior as indicated by the findings in the vast majority of studies reported. Summing up the problem with respect to the so-called clinical judgments Meehl says:

> Is any clinician infallible? No one claims to be. Hence, sometimes he is wrong. If he is sometimes wrong, why should we pay any attention to him? There is only one possible reply to this "silly" question. It is simply that he *tends* (read: "is likely") to be right. "Tending" to be right means just one thing—"being right in the long run." Can we take the clinician's word for this? Certainly not. As psychologists, we do not trust our memories, and we have no recourse except to record our predictions at the time, allow them to accumulate, and ultimately tally them up. We do not do this because we have a scientific obsession, but simply because we know that there is a difference between veridical knowledge and purported knowledge, between knowledge which brings its credentials with it and that which does not. After we tally our predictions, the question of success (hits) must be decided upon. If we remember that we are psychologists, this must be done, either by some objective criterion, or by some disinterested judge who is not aware of the predictions. . . . We have carried out a validation study of the traditional kind! I am led by this reasoning to the conclusion, in complete agreement with Sarbin, that the introduction of some special "clinical utility" as a surrogate for validation is inadmissible. If the clinical utility is really established and not merely proclaimed, it will have been established by procedures which have all the earmarks of an acceptable validation study. If not, it is a weasel phrase and we ought not to get by with it. [*pp. 137-138*]

As we indicated above, however, there are many situations in which test scores are unavailable, where the interviewer's judgment must be the sole basis for obtaining estimates of personality characteristics. It is therefore important that the problems inherent in such judgments be considered.

Asch (3) and Gollin (23) have described how forming an impression of a personality is an organized process, and to know a person is to have a grasp of a particular structure. From his experimental study Gollin found confirmation that the formation of an impression of the personality of another is a function not only of the characteristics of the person being observed but "also to a considerable extent a function of the underlying perceptual-cognitive organizing process in the observer." Similar studies completed later by Gollin and Rosenberg (24) also lend support to the hypothesis of generality of cognitive type. A relationship is apparent between organizing tendencies in impression formation and the individual's tendencies in concept formation.

Several studies have been made of the contribution of an interview to personality assessment, particularly its value in supplementing more objective measures. A study, under the direction of E. L. Kelly, was made of the use of tests, interviews, and other methods in the selection of candidates and the prediction of their success in clinical psychology. The interviews apparently added little to the predictions. Tupes (60) studied the contribution which an unstructured appraisal interview added to the validity of personality-trait ratings based on an interview plus psychological tests and found that the interview added very little. Longer probing interviews with the objective of uncovering personality dynamics contributed little, if any, more to the validity of personality trait ratings than do shorter interviews in which the objective was to elicit information.

There are some studies which indicate that interviews properly structured and skillfully used may have significant validity for the selection of personnel. An evaluation of a "guided" interview for selection of doctoral candidates was made by the Center for Research and the faculty of the School of Education of New York University in 1950, and reported by Anderson (2). Scales were prepared for rating ten desirable qualities, and twelve types of questions were developed. Two hours of training was given in the use of the questions and scales and in presenting sample recorded interviews. A group of 278 applicants for doctoral candidacy were interviewed and rated in thirty-minute periods, once by one interviewer. Faculty members made ratings on the basis of the recordings of the interviews; and these ratings correlated with the face-to-face interviewer ratings, r .85. Reratings by the original interviewer on the basis of his recordings some weeks later gave a reliability of .9. Correlations of ratings by interviewers with ratings by two faculty members who knew the candidates well gave a correlation of .51, which was much better than tests or grades correlated with faculty ratings.

Symonds and Dietrich (57) investigated the effect of variations in the time interval between an interview and its written recording. Three interviews were recorded by three groups of four persons, each at different intervals after the interview—immediately, after two days, and after seven days. An interview recorded immediately contained the maximum of details such as dates and places, and was more complete in general. The significant parts of the interview, however, were not quickly forgotten. The more meaningful the material is, the more likely that it will be remembered and reported later. "One may surmise that there may be a process of integration and consolidation with the less significant material being forgotten. For insight and interpretation there may be gain from later recording."

Recorded Interviews

More penetrating analysis of interviews was made possible by the improvement of techniques for recording sound. Recorded interviews and counseling processes were studied at Ohio State University by Carl Rogers and Francis Robinson and their graduate students. Covner (13) in 1942 described early experiments in the use of phonographic recording equipment, and reported the negligible effect of its use on interviewers and interviewees. He also compared written reports with electric recordings. Although most material found in the written reports was accurate, 75-95 per cent, much of the actual interview material, over 70 per cent, was omitted. Often the sequence of items was changed, giving a false implication that one statement or idea led to another. Covner concluded that written notes will continue to be needed for many interviews, particularly for employment and for fact finding of employee attitude; but for counseling, especially in the training and supervision of counselors, the electrically recorded interviews are essential for improving techniques.

Rogers (49) has described more specifically how electrically recorded interviews may be used for improving psychotherapeutic and counseling techniques. Analytical discussions of recorded interviews reveal to most counselors that they are more directive than they realized. Recordings almost always give the clues to such phenomena as resistances, antagonisms, and slumps occurring in the interview. Recorded interviews reveal those techniques which lead toward insight and reorientation. Finally, recorded interviews provide objective data for research and for developing scales and other instruments for research. These statements have been supported by empirical results in extensive use of recordings in training and supervision.

Bugental (11) has designed a program of research to develop techniques for the objective description of interviewing, which he has named "explicit analysis." He proposed five descriptive dimensions:

1. Topical content.—What is talked about.

2. Idea-feeling balance.—Relative amount of attention to ideas and to feelings in what is talked about.

3. Focus.—How specifically is it spoken of.

4. Intensity.—How much does the speaker attempt to manipulate what will be said in response.

5. Concurrence.—How well does each party to the interview agree with the other in relation to each dimension.

Bugental has described a procedure for the "explicit analysis of topical concurrence" as follows:

A verbatim typescript of an interview is analyzed into its constituent thought units. Then each thought unit is examined to determine the extent to which it accords with or departs from the subject matter of what the preceding speaker has said. A five-level scale is employed for categorizing the level of topical concurrence.

Level I. Passive: No variation from the preceding response. Simple agreement, bridging, requests for clarification.

Level II. Responsive: Normally replying and contributing to the discussion. Answers to questions.

Level III. Developing: Addition of new aspects of topic but staying directly with the point of the referent response. Explanation, illustration, etc.

Level IV. Diverging: Changing the emphasis of the direction of the discussion rather clearly but without completely changing the topic. Bringing in explicitly related but tangential material.

Level V. Changing: No explicit connection to the topic of the preceeding speech is evident.

Each of these levels may be illustrated by typical alternative responses to the following client statement: "And so my childhood was happy enough but after my parents died, things got much tougher and much less pleasant."

IR-I: "I see."

IR-II: "After your parents' death, things didn't seem to go so well as they had before."

IR-III: "Tell me some more about that period after your parents' deaths."

IR-IV: "Did your parents' deaths affect your sister as strongly as they did you?"

IR-V: "Now, suppose you tell me something about your education."

Other investigators have wrestled with methods of analyzing interviews. Muthard compared the relative effectiveness of using different types of units in the analysis of counseling interview transcripts. One unit, the *discussion topic,* represents all the conversation of both client and counselor about the same topic or subject. A *problem-area unit* consists of all the contiguous statements dealing with the same kind of problem. The *fraction unit* consists of a definite percentage, such as twenty per cent, of the total remarks within a series of counseling interviews. The three criteria used to examine the effectiveness of the different types of units were (a) reliability, (b) sensitivity, and (c) the degree to which the unit brings together related material and separates out the less related. All units were found to be reliable. For sensitivity and for bringing together related material, the methods of the problem-area units and the discussion-topic units were equally more effective than fifths of the interview series.

Several investigators have found wide variation in the extent to which different interviewers probe a respondent, as well as in the length of the interview. The influence of the fullness or length of an interview on the judgments based on the interview were studied by Harry Levin (34). The judgments were analyzed for reliability, discriminability, and validity. Interviews with fifty respondents, each lasting two and a quarter hours or more, were compared with interviews from twenty-five respondents lasting only one and a quarter hours or less. When judgments are made on a specific section of the interview, reliability, as measured by agreement of judges, is higher on the short interviews. There are no differences in reliabilities between judgments on long and short interviews when the appropriate material is based on a group of questions scattered throughout the interview. There are no differences in the extent to which judgments based on short interviews and those based on long interviews discriminate among respondents. When validity is judged by the utility of the ratings in generating relationships with other variables, long and short interviews are equally valid on lengthy and scattered materials in the interviews. There is a suggestion that judgments on a specific section of the interview are more valid in the short interviews, although this may be a reflection of the higher reliabilities of these judgments.

One of the most disconcerting sources of error in judging personality is the tendency for the judgments on specific traits to be reflections of the interviewer's general impression of the person. This phenomenon was described by Wells in 1907 and christened "the halo effect" by Thorndike in 1920 (58). Thorndike strongly emphasized the practical implications of this common tendency among raters:

The writer has become convinced that even a very capable foreman, employer, or teacher, or department head is unable to treat an individual as a compound of separate qualities and to assign a magnitude to each of these in independence of the others. The magnitude of the constant error of the halo, as we have called it, also seems surprisingly large, though we lack objective criteria by which to determine its exact size. As a consequence science seems to demand that in all work on ratings for qualities the observer should report the evidence, not a rating, and the rating should be given on the evidence as to each quality separately without knowledge of the evidence concerning any other quality in the same individual.

Various studies, such as those by Symonds (55), Allport (1), and Bruner and Goodman (10) highlight the major factors involved in the errors made by observers, their unnoticed biases and preferences. When halo was first identified, psychologists were somewhat more optimistic than at present about the possibilities of reducing or removing it. Recognizing that ratings are the end product of rater perceptions and realizing that these perceptions are extremely sensitive and idiosyncratic, motivated strongly by conscious and unconscious factors, attention has been turned to ways of calibrating, of correcting for biases due to halo effects. That is, there has been a recognition that it is a virtual impossibility to control the many motivational aspects of perception on which ratings are based; instead, attempts have been made to adjust ratings for such effects.

There have been, however, a number of methods devised for improving ratings, for reducing the effects of unwanted variables. One of the writers (26) has discussed these as they apply to the ratings made by supervisors. Since ratings are part or all of so many criteria, recent work on the development of criteria is relevant to this problem. Flanagan (20), for instance, has proposed what he calls the "critical incidents technique" as a way of describing criterion behavior which avoids many of the problems, including halo.

Even after interviewers have been cautioned against allowing general impressions to masquerade under the guise of specific trait ratings, after they have been trained in drawing out and noting behavior indicative of the traits to be appraised, and after due allowance has been made for the correlations known to exist among common traits there still remains a general, positive correlation between overall evaluation of the person and specific trait ratings—a halo which cannot and perhaps should not be eliminated because it is inherent in the judgment of personality, in the perceptual process, and in the very act of judgment.

Consider what happens when an interviewer rates an individual's speaking voice. His judgment is an estimate based on a configuration in which the trait under consideration is but an aspect of a total pattern of behavior. The observer's perception and rating varies, not independently, but with the setting within which it is observed. This is an example of the context problem which is of so much concern particularly in Gestalt psychology. A clear feminine voice may be rated "excellent" when coming from a young woman, while a similar voice, coming from a stocky, athletic male might be judged as "bad" or "requiring extensive retraining." *The trait is and should be rated as a characteristic of the individual.*

However, this background, this context, does not change when the rater shifts from rating on voice quality to rating on general appearance, freedom from bias, or emotional stability. Presumably, different (in part) behaviors are considered, but the overlap is extensive. The problem is complicated by the fact that ratings are usually not made in the abstract but as indications of the person's suitability for some kind of activity or job. The rater therefore sees these traits against a still wider "ground" or context which includes the total personality pictured in relation to the duties in question. This context remaining constant, some halo in the ratings by skilled interviewers is to be expected and perhaps welcomed.

One of the writers (6) has distinguished between valid and invalid halo. By valid halo is meant the tendency of ratings to reflect the actual correlation among themselves. Thus, for example, there probably should be some relationship between the ratings of any individual on such traits as emotional maturity and dependability since the two are, in fact, correlated. By invalid halo is meant the excess of overlap beyond that which is to be expected due to the correlation among the traits under consideration. One would not expect a particularly close relationship to obtain between ratings of friendliness and intellectual ability although some raters might be so favorably impressed by the one that they would attribute a good deal of the other to the person rated.

Walter Lippmann drew attention years ago to the fact that there are commonly certain "pictures in our heads" of the supposed appearance of individuals of a given race, class, occupation, or social group. These he called "stereotypes." Many of these are so common and well entrenched that they can be caricatured and used freely in literature and the theater. J. Roaringham Fatback and General Bullmoose, cartoon characters created by Al Capp, are used to satirize the capitalist of a certain type. Their usefulness for this purpose rests in large part on the existence of stereotypes about capitalists. Other common stereotypes include the tough sergeant, the prostitute with a heart of gold, the dull but funny Negro, the smart kid from Brooklyn, and the shaven-headed, monocle-adorned Prussian general. Rice (45) once made a study which clearly demonstrated the power of these stereotypes. He asked 258 Dartmouth undergraduates and 31 members of the Grange to identify nine portraits. Included among these were a bootlegger, a European premier, a Bolshevik, a United States Senator, a labor leader, an editor-politician, two manufacturers, and a financier.

The replies, when tabulated, showed marked consistencies which included amusing confusions of identification. Other groups rated the same portraits, presented purposely with wrong identifications, first according to intelligence and second according to craftiness. Some of the more general conclusions of the study were:

1. The existence of certain common stereotypes concerning the appearance of various classes of persons (bootleggers, senators, etc.) is clearly indicated.

2. The stereotypes found among college students and Grange members are similar, but there appeared to be somewhat greater uniformity among the latter.

3. Estimates of intelligence and craftiness, presumably based on the features portrayed, are in reality influenced by the supposed identity of the portrait—that is, by the stereotype of the supposed social or occupational status held in the mind of the rater.

In his extensive study of convicts, Goring (25) demonstrated that a composite of *sketches* of criminals gave the appearance of abnormality, whereas a composite of *photographs* shows *no* appearance of abnormality. "An examination of these contrasted outlines," he says, "shows most strikingly the difference between criminal types, as registered by the mechanical precision of the camera, and as viewed by the imagination of an enthusiastic, but uncritical, observer." The sketches were biased in a constant direction, in the direction of the artist's conception of criminals.

Two recent studies are relevant here. Edwards (16) studied the relationship between the judged desirability of a trait and the probability that it will be endorsed. That is, he was concerned with whether "good" characteristics (honesty, fairness, etc.) would be used as self descriptions more often than they ought, considering the real facts of the case. He found a correlation of .871 between the tendency to judge a trait as good or desirable and the tendency to appropriate that trait to one's self. Wyatt and Campbell (63) showed that interviewer expectation was a source of some bias. It stereotypes constitute a kind of bias for expectation, it can be seen that their effects on the interview may be serious. One of the writers once talked with the personnel manager of a plant in the South, a man with strong anti-Negro feelings. This personnel man indicated that he could use a very brief, two or three minute interview in selecting men for laboring jobs because all of the applicants were Negroes. He was supposed to be looking for individuals with abilities which would enable them to perform as stock clerks and on other clerical jobs. He was so sure that Negroes were of low intelligence that he never found any with enough ability for the better jobs. The writer was particularly interested because he knew that one of the applicants recently interviewed was a senior in college, a very intelligent young man. He, however, had been judged as having low intelligence also.

In estimating another's personality, either as a whole or on certain traits, few interviewers are completely aware of their reasons for assigning ratings. Landis (33) found that, of the reasons given in justification for the judgment made, half were nonspecific. He also found that a specific reason was more likely to be cited when the judge believed that his rating implied undesirability. The so-called reason was frequently a rationalization or plausible explanation which covered up the real reason. Crissy and Regan (14) obtained essentially the same results in a later study. They found that a good bit more evidence was presented to support ratings of rejected applicants and that interviewers found significantly more data to support low ratings than high ones.

The impression that personality can be judged from physical appearance is a myth which stubbornly defies extinction. The ancient ideas that red hair signifies a hot temper or that a square jaw denotes stubbornness or inflexibility are but two examples. These ideas were even popular among scientists for a time. The classic book, *Physique and Intellect,* by Paterson (41) did a lot to lay many of these troublesome ghosts as far as psychologists were concerned, but the notions are still widely current among people whose judgments have substantial effects on the lives of others. One has to do only a little reading in popular magazines and novels to see these physical stereotypes in action. Criminals with slack jaws and shifty eyes; slender, sensitive writers; blue steely-eyed heroes; high-spirited, redheaded heroines abound. These stereotypes, based on physical characteristics, are relatively harmless in literature (except that they reinforce popular misconceptions), but they can be very troublesome when they are part of the belief patterns of personnel managers, employers, and other interviewers.

These beliefs have their origins in one or more of the following reasons for associating physical characteristics with a particular personality trait:

1. Resemblance to some lower animal thought to have certain traits, as in the case of a bulldog's jaw (stubborn) and a snake's beady eyes (cruel).

2. Fixed resemblance to transitory expressional states commonly associated with particular emotions, such as merriment suggested by upturned corners of the mouth or fine lines about the eyes.

3. Appearance of physiological conditions associated with certain temperamental traits, such as melancholy or cheerfulness with dyspepsia or good health.

Ever since the days of the phrenologists—Gall and Spurzheim in Europe, the Fowler brothers in this country—there have existed popular systems of character analysis grounded on some theory or other regarding the connection between personality traits and physical characteristics. These systems are intriguing to many because, if true, they would make the work of the interviewer, the personnel man, and others, relatively simple. If it were possible to tell what a person is like merely by looking at him, a lot of the labor of extensive interviewing, checking records, and testing could be dispensed with. Unfortunately, the data do not support any of these systems.

There may well be some connection between anatomy and physiology on the one hand with temperament and ability on the other, but these connections are not obvious or readily observable. Rather, they lie in the relations existing between billions of cells, particularly nerve cells, all of which are hidden from view except to the anatomist and physiologist. The brain itself is made up of nerve cells which, unlike muscles, do not increase with exercise. Moreover, personality traits are only very generally associated with areas of the brain. Studies of individuals with damaged brains have shown that there are effects on personality, but these are quite general, not specific as would be demanded by the phrenologists. One of the earliest studies, for instance, was performed on a soldier whose skull had been blown open by a bullet. When the physician stimulated what the phrenologists had labelled the area of "amativeness," the soldier's big toe moved! Further, it is known that men's brains are, on the average, larger than women's, yet there is no difference between the sexes in measured intelligence. These data and others suggest some of the extreme difficulties inherent in drawing inferences about ability or personality from physical appearance. The interviewer who looks to bodily shape for clues to personality merely diverts his attention from significant essentials on which valid ratings can be made.

Realizing that morphological data have little if any relationship to personality and ability, scientific investigators have long since turned to the study of actual behavior as a better index to personality. The ways of measuring personality have been described in a number of excellent works including those by Ferguson (18), Cattell (12), Eysenck (17), Super (54), and others. The interviewer should be thoroughly familiar with these before attempting to deal with either rating or measuring personality and abilities. Many tests, such as the Stanford-Binet, a measure of intelligence, are essentially standardized interviews.

Turning our attention from the interviewer to the person being interviewed, we may ask: To what extent does he answer questions inaccurately, even when his intentions are the best; what is the nature of his errors; how can these sources of unreliability in the interview be minimized?

Two particular kinds of error are of concern: variable errors and constant errors. The existence of variable errors is easily detected by the mere fact of the scatter, the inconsistency of answers. Borgatta and Bales (9) have indicated that interviewee behavior is relatively consistent. This does not eliminate the possibility of variable error, however. Vaughan and Reynolds (61) studied the reliability of reporting of such objective data as age, education, and socio-economic status. Retesting three months after the first interview, they found that the coefficient of reliability of reporting for age was .85 in one sample, .80 in another; for education, the coefficients were .82 and .67; for socio-economic status, .61 and .42. Even at best, it can be seen that there was approximately 35 per cent error in these data, objective as they are.

Constant error, on the other hand, refers to a consistent tendency for the reported facts to vary in one direction from the objectively determined facts. Woodworth (62) has illustrated the difference as follows:

Witnesses in court may be required to testify as to the length of time elapsing between two events, say a cry of terror and the sound of a pistol. One observer reports fifteen seconds; one, half a minute; one, a minute. We take a rough average of these estimates, and conclude that the time must have been something like half a minute. But is there a constant error in this sort of estimation? An experiment may tell. Take out your watch before an audience, and say, "I want you each to estimate the time between the moment I say 'Begin' and the moment when I say 'Stop.'" Allow fifteen seconds to elapse, and you will find that the estimates range from perhaps fifteen seconds as a lower limit to a minute or a minute and a half, with an average of about 25 or 30 seconds. There is then a large constant error, in the direction of overestimation of time, under certain conditions. Change the conditions, and you alter the amount of the constant error, and may even reverse its direction.

The two kinds of error, constant and variable, may be seen in judgments of personality. A variable error appears in the diverging opinions held by different persons in regard to a trait in any one individual. A constant error, on the other hand, is seen in the tendency of people, when rating themselves, to overestimate their desirable traits and to underestimate less desirable ones.

The pervasive effect of a general set as well as of a particular preconception in controlling an interviewee's interpretation of events is illustrated by experiments in the psychology of report in which a little scene is enacted before an audience in such a way that it gives them the impression that it really happened. Later, each member of the group writes a description of the incident and answers questions about it. The scene must be rehearsed in advance so that there may be independent knowledge of the actual facts. Woodworth describes such an experiment in which he himself took part and which brings out the fact of the constant error.

I conspired with two of my students, out of a college class of about thirty young men, to enact this little scene before the class. I interrupted my lecture at a predetermined point to say that Mr. A (one of my fellow conspirators) had prepared a memory experiment for the class to try. Mr. A then came to the desk, and placed behind the screen several objects from underneath the desk. Mr. A then said, "We shall need to light the desk light," which stood behind our screen. I turned the key on the socket, but no light came. Mr. A went to the wall switch, but still no light. Both of us stood registering perplexity, when Mr. B, the other conspirator, who was sitting in the front row, started up, extended his arm over the screen, and screwed in the bulb, producing light. As Mr. B. took his seat again, I from behind gave the screen a push, and it fell to the floor, revealing the objects behind it. Mr. A and I registered annoyance, I remarked that we couldn't continue with the experiment now, hastily removed the objects from the desk top, and resumed my lecture.

Two days later, a free report of the scene was written by each of the witnesses, and a number of specific questions were also answered. I will mention only one fact which came out. The members of the class were practically unanimous in reporting that Mr. B., "butting into the experiment," had spoiled it by knocking down the screen. Some witnesses told exactly how Mr. B. had done it. He was a senior, and the seniors were wearing gowns, more or less, at this time: One witness explained that Mr. B's gown became entangled with the screen and pulled it down. As a matter of fact, Mr. B. was not wearing his gown that day.

Now here we have a constant error in a mass of harmonious testimony, and we can see, roughly, the source of the constant error. Mr. B certainly seemed to be an outsider, "butting in" though with good intentions. That conception of his action was almost forced upon the witnesses from the instant he rose from his seat. What followed was seen in the light of this preconception. The conception which the witness brings to the scene, or which is aroused in him by the early stages of its occurrence, has much to do with his interpretation of what is enacted before him.

A common but subtle form of mental set is that produced from the form of the question, as we have seen. It has long been recognized that the way in which a question is asked has a lively influence on the answer made to it. The legal profession has recognized this for centuries. A court does not permit an attorney examining a witness to ask a "leading question" because its very form conveys a suggestion which markedly decreases the accuracy of report among children and to a lesser extent among adults. It is also known that people vary widely in their susceptibility to suggestion. Some are highly suggestible while others are very hard to influence. The recent work by Hyman *et al.* (30) discusses such problems in considerable detail. The personality characteristics which account for differences in suggestibility have already been mentioned. The so-called dynamics of personality, the motives and the needs, combine to make some people susceptible, others not so. It must also be recognized that many respondents, be they witnesses or interviewees in other situations, will give what they think the interviewer wants to hear. They may be trying to be agreeable; they may fear censure if they express their own opinions; they may be afraid of being contradicted or made to appear ridiculous, etc. This is not the kind of suggestibility denoted above although it is related.

We have seen that limits to the utility of the interview are imposed by the purposes of the interview, the uses to which the obtained data are put, and the personality characteristics of the participants in the interview, as well as by the methods employed. The weaknesses, the sources of error in the interview must be forthrightly recognized and, insofar as possible, forestalled.

By no means all of the problems involved in the interview can be dealt with in a book such as this. We have therefore selected a few of what we believe to be the most important questions which will be kept uppermost:

For what uses is the interview feasible and reliable?

What needs for fact finding are served better by the interview than by other available procedures?

What special contributions to understanding the interview process have been made by the various special groups active in its use?

What general principles of interviewing can be formulated?

What are the common errors or pitfalls in interviewing, and how can they be avoided?

How can interviewers best be trained so that their work is as sound and reliable as possible?

What is the nature of the interaction between the participants in the interview, and how does this affect the results?

This chapter has dealt with certain fundamental problems. Some sources of difficulty have been brought into the open, such as the often astonishing difference between what the interviewer means by his question and the meaning which the interviewee attaches to the question; distortions of statement motivated by conscious and unconscious processes; errors of observation and of recall which affect the data obtained in the interview. The successful interviewer must, somehow, control these factors. He must appreciate and control his own biases and predilections while recognizing those of the interviewee. Frank sincerity on his part tends to engender confidence and frankness in the person interviewed. Attempts to be clever or surreptitious in his questioning make it hard to establish the kind of working relationship, the close cooperation between the two participants in trying to solve a mutually agreed upon problem, without which any interview tends to be halting and ineffective. Once a sound relationship has been established, the interviewer can function best, and the interview can best reach its goals, if he has at his command an understanding of those available techniques, those insights into personality, both normal and abnormal, which have been developed from carefully controlled research and experienced clinical judgment. In the chapter to follow, the interaction, the relationship between the participants, will be discussed as one of the central issues in learning How to Interview.

REFERENCES

1. ALLPORT, G., *Personality*. New York: Holt, 1937.
2. ANDERSON, R., The guided interview as an evaluative instrument. *J. educ. Res.*, 1954, 48, 203-209.
3. ASCH, S., Forming impressions of personality. *J. Abnorm. Soc. Psychol.*, 1946, 41, 258-290.
4. BACK, K., HILL, R., and STYCOS, J., Interviewer effect on scale reproducibility. *Amer. Soc. Rev.*, 1955, 20, 443-446.
5. BERDIE, R., Psychological processes in the interview. *J. Soc. Psychol.*, 1943, 18, 3-31.
6. BINGHAM, W. HALO, Invalid and valid. *J. appl. Psychol.*, 1939, 23, 221-228.
7. BLANKENSHIP, A. The effect of the interviewer upon the response in a public opinion poll. *J. consult. Psychol.*, 1940, 4, 134-136.
8. BLUM, G., *Psychoanalytic Theories of Personality*. New York: McGraw-Hill, 1953.
9. BORGATTA, E. and BALES, R., The consistency of subject behavior and the reliability of scoring in interaction process analysis. *Amer. soc. Rev.*, 1953, 18, 566-569.

10. BRUNER, J. and GOODMAN, C., Value and need as organizing factors in perception. *J. abnorm. soc. Psychol.*, 1947, 42, 33-44.

11. BUGENTAL, J., Explicit analysis: a design for the study and improvement of psychological interviewing. *Educ. psychol. Measmt.*, 1954, 14, 552-565.

12. CATTELL, R., *Personality*. New York: McGraw-Hill, 1950.

13. COVNER, B., Studies in phonographic recording of verbal material: I The use of phonographic recordings in counseling practice and research. *J. consult. Psychol.*, 1942, 6, 105-113.

14. CRISSY, W. and REGAN, J., Halo in the employment interview. *J. appl. Psychol.*, 1951, 35, 338-341.

15. CRONBACH, L., *A Consideration of Information Theory and Utility Theory as Tools for Psychometric Problems*. Urbana: Univ. of Illinois, College of Education, 1953.

16. EDWARDS, A., The relationship between the judged desirability of a trait and the probability that the trait will be endorsed. *J. appl. Psychol.*, 1953, 37, 90-93.

17. EYSENCK, H., *The Structure of Human Personality*. New York: Wiley, 1953.

18. FERGUSON, L., *Personality Measurement*. New York: McGraw-Hill, 1952.

19. FIEDLER, F., The concept of the ideal therapeutic relationship. *J. consult. Psychol.*, 1950, 14, 239-245.

20. FLANAGAN, J., Critical requirements. In Dennis, W. (Ed.) *Current Trends in Industrial Psychology*. Pittsburgh: University of Pittsburgh Press, 1947.

21. FRIEDMAN, P., A second experiment on interviewer bias. *Sociometry*, 1942, 5, 378-381.

22. GOLDMAN-EISLER, F., Individual differences between interviewers and their effect on the interviewees' conversational behavior. *J. ment. Sci.*, 1952, 98, 660-671.

23. GOLLIN, E., Forming impressions of personality. *J. Pers.*, 1954, 23, 65-76.

24. GOLLIN, E. and ROSENBERG, S., Concept formation and impressions of personality. *J. abnorm. soc. Psychol.*, 1956, 52, 39-42.

25. GORING, C., *The English Convict*, London: Darling and Son, 1913.

26. GUSTAD, J., Rating and the supervisor. In Ayers, A. (Ed.) *Proceedings of the third annual industrial relations conference*. Department of Psychology, University of Maryland, 1954. Mimeographed.

27. GUSTAD, J. and TUMA, A., The effects of different methods of test introduction and interpretation on client learning in counseling. *J. couns. Psychol.*, 1957, 4, 313, 317.

28. GUTTMAN, L., The Cornell technique for scale and intensity analysis. *Educ. Psychol. Measmt.*, 1947, 7, 247-280.

29. HOLLINGWORTH, H., *Vocational Psychology and Character Analysis.* New York: Appleton-Century, 1929.

30. HYMAN, H. *et. al., Interviewing in Social Research.* Chicago: University of Chicago Press, 1954.

31. HYMAN, H., Isolation, measurement, and control of interviewer effect. New York: Social Science Research Council *Items*, 1949.

32. JENKINS, J., The questionnaire as a research instrument. *Trans. N.Y. acad. Sci.*, Series II, vol. 2, no. 5, 1940.

33. LANDIS, C., The justification of judgments. *J. personnel Res.*, 1925, 4, 7-19.

34. LEVIN, H., The influence of fullness of interview on the reliability, discriminability, and validity of interview judgments. *J. consult. Psychol*, 1954, 18, 303-306.

35. LINDZEY, G., A note on interviewer bias. *J. appl. Psychol.*, 1951, 35, 182-184.

36. MEEHL, P., *Clinical Versus Statistical Prediction.* Minneapolis: University of Minnesota Press, 1954.

37. MILLER, G., *Language and communication.* New York: McGraw-Hill, 1951.

38. MONROE, R., *Schools of Psychoanalytic Thought.* New York: Dryden, 1955.

39. MUSCIO, B., The influence of the form of the question. *Brit. J. Psychol.*, 1916, 8, 351-389.

40. OLDFIELD, R., *The Psychology of the Interview.* London: Methuen, 1941.

41. PATERSON, D., *Physique and Intellect.* New York: Appleton-Century, 1930.

42. PATTON, R. (Ed.), *Current Trends in Information Theory.* Pittsburgh: University of Pittsburgh Press, 1953.

43. POFFENBERGER, A., *Applied Psychology, Its Principles and Methods.* New York: Appleton-Century, 1927.

44. REUSCH, J. and KEES, W., *Non-Verbal Communication.* Berkeley: University of California Press, 1956.

45. RICE, S., Stereotypes. *J. personnel Res.*, 1926, 5, 267-276.

46. RICE, S., Contagious bias in the interview: a methodological note. *Amer. J. Sociol.*, 1929, 35, 420-423.

47. ROBINSON, F., The dynamics of communication in counseling. *J. couns. Psychol.*, 1955, 2, 163-169.

48. ROGERS, C., *Counseling and Psychotherapy.* New York: Houghton-Mifflin, 1942.

49. ROGERS, C., Electrically recorded interviews in improving psychotherapeutic techniques. *Amer. J. Orthopsychiatry,* 1942, 12, 429-435.

50. SASLOW, G., MATARAZZO, J., and GUZE, S., The stability of interaction chronograph patterns in psychiatric interviews. *J. consult. Psychol.,* 1955, 19, 417-430.

51. SHANNON, C. and WEAVER, W., *The Mathematical Theory of Communication.* Urbana: University of Illinois Press, 1952.

52. STANTON, F. and BAKER, K., Interviewer bias and the recall of incompletely learned materials. *Sociometry,* 1942, 5, 123-134.

53. STRONG, E., *Psychology of Selling and Advertising.* New York: McGraw-Hill, 1925.

54. SUPER, D., *Appraising Vocational Fitness.* New York: Harper, 1949.

55. SYMONDS, P., *The Dynamics of Personal Adjustment.* New York: Appleton-Century, 1946.

56. SYMONDS, P., *Diagnosing Personality and Conduct.* New York: Appleton-Century, 1931.

57. SYMONDS, P. and DIETRICH, D., Effect of variations in the time interval between an interview and its recording. *J. abnorm. soc. Psychol.,* 1941, 36, 593-598.

58. THORNDIKE, E., Constant error in psychological ratings. *J. appl. Psychol.,* 1920, 4, 25-29.

59. TUMA, A. and GUSTAD, J., The effects of client and counselor personality characteristics on client learning in counseling. *J. couns. Psychol.,* 1957, 4, 136-143.

60. TUPES, E., An evaluation of personality-trait ratings obtained by unstructural assessment interviews. *Psychol. Monogr.,* 1950, 64 (11), No. 317.

61. VAUGHAN, C. and REYNOLDS, W., Reliability of personal interview data. *J. appl. Psychol.,* 1951, 35, 61-63.

62. WOODWORTH, R., Psychological experience with the interview. *J. Personnel Res.,* 1925, 4, 162-165.

63. WYATT, D. and CAMPBELL, D., A study of interviewer bias as related to interviewers' expectations and own opinions. *Int. J. Opin. Attit. Res.,* 1950, 4, 77-83.

2. The Participants in the Interview

Interview as a relationship of interaction

WHILE some interviewing is done in groups, in the overwhelming proportion of instances it is a matter of two individuals, the interviewer and the interviewee, talking together. For all practical purposes, we can amend our definition of the interview as a serious conversation with a purpose by adding this feature: that it is a conversation between two persons. The implications of this fact, that the interview is a relationship between two persons, are just now beginning to be seen.

The key word above is "relationship." The interviewer and the interviewee both bring into the interview their own characteristics, their own life histories, their own personalities. What happens in the interview, however, cannot be understood merely by studying these two participants as separate entities. Rather, it is essential to realize that they relate, that they interact, that this relationship, this interaction, a product of their two personalities, is what determines the outcome of the interview.

We shall discuss certain guides to the conduct of the interview in the next chapter. These rules by themselves, however, cannot guarantee a well conducted, productive interview. One person may follow the rules religiously and still fail as an interviewer. Another person may actually or apparently flout these rules and still be successful. Just knowing the rules, even having impressive knowledge of human behavior, is no guarantee of success as an interviewer. Success as an interviewer is a function not only of what is done but *how* it is done.

The problem is even more complicated by the fact that an interviewer may be successful with some interviewees, unsuccessful with others. This fact is widely recognized among those who do interviewing and those who train interviewers. If this is so, it suggests that the interviewer alone is not our sole concern. It suggests, rather, that we must study the interviewer *in interaction* with different kinds of interviewees if we are to understand the interview process. We must, in other words, see whether we can determine what kinds of people produce what kinds of results from an interview. This involves studying the interviewer, the interviewee, *and the relationship between them.*

This problem has been recognized for many years by several groups of interviewers, especially those engaged in therapeutic interviewing. Unfortunately, research has just begun to appear in any significant amount. A good illustration is found in the field of psychoanalysis. Very early in its development as a therapeutic technique, it was recognized that often the patient's reactions were not appropriate to what the analyst had been doing or saying. Some patients became unaccountably angry at the analyst; others were effusive in their admiration or affection. To explain this phenomenon, the psychoanalysts introduced the concept of *transference.*

By this was meant the tendency for the patient to project onto the analyst ideas and feelings which really belonged elsewhere. Childish temper tantrums, infantile demands for affection and security were exhibited toward the analyst who was, unconsciously, seen as a parent substitute.

Similarly, it was soon clear that the analyst himself was not free from these tendencies despite the fact that he had been psychoanalyzed and was presumably aware of his own personality make-up. Analysts noticed themselves becoming angry at patients, or developing strong, positive feelings toward them, all for no apparent reason. This tendency on the part of the analyst was called, to distinguish it from the patient's reaction, *counter-transference.*

Initially, these transference reactions were seen as hindrances to the successful handling of the therapy. Gradually, however, it was recognized that they were an essential element in treatment, for it was through dealing with these childish tendencies that the analyst was able to help the patient to reach a better adjustment.

For our purposes, the point of discussing transference reactions is to indicate how the personalities of the participants in the interview can and do interact in subtle, complicated, and extremely important ways. There is some argument about whether transference, in the classical, psychoanalytic sense, actually takes place in many kinds of interview situations. Psychoanalysis ordinarily requires a long time, frequently two, three, or more years. This provides an opportunity, indeed, makes it virtually certain, for the participants to become very well acquainted. In personnel selection interviewing, in much guidance and counseling, in public opinion polling, the interview relationship is much shorter. Because of this, some have felt that transference, or at least subtle, unconscious personal interaction, is of no concern in these areas. While it may be true that transference, in the usual sense of the term, does not occur in brief interviews, there is growing evidence that unconscious reactions do have marked effects even on such interviews.

A personnel interviewer, selecting job applicants, may find that he reacts badly to some people even on first contact. This reaction cannot usually be explained by things that the interviewee has done or said. More likely, the interviewer is reacting on some other basis, probably unconscious. Most of us have had the experience of liking or disliking, of feeling comfortable or uncomfortable with people on first acquaintance, long before we have had a chance to make a conscious, rational decision about them. Often, too, our liking or disliking is transmitted to the other person by subtle processes such as gestures, posture, voice intonations, or choice of words. The point to be kept in mind is this: the relations between people are complex and occur at several levels from the conscious to the unconscious. This is true whether the relationship is brief or long, formal or informal.

We now consider some aspects of this problem. We shall try to compare and contrast various levels of interaction; we shall discuss methods of describing these; we shall consider the personalities of the interviewer and the interviewee; we shall, finally, try to describe some of the problems involved in and resulting from the interaction between persons in the interview.

Dynamics of personality

The necessary starting point for this discussion is in the area of personality dynamics. Mention was made in the first chapter of some of the major dynamics of personality such as projection, sublimation, rationalization and repression. Encountering these for the first time, one is apt to think of them as representing pathological states. In the extreme, they undoubtedly are, but they exist so universally that we must consider them also to be parts of normal personality.

Without necessarily subscribing to any of the numerous theories of personality, it is possible to describe personality in terms of certain important aspects or elements. We are all aware of ourselves as thinking organisms. This aspect of personality, the conscious part, is important for understanding human behavior, but it is not enough. Many find it hard to accept the notion that each person also has an *unconscious*. The existence of the unconscious is no longer a matter of debate; it has been demonstrated to exist in all of us and to play an enormously important role in our behavior. It is not possible to estimate at all precisely what proportion of our total psychological life is conscious, what proportion unconscious. Everyone who has studied the problem, however, agrees that consciousness is the smaller part of personality. Most of what we are and do is a result of unconscious processes. To ignore this, particularly in enterprises involving intimate interpersonal relationships, is to risk serious mistakes.

Another aspect of behavior which must be discussed briefly is *motivation*. There are many theories of motivation available (35) (36) (44) (48), none of which is universally accepted. Motivation is the internal part of the answer to the question, "Why do people do what they do?" It has always been recognized that people, as well as animals, do things for a reason or for several reasons. Faced with a choice between food and water, a hungry animal or human will choose food. From this, we say that the animal is hungry, that he is motivated to obtain food.

These motives may be divided into two major types or categories: physiological and social. Hunger, thirst, sexual drive, and maternal drive are included among the physiological motives. Deprive an animal of food, and he will seek it; deprive him of water, and he will try to find it, and so on. He is motivated to seek what he needs. In addition to these basic, physiological motives, however, there are social motives. These are largely learned. Because humans are probably the best learners among all the species, their behavior contains more learned elements than any other. We learn to want money, to want security, friends, prestige, and many other things. Since few of us in this country ever face severe deprivation of food or water, these motives do not seem to play the same role in human behavior that they do in animal behavior. Because learning enables the individual to acquire many more abilities and desires, human behavior is considerably more flexible and complex than that of any other organism.

Security is a good example of a learned motive. As an infant, the person's basic needs for food, water, warmth, and protection are provided by the parents, most directly and usually by the mother. The child quickly learns that the mother is the primary source of good and necessary things, is the source, in short, of security. Later, he learns that the father is also a source of security. As he grows older, siblings, schoolmates, friends also provide different kinds of security. In order to obtain what he feels to be the needed amount of security, the individual learns to do certain things: to obey parents in order to retain their love and support; to get along with (or dominate) siblings and friends in order to obtain security from them; to store up such tangible symbols of security as money and property or power so that needs, when they arise, may be satisfied.

One other major aspect of personality must be discussed. We have all experienced fear. We may have been in an automobile accident; we may have been in military combat; we may have been severely reprimanded by parents, teachers, or others in authority. There are many things which produce fear. Fear is a motive also in that it makes people do something. Running away is a common reaction, designed to get the person out of the way of the feared situation or object. Closely related to fear, and in many ways more important for understanding human behavior, there is *anxiety*. Like many other personality dynamics, anxiety may, in extreme cases, be pathological. It is, however, so common, so nearly universal that we must consider it also as an aspect of normal personality.

To understand the difference between fear and anxiety, it is necessary to refer to the conscious and the unconscious. When we are afraid, we ordinarily know what it is that is frightening us. Often, however, we experience many of the same symptoms of fear in situations where there seems to be no reason for them. In many cases, the heart rate accelerates, hands perspire, breath becomes more rapid, and other physiological reactions appear. These are some of the symptoms of fear, but they also can be symptoms of anxiety. Mowrer (50) has said that anxiety presupposes the existence of materials in the unconscious which are disturbing to the individual. Without attempting to explain here how these get into the unconscious, it seems fair to say that the difference between fear and anxiety is that *fear is a response to something which is known, anxiety is a response to something which is (at least consciously) unknown.*

Most of the things which are in the unconscious and which produce anxiety are unpleasant and undesirable. Memories of acts or ideas of which the individual is ashamed (guilt), and feelings of anger, especially toward parents (hostility), are commonly found at the root of anxiety reactions. The individual is unaware of their existence; he has built defenses against their appearing undisguised in his behavior or his consciousness, but they keep threatening to break out into the open and into view or expression. He fears this, and this fear is anxiety. Getting at the roots of anxiety is the task of the skilled psychologist or psychiatrist, not the layman. Yet the layman, if he is to understand human behavior, must realize that these facets of personality do exist, that in very large measure they account for what people do.

Hall (30) described a series of situations in which unconscious motivation seemed to be operating. He made appointments with a number of municipal officials to get their opinions on a very touchy topic, segregation. He related such things as broken appointments and unnecessarily long waits to see these men after the appointment hour, to their attitudes on segregation. When he reported that several city officials were opposed to integration, there was a chorus of denials. Yet their behavior, indicating that they did not wish to discuss this topic, did seem to give credence to his conclusions. Hall was following up ideas expressed by Freud (23) in his discussion of the psychology of errors. Freud insisted that such things as slips of the tongue or forgetting of engagements were indications of unconscious reactions. Freud cited an incident which he thought illustrated this. A professor, angry at the students in his class for their failure to understand the course, said that he could count the number of people who understood what he was saying *on one finger*. He had meant to say on the fingers of one hand, but his real meaning, that *only* he understood the material, slipped out despite his intentions to do otherwise. Freud's point, like Hall's, was that errors are motivated, that they provide cues to the unconscious processes of the individual.

Recording interaction in the interview

If it is true that the interaction between the interviewer and the interviewee is the critical area for study, then methods must be devised to describe this interaction, to record it for subsequent analysis. The trouble with an interview is that things happen so rapidly that the interviewer, even a highly trained and experienced one, has trouble in recalling and recording the significant elements.

An effective method for obtaining information about the interaction in the interview is to record it electrically. Rogers recommended this a number of years ago, and one of his students, Porter (54) (55), first developed the method so that it was functionally useful. Recording the interview provides a permanent record. This record may be played back repeatedly or, more commonly, may be transcribed by a typist. With a typescript in hand, it is possible to analyze the interview in a number of ways. Robinson (56) has reviewed a number of studies dealing with this process and has suggested several dimensions of the interview. Berdie (7), in connection with his discussion of psychological processes in the interview, also dealt with recording as a method for studying the interview, and Heyns and Lippitt (31) have provided an excellent review of work dealing with recording.

The principal difficulty in using electrical recording as a way of studying the interview is that it yields both too much and too little information. The typescript of even a single interview runs to thousands of words, hundreds of conversational exchanges between the interviewer and the interviewee. Numerous attempts have been made to devise ways for reducing this vast pool of information to manageable proportions. Robinson and several of his pupils (16) (17) (52) (39) have done especially fine work on this problem as have Bales (3), Bugental (12) and Matarazzo et al. (47) There is so far no generally accepted way for reducing the information obtained from a recording to the point where it can be conveniently analyzed.

At the same time, the electrical recording misses some putatively important things. While the words, voice qualities, and inflections of the participants are captured on tape, there is no record of gestures or facial expressions, some of which are probably very important. It has been suggested that motion pictures be made simultaneously, and this is being done on an experimental basis in a few places, but it is too early to tell whether the additional mountain of information made available on film will be worth the cost and trouble of collecting it.

Analyzing effects of the interview

Another method for studying the interview process uses indirect, *post hoc* data. Devised originally by Stephenson (63), it is called the Q-sort technique. Those interested in a detailed discussion of the method and its numerous modifications are referred to Stephenson's book. Basically, the method involves asking subjects, be they interviewers, interviewees, or others, to sort or classify descriptive statements. Having selected a fairly large pool of items or statements which cover the range of a particular kind of behavior or attitude, the experimenter sets up a number of categories which range from most correct or most descriptive to least correct or descriptive. The subject is instructed to sort the items into these categories, putting a specified number (so as to produce a symmetrical, if not necessarily normal distribution) into each category. He may be asked to sort the statements in terms of how they would apply to him (self-sort), to the kind of person he would most like to be (ideal self-sort), to his interviewer, or to others. Because of the way in which the statements have been sorted into categories, it is then possible to correlate for each individual the sorts for self and ideal self, or for self and interviewer. The principal advantage of this technique is that it provides a method for studying individuals and pairs of individuals. The experimenter does not have to lose sight of his individuals in the midst of masses of data. The soundness of this technique is not accepted by all, but it has been put to use in a number of interesting studies. Fiedler (19) (20) (21) and Berenson (9) have used it to study the interaction between the participants in therapeutic interviews.

Probably the most widely used method for studying the interview involves pretesting the client, the counselor, or both and then retesting after the interviews are completed. This method, exemplified by studies by Williamson and Bordin (71) (72), Magoon (41), Jesness (34), and Hoyt (32), permits the experimenter to find out what effects the interview series has had on the participants, although it does little to shed light on the interview process itself.

Research by Tuma and Gustad (29) (68) illustrates this method. They were concerned with two general problems: the effects of certain methods of introducing and interpreting tests in vocational counseling and with the impact on the results of certain personality characteristics of the participants. They found that methods as such made no difference; all groups studied improved equally (and significantly). The personality measures, however, yielded some interesting results. It was found that, when the client and his counselor were quite similar on three of the measures used, the outcomes of counseling were better than if there were differences between the participants. The three scales were: dominance, social presence, and social participation. These are all scales on the California Personality Inventory. More will be said about this kind of study in a later section as counselor and client traits are discussed. The study was cited here to illustrate one kind of study of the interview.

A new and intriguing approach to the study of interview behavior is one being followed by Malmo and his colleagues at McGill University (42) (43) (60). Here, electrical recordings of a number of physiological processes are made during the interview. For instance, muscle tension, galvanic skin response, and heart rate are recorded. They have yet to conduct a study with sufficient numbers of subjects to allow for the emergence of dependable results, but their exploratory work has been highly suggestive. Goldman-Eisler (24) (25) (26) has recorded certain speech activities, such as inspiration and expiration time, and related these to interview behavior. The results of these studies will also be discussed later.

Attention is turning more and more to the interaction between the participants in the interview and the effects of such interaction on interview outcomes. Hopefully, the next few years will add enough to what is already known so that dependable generalizations may be developed about processes in the interview. The few studies already available are suggestive and extremely stimulating. A few of these will be presented next.

If the interaction between the participants in the interview is the crucial problem, it is necessary to consider first the variability of the behavior under examination. If this varies widely, is at the mercy of the situation, then the problem of accounting for it becomes enormously complicated. If, however, there is some consistency, some stability, then the search for correlates of such behavior is a more promising enterprise.

Saslow, Matarazzo, and Guze (59) employed Chapple's interaction chronograph to study this problem. They studied twenty standardized psychiatric interviews which were conducted by two psychiatrists. They found that the instrument was highly reliable, that there was a marked stability of patient patterns of behavior when the stimulus conditions remained constant, and that there was considerable flexibility in interaction patterns when the stimulus conditions changed. These same writers (45) replicated the study by having an additional twenty patients interviewed by two different psychiatrists. They concluded from this second study that a single patient's interaction pattern with the interviewer is both susceptible to planned changes and is also remarkably stable from one interviewer to another.

Bugental, employing his own method for analyzing the interview, reported that interviewees were relatively consistent, *more so than were the interviewers*. Goldman-Eisler (24), on the other hand, reported that her interviewers were consistent in their behavior regardless of the patient being interviewed. The difference between these studies may be due to the methods of analysis since Goldman-Eisler was studying rather molecular aspects of speech behavior while Bugental was concerned with larger units of interview interaction. Goldman-Eisler also reported that the interviewees were quite consistent although their verbal behavior showed influence of the therapists.

While consistency of behavior makes the task of analyzing the interview simpler, it may be asked whether there are desirable limits to such consistency. Back (2) studied this dimension in interviewing. All of his interviewers, who were interviewing for factual information, took Luchins' Einstellung Test which is a measure of rigidity. The criterion with which test scores were correlated was an index of the efficiency of their obtaining information. He set up two hypotheses: (1) the interviewer who adjusts to short range situations is inferior; (2) the interviewer who has an over-all plan but employs several methods is superior. Both hypotheses were substantiated by the data.

Empathy in interviewing

The available data seem to suggest that there is substantial consistency of behavior on the part of both the interviewer and the interviewee. At the same time, both vary their behavior in accordance with the demands of the situation. This leads to a further question: how are the demands of the situation communicated between the participants? One possibility which is receiving considerable attention is empathy. Empathy is difficult to define precisely. Roughly, it refers to the ability of one individual to respond sensitively and imaginatively to another's feelings. Kerr (38) and Dymond (18) have attempted with indifferent success to develop measures of this ability. Cronbach and Gleser (15) and Bender and Hastorf (5) have discussed the methodology employed in studying and measuring empathic ability. The former authors in particular are highly critical of the research so far available. Yet few who have studied the interview doubt that this ability, whatever it is and however it may operate, seems to be important as an ingredient in successful interviewing.

The most popular method for measuring empathy at present calls for one individual to try to predict how another would answer a series of questions. The assumption is that, if the first individual really has some feeling for the personality make-up of the other, he should be able to predict this person's behavior in certain situations, specifically in response to test items. Bender and Hastorf (5), on the basis of some interesting research, have pointed up several areas of caution. Students were asked to complete three tests for another person, chosen by them on the basis of acquaintance. The three tests were the Minnesota Social Behavior scale, the A-S Reaction, and the Study of Motives. Then, the individuals themselves took the tests, and the predicted scores were correlated with the obtained or real scores. The correlations were quite interesting. They were: .38 for the Minnesota Social Behavior Scale; .47 for the A-S Reaction; .07 for the Study of Motives. The last test in particular showed considerable influence of projection, for the correlation between each individual's own score and the score of the test he "took" for someone else was .71. In addition, there was a suggestion that an individual may be empathic in one situation or on one dimension, not so on another.

They also followed up the matter of projection and empathy. They took two discrepancy scores for each pair of subjects: one was the difference between the rater's prediction and the subject's actual score (empathy); the other was the difference between the rater's prediction and his own score (projection). They found that more of their subjects were projectors than empathizers!

Lindgren and Robinson (39) studied Dymond's measures of insight and empathy. They found that scholastic aptitude, as measured by the ACE, correlated only .14 with empathy, .02 with insight. They then obtained the profiles, on the Minnesota Multiphasic Personality Inventory (MMPI), of individuals classified by the Dymond test as good and poor empathizers. MMPI scales on which there were T-score differences of at least five points were: F*, K, Pd*, Pa*, Pt*, and Ma*. (The abbreviations stand for the following: F—fakes bad or misunderstands; K—suppressor; Pd—psychopathic deviate; Pa—paranoia; Pt—psychasthenia; Ma—hypomania) Asterisks indicate that the *poor* empathizers had higher or more deviant scores. The authors conclude that their poor empathy group tended to appear less well adjusted on the MMPI. If this is in fact true, it brings the results of Back's study, cited above, into focus, for rigidity is generally considered to be a sign of personality disorganization or difficulty. It must be kept in mind, however, that there is serious question about the validity of the method used to measure empathy in which one person is asked to answer questions for another. The Bender and Hastorf work raises the question as to whether what is being measured is not largely projection. It is, of course, quite possible that empathy is a kind of controlled projection. Murray's concept of recipathy, which refers to a diagnostic technique based on how the therapist is made to feel in the interview, suggests that this may possibly be so.

Astin (1) conducted an investigation in which she compared the projective method for measuring empathy with the situational method. She asked her judges, graduate students in psychology, to predict the Allport-Vernon-Lindzey profiles of undergraduate students after reading case histories and listening to a recorded interview. In the situational test, she had the same judges respond to recorded client statements. Their responses were then rated for empathy by a group of experienced psychologists. The reliability of both methods was good, but the correlation between the approaches was zero. Internal evidence suggested the superiority of the situational test approach.

We will next discuss the more general matter of inter-personal perceptions and the control of behavior. It is these perceptions, correct or incorrect, which mediate the interaction, which determine so largely its quality and its outcomes. Mellinger (49), for instance, reported that a communicator who does not completely trust the person to whom he is telling something tends to conceal his own true attitudes. The result of this is that the recipient of the information does not perceive accurately the material communicated. Such lack of trust or confidence on the part of either the interviewer or the interviewee could have substantial effects on the relationship. If both persons felt such mistrust and if each inadvertently misled the other, it is unlikely that a successful interview could take place.

Mind set or focus of attention

Several studies have been concerned with the effects of certain kinds of interaction on perceptions and attitudes. Lundy (40) reported such a study. In it, subjects were introduced to each other in pairs and then were asked to complete Allport-Vernon tests on each other. Two weeks later, they met again and were assigned a topic for discussion. One group of subjects was instructed to concentrate on themselves (A); the other group was instructed to concentrate on the other person (B). Afterward, the pairs again filled out the Allport-

Vernon on each other. On retest, group A's answers showed that they were more like themselves, less like the persons they were supposed to be describing; the reverse was true for the members of group B. This suggests that inaccuracy in judging another's personality is a function of not really paying attention to him, of concentrating rather on one's own feelings and reactions. The difference might be related to the study discussed earlier (Bender and Hastorf, *op. cit.*) in suggesting that group A was actually projecting while group B was reacting on the basis of empathy. Lundy's results are partly substantiated by Bieri's (10). Bieri had subjects fill out a Rosenzweig Picture-Frustration Test under two conditions: (1) for themselves and (2) for a stranger. There followed two opportunities for social interaction after which there was a retest. On the second administration, "others" were described as more like selves than they were the first time.

The Lundy study suggests that the mind set induced or held, that is the focus of attention of the observer, is crucial. Not only is the focus of attention apparently susceptible to manipulation but the quality of the reaction may be altered by this set. Gollin and Rosenberg (27), for instance, were concerned with the conceptualizations formed by subjects under various conditions. They found that subjects who do *not* form hierarchic concepts (taking into account molar features, integrating the entire stimulus situation) are markedly more extreme in their judgments (of social distance in this study). Similarly, Kelley (37) conducted a study in which students were told that they would have a "substitute" instructor. A description of him was given, and he was later rated by the students after he had taught the class. Those who had heard a "warm" or favorable description of him beforehand tended to rate him more favorably than did those who had heard a "cold" description. Thus it may be seen that judgments of the same behavior may vary depending on the expectations or the sets of the observers.

Personality Factors

Weiss and Fine (70) have also reported similar results but have related their results to measures of the personalities of the observers. They first administered three measures, the Thematic Apperception Test (TAT), Picture—Frustration Test (PF) and an attitude scale, to a group before reading an "article" advocating harsh treatment of delinquents. They found that the article was most effective in those subjects whose extrapunitive tendencies as measured by the PF were high, in those subjects whose TAT scores indicated high aggressive needs, and most effective in those cases where both of these scores were high. In other words, people with strong needs to express hostility responded quite markedly to suggestions that delinquents be treated harshly.

A related issue has to do with the needs of the individual to have a structured situation, one in which all of the issues are readily apparent and are surrounded by rules for dealing with them. Some people are thrown into a panic, experience extreme anxiety, whenever the situation is too flexible, too fluid. Since so many interviews are of this nature, it is important to understand the need for structure, the intolerance of ambiguity. Wispé and Lloyd (73) studied a group of life insurance salesmen. They interviewed these men and rated them on relevant variables. They also had available their sales records. It was found that the men who were both better salesmen and also most secure as individuals tended to prefer less structured relationships. It is doubtful whether these results can be applied directly to the interview, but they are certainly suggestive and may explain why some people can and others cannot deal comfortably and effectively with the fluid, unstructured interview situation.

This problem has been further explored by Smock (62). He was specifically concerned with the problem of the tolerance of ambiguity. He presented a group with an ambiguous stimulus under both stress and security conditions. Stress seemed to produce earlier, more rapid responses; it also resulted in getting the correct response late. In other words, under stress conditions, individuals began responding earlier but got the correct response later than under security conditions. On the other hand, under security conditions, practice effects were noted. The subjects were able to profit from experience more readily.

These studies are too scattered in their coverage, occasionally too tenuous in their methods, but they are suggestive of the importance of flexibility and objectivity as well as sensitivity. They suggest that experience alone is not enough, that the determining factor in experience in interpersonal relations is the attitude, the set, the over-all personality of the observer. If he is capable of getting outside himself, of really concentrating on the other person and if he can deal with the highly ambiguous situation which is the interview, then perhaps he can learn to understand the person being observed. If, on the other hand, he refers all stimuli to himself, is entirely or largely egocentric, and if stress or ambiguity turn him inward, then no amount of experience, no opportunity to observe will enable him to become a sensitive interviewer.

The generalizations just described are really hypotheses. They must remain such until further evidence is brought to bear upon them, but they do seem to lead in to the core of the problem of the interview. If they are tenable, they suggest quite clearly that the crucial issues are bound up in the personality characteristics of the participants. More, they suggest that the personality of the interviewer is at or near the heart of the problem of the interview.

One study which illustrates this problem especially well was done by Cohen (14). Having tested his subjects with the Blacky Test, he paired them in terms of (a) defenses, (b) psychosexual adjustment, and (c) intensity of disturbance. His results are summarized below:

1. When the interaction between pairs involves a task arousing a common psychosexual problem, two projectors (that is, subjects preferring projection as a defense) tend to see the situation as bad;

2. This situation is not as marked when one of the partners employs a defense system other than projection;

3. When both partners are high in disturbance intensity, there is more negative interaction;

4. The similarity of defense employed per se makes little or no difference;

5. The kind of defense system employed was associated with the interaction; that is, those employing avoidance reported the most positive interaction; those using reaction formation were next; those employing repression were next; those utilizing projection reported the worst interaction.

6. There was also a hierarchy associated with the psychosexual dimension involved; that is, sibling rivalry created the most problems; castration anxiety was the next worst, oral sadism, expulsiveness, and oedipal intensity were, in that order, less and less troublesome.

Since the Blacky Test gets at largely unconscious material, the Cohen study indicates that the quality of the interview relationship may be markedly affected by such reactions, unknown both to the interviewer and the interviewee. These results could explain in part why some interviewers get along well with some interviewees but badly with others who, on the surface, are quite similar. It also suggests that interviewers should be selected on the basis of and trained in the light of their personality characteristics. This is not to say that every interviewer must necessarily undergo intensive psychoanalytic therapy, although there are some who would advocate this. It is to say, however, that the selection and training of interviewers must take these possibilities into account. Precisely how this is to be done rests on the collection of further and more definitive data.

Several studies have been concerned with the interviewer. Hyman (33) has discussed some of the issues as they appear in public opinion interviewing. A number of studies have dealt with what might be called "deeper" aspects of the interviewer's personality and behavior. Strupp (65) (66), for instance, has compared analyzed and non-analyzed interviewers in a variety of situations. His sample included psychiatrists, psychologists, and social workers. He asked all of his subjects to respond to suicide threats, schizoid reactions, and transference situations. The statements which they made were analyzed by the Bales technique. He found some significant differences between analyzed and non-analyzed interviewers. Those who had been analyzed tended to be more active; in the transference situation, they preferred interpretation, silence, and structuring; they reacted to schizoid productions with less silence and more activity.

A related study by Sheehan (61) is concerned with much the same problem. Having given Rorschachs to both patients and therapists before and after therapy, he found, on the retest, that the patients' Rorschachs had become more like their therapists' *even where the therapists' contained pathological signs.*

The analyzed-non-analyzed dimension is somewhat different from the one explored by Fiedler (19) (20) (21). He was concerned with the relationship established by therapists of different theoretical persuasions. The subjects for these studies included Rogerian, Rankian, and Freudian therapists. He found that experienced therapists of all three schools were more like each other than they were like the neophytes of their own schools. Strupp (65) has also compared Rogerian and psychoanalytically oriented therapists. He found significant differences at first, the Rogerians preferred reflection and used little else while the analytically oriented therapists employed a variety of techniques. With experience, the Rogerians studied by Strupp employed fewer reflective responses and more evaluative and analytic ones. Analyzed Rogerians showed fewer passive responses and more activity. Strupp concludes by saying, "Exclusive reliance on one technique appears to be a correlate of inexperience." (p. 7) In this, he is in agreement with Fiedler. In another study concerned with the experience dimension, Strupp (66) again reported that there were differences between experienced and inexperienced therapists.

If, as suggested by the above studies, there are differences in the behavior, particularly in the verbal behavior, of the therapists, it would be of interest to explore this matter further. Goldman-Eisler (24) (25) (26) has studied the problem extensively. She compared ten patients, five of whom were considered talkative, five quiet, in their reactions to three psychiatrists. The psychiatrists tended to be quite consistent in their behavior. The patients were also quite consistent although their speech behavior showed some effects in response to the psychiatrist. The psychiatrist with the highest activity level and speech tempo was found to have the greatest effect on the speech activity of the patients.

Benton, Hartman, and Sarason (6) studied a similar problem but extended it somewhat. They were concerned with speech behavior and anxiety levels. They compared the responses to the TAT of individuals high and low on the Taylor Anxiety Scale. Employing a number of measures of speech activity (such as verb-adjective ratio, number of adjectives per 100 words, total number of words, etc.), they found that the subjects with high anxiety scores were highest on *all* measures. This points up an interesting and puzzling contradiction. In the Strupp studies cited above, it was reported that the analyzed therapists were more active (and presumably more verbal) in the interview. Benton, Hartman, and Sarason, however, seem to suggest that high verbal output is associated with high anxiety.

A study by Bandura (4) is related to this apparent contradiction. He had forty-two therapists rate each other and themselves on several variables. The discrepancy between self-rating and others' ratings was taken as an index of insight. He found that there was a significant negative relationship between anxiety level and (rated) therapeutic competence. He also reported that there was no relationship between insight and competence and none between self-rated anxiety and competence. Insight is apparently not enough. Bandura's study spins even tighter the web of contradictions, because it suggests that insight, which is so often the goal of psychoanalysis, is not sufficient for effective interviewing. Left unresolved is the question about the anxiety level, on the one hand, and high speech activity and competence on the other.

Parloff (53) had two experienced therapists work alternately with the same two groups. The therapists' personalities were rated by twelve subordinates. He found that the therapists who established better social relationships also established better therapeutic relationships. Further, Parloff reported that the therapist who perceived his patients as close to his own ego ideal established the better relationships. This finding is related to the conclusion reached by Sarbin and Jones (58) who found that role-taking ability and social adjustment were positively correlated. This in turn recalls Fiedler's suggestion (21) that successful therapy is largely a matter of being able to establish good social relationships.

Fiedler and Senior (22), employing the Q-sort technique with fifteen patient-therapists pairs, reported a number of interesting results. Better therapists are superior in predicting patients' self-sorts; better therapists tend to be *less* satisfied; the better the therapist, the more the patient is likely to see him as an ideal; conversely, the more satisfied the therapist is, the less likely is the patient to see him as an ego ideal; the more the therapist resembles the patient's *ideal* sort, the less he likes or empathizes with the patient; the more the patient resembles the therapist's ideal sort, the more the therapist is likely to see him as maladjusted; the more satisfied the patient, the less likely he is to feel that the therapist is well adjusted; more self-satisfied patients tend to resemble closely the therapist's ideal self-sort; the more the therapist, in the patient's eyes, resembles the patient's ideal self, the less likely is the patient to feel that the therapist is maladjusted like himself.

The implications of this study are many. It is extremely fruitful of ideas about the interview situation, at least the therapeutic interview. Rephrasing and reclustering the above results, we may make several generalizations. Good therapists tend to be empathic (able to predict patients' self-sorts) and dissatisfied with (critical of) their work. Better therapists are seen as resembling the patients' ideal selves, but if the therapist sees himself as actually resembling the patients' ideal selves, he finds it hard to empathize, to like the patient. In other words, it is all right for the patient to see him as an ideal, but if the therapist sees himself as actually like this ideal, it creates a barrier. If the patient resembles the therapist's ideal self, he is likely to be seen as maladjusted; yet, more satisfied patients tend to resemble the therapist's ideal self-sort. We could go on, for the permutations—and contradictions—are numerous. The above will have to suffice, however, to indicate the difficulties involved in trying to conceptualize the interaction process in the interview. Although we shall, later in this chapter, attempt to set up certain general principles, certain working hypotheses, the contradictions contained in some of the studies above must be kept in mind, for they keep all serious students of the interview from becoming dogmatic, from laying down any ironclad rules about the conduct of the interview.

Exploring further the area of personality as it relates to social (i.e., interview) behavior, Berger (8) reported a correlation of .70 between self-acceptance and acceptance of others. Yet there is, as indicated by the Fiedler and Senior study (*op. cit.*), a question as to what is meant by self. We must ask, which self are we talking about? Borgatta (11), for instance, factor analyzed a large number of variables and found three which showed up on all eight factors: actual social performance, role playing, and projected (conversational) performance. This study, along with the one by Fiedler and Senior, must serve to caution us against too ready generalization about the relationships obtaining in the interview.

The level of interaction is exemplified by two studies done at Indiana University. Greenspoon (28) made a study in which he simply said, "Uh-huh," every time the subject spoke a noun. Subjects had been instructed to speak single words in fairly rapid order. Greenspoon's verbalization, of which the subjects were unaware, resulted in an increase in the number of nouns spoken. In other words, even so apparently innocuous a response as giving a gutteral affirmative, something which most of us do without thinking, had marked effects on the verbal behavior of the other person involved. Verplanck (69) extended the Greenspoon study. He divided fifteen minute interviews into three parts. In the first part, he simply noted the opinions of the subject. In the second part, he reinforced these by methods like Greenspoon's, found that the opinions were strengthened. In the last part, he extinguished these same opinions simply by not responding to them in any way. With agreement, subjects increased their rates of speaking; with non-agreement, their rates decreased. Remembering the extremely simple reinforcement employed —saying "Uh-huh"—and recalling that most of us use this either without thinking or as a filler for silent spaces in the interview, we are led to consider what are the effects of such other unintentional, unplanned behavior as gestures or postures. It also suggests that the participants in the interview are reacting to one another without necessarily being aware of all of the stimuli to which they are responding.

We have not attempted to present all of the relevant studies. Even though significant research on many of these problems has just begun, the literature is already too extensive to be dealt with here. Instead, we have tried to present some of the more stimulating studies whose results either suggest new ways of thinking about the interview relationship or call into question some fondly held notions.

It should be easier a decade from now to see the proverbial forest through the ubiquitous trees. At the present writing, only one generalization seems reasonably safe and sound: the interviewer, to be successful, must (a) be fairly well put together himself; (b) capable of reacting empathically to the other person, unhampered by his own predispositions; and (c) widely read and extremely thoughtful about personality and its dynamics. Beyond this, however, there are certain other ideas, certain currents, which seem worth considering.

The verbal interchange which is the major aspect of the interview is a reflection of both the conscious intent and the unconscious processes of the participants. Because the interviewee's insights and understandings must be dealt with as they are encountered, it behooves us to prepare interviewers as carefully as possible to be aware of their own dynamics, to learn (insofar as it can be taught) to respond to the interviewee as he is and not through the dark glass of personal projections, and to be sensitive to both what the interviewee says and what lies behind what he says.

The interaction in the interview is partly conscious and intentional. It is also significantly unconscious and unintentional. Yet this aspect of the interaction very likely carries much of the weight in informing the participants about the other's feelings, attitudes, and ideas. Again, this points clearly to a need to train interviewers to be sensitive to themselves, to their liminal and subliminal stimulus value, and to the reduced cues they give out and react to.

The interview seems to be not something highly special, something encapsulated and different from all other interpersonal relationships, but rather simply another example, another instance of these. Therefore, the ability of the interviewer to deal effectively with social situations of other kinds may yield cues about his ability to handle the interview. There is a growing consensus of opinion that the interview depends on the ability to establish sound social relationships of warmth and trust.

REFERENCES

1. Astin, H., *A comparative study of the situational and predictive approaches to the measurement of empathy.* Unpublished Ph.D. dissertation, University of Maryland, 1957.
2. Back, K. V., The einstellung test and performance in factual interviewing. *J. abnorm. soc. Psychol.,* 1956, 52, 28-32.
3. Bales, R., *Interaction Process Analysis.* Cambridge: Addison-Wesley, 1950.
4. Bandura, A., Psychotherapist's anxiety level, self-insight, and psychotherapeutic competence. *J. abnorm. soc. Psychol.,* 1956, 52, 333-337.
5. Bender, I. and Hastorf, A., On measuring generalized empathic ability (social sensitivity). *J. abnorm. soc. Psychol.,* 1953, 48, 503-506.
6. Benton, A., Hartman, C., and Sarason, I., Some relations between speech behavior and anxiety level. *J. abnorm. soc. Psychol.,* 1955, 51, 295-297.
7. Berdie, R., Psychological processes in the interview. *J. soc. Psychol.,* 1943, 18, 3-31.
8. Berger, E., The relationship between expressed acceptance of self and expressed acceptance of others. *J. abnorm. soc. Psychol.,* 1952, 47, 778-782.
9. Berenson, B., *Level of counselor experience and its relation to selected aspects of counselor-client interaction.* Unpublished M.A. dissertation, University of Maryland, 1957.
10. Bieri, J., Changes in interpersonal perceptions following social interaction. *J. abnorm. soc. Psychol.,* 1953, 48, 61-66.
11. Borgatta, E., Analysis of social interaction: actual, role-playing, and projective. *J. abnorm. soc. Psychol.,* 1955, 51, 394-405.
12. Bugental, J., Explicit analyses of topical concurrences in diagnostic interviewing. *J. clin. Psychol.,* 1953, 9, 3-6.
13. Cofer, C., An analysis of the concept of "clinical intuition." In Kelly, G. (Ed.) *New Methods in Applied Psychology.* College Park: University of Maryland Press, 1947.

14. COHEN, A., Experimental effects of ego-defense preference on inter-personal relations. *J. abnorm. soc. Psychol.*, 1956, 52, 19-27.
15. CRONBACH, L. and GLESER, G., *Psychological Tests and Personnel Decisions.* Urbana: University of Illinois Press, 1957.
16. DANSKIN, D. and ROBINSON, F., Differences in "degree of lead" among experienced counselors. *J. couns. Psychol.*, 1954, 1, 78-83.
17. DIPBOYE, W., Analysis of counselor style by discussion unit. *J. couns. Psychol.*, 1954, 1, 21-26.
18. DYMOND, R., A preliminary investigation of the relation of insight and empathy. *J. consult. Psychol.*, 1948, 12, 228-233.
19. FIEDLER, F., Comparison of therapeutic relationships in psycho-analytic, non-directive, and Adlerian therapeutic relationship. *J. consult. Psychol.*, 1950, 14, 436-455.
20. FIEDLER, F., Factor analysis of psychoanalytic, non-directive, and Adlerian therapeutic relationship. *J. consult. Psychol.*, 1951, 15, 32-38.
21. FIEDLER, F., The concept of the ideal therapeutic relationship. *J. consult. Psychol.*, 1950, 14, 239-245.
22. FIEDLER, F. and SENIOR, K., An exploratory study of unconscious feeling reactions in fifteen patient-therapist pairs. *J. abnorm. soc. Psychol.*, 1952, 47, 446-453.
23. FREUD, S., *A General Introduction to Psychoanalysis.* New York: Garden City, 1943.
24. GOLDMAN-EISLER, F., Individual differences between interviewers and their effects on the interviewees' conversational behavior. *J. ment. Sci.*, 1952, 98, 660-671.
25. GOLDMAN-EISLER, F., A study of individual differences and of inter-action in the behaviour of some aspects of language in interviews. *J. ment. Sci.*, 1954, 100, 177-197.
26. GOLDMAN-EISLER, F., Speech-breathing activity and content in psy-chiatric interviews. *Brit. J. Med. Psych.*, 1956, 29, 35-48.
27. GOLLIN, E. and ROSENBERG, S., Concept formation and impressions of personality. *J. abnorm. soc. Psychol.*, 1956, 52, 39-42.
28. GREENSPOON, J., The effect of verbal and mechanical stimuli on verbal behavior. Cited as personal communication in Dollard, J. and Miller, N. *Personality and Psychotherapy*, Chapter 3.
29. GUSTAD, J. and TUMA, A., The effects of different methods of test introduction and interpretation on client learning in the interview. *J. coun. Psychol.*, 1957, 4, 313-317.
30. HALL, E., The Freudian error as an aid in determining attitudes. *Int. J. Opin. Attit. Res.*, 1949, 3, 113-122.
31. HEYNS, R. and LIPPITT, R., Systematic observational techniques. In

Lindzey, G. (Ed.) *Handbook of Social Psychology.* Cambridge: Addison-Wesley, 1954.

32. HOYT, D., *Differential outcomes of counseling with college men.* Unpublished Ph.D. dissertation, University of Minnesota, 1954.
33. HYMAN, H. *et. al., Interviewing in Social Research.* Chicago: University of Chicago Press, 1954.
34. JESNESS, C., *Effects of counseling on clients self perception.* Unpublished Ph.D. dissertation, University of Minnesota, 1954.
35. JONES, M. (Ed.), *Current Theory and Research in Motivation.* Lincoln: University of Nebraska Press, 1953.
36. JONES, M. (Ed.), *Nebraska Symposium on Motivation.* Lincoln: University of Nebraska Press, 1954, 1955, 1956, 1957.
37. KELLEY, H., The warm-cold variable in first impressions of persons. *J. Personality.,* 1949, 18, 431-439.
38. KERR, W. and SPEROFF, B., *The Empathy Test.* Manual of instructions. Chicago: Psychometric Affiliates, 1955.
39. LINDGREN, H. and ROBINSON, J., An evaluation of Dymond's test on insight and empathy. *J. consult. Psychol.,* 1953, 17, 172-176.
40. LUNDY, R., Assimilative projection and accuracy of prediction in inter-personal perceptions. *J. abnorm. soc. Psychol.,* 1956, 52, 33-38.
41. MAGOON, T., *General and specific outcomes of counseling with college men.* Unpublished Ph.D. dissertation, University of Minnesota, 1954.
42. MALMO, R., SHAGASS, C., and DAVIS, F., Symptom specificity and bodily reactions during psychiatric interviews. *Psychosom. Med.,* 1950, 12, 362-376.
43. MALMO, R., SMITH, A. and KOHLMEYER, W., Motor manifestations of conflict in interview: a case study. *J. abnorm. soc. Psychol.,* 1956, 52, 268-271.
44. MASLOW, A., *Motivation and Personality.* New York: Harper, 1954.
45. MATARAZZO, J., SASLOW, G. and GUZE, S., Stability of interaction patterns during interviews: a replication. *J. consult. Psychol.,* 1956, 20, 267-274.
46. MATARAZZO, J., SASLOW, G., MATARAZZO, R., and PHILLIPS, J., Stability versus modifiability of personality patterns as manifested during a standardized interview. Paper read before Amer. Ortho-Psychiatric Association, New York City, 1956.
47. MATARAZZO, J., SASLOW, G., and MATARAZZO, R., The interaction chronograph as an instrument for objective measurement of interaction patterns during interviews. *J. Psychol.,* 1956, 41, 347-367.
48. MCCLELLAND, D., ATKINSON, J., CLARK, R., and LOWELL, E., *The Achievement Motive.* New York: Appleton-Century-Crofts, 1953.

49. MELLINGER, G., Interpersonal trust as a factor in communication. *J. abnorm. soc. Psychol.,* 1956, 52, 304-309.

50. MOWRER, O., Anxiety theory as a basis for distinguishing between counseling and psychotherapy. In Berdie, R. (Ed.) *Concepts and Programs of Counseling.* Minneapolis: University of Minnesota Press, 1951.

51. MOWRER, O., *Learning Theory and Personality Dynamics.* New York: Ronald, 1950.

52. MUTHARD, J., The relative effectiveness of larger units used in interview analysis. *J. consult. Psychol.,* 1953, 17, 184-188.

53. PARLOFF, M., Some factors affecting the quality of therapeutic relationships. *J. abnorm. soc. Psychol.,* 1956, 52, 5-10.

54. PORTER, E., The development and evaluation of a measure of counseling interview procedures: I. The development. *Educ. psych. Measmt.,* 1943, 3, 105-126.

55. PORTER, E., The development and evaluation of a measure of counseling interview procedure: II. The evaluation. *Educ. psych. Measmt.,* 1943, 3, 215-238.

56. ROBINSON, F., The dynamics of communication in counseling. *J. couns. Psychol.,* 1955, 2, 163-169.

57. ROGERS, C., *Client Centered Therapy.* New York: Houghton-Mifflin, 1951.

58. SARBIN, T. and JONES, D., An experimental analysis of role behavior. *J. abnorm. soc. Psychol.,* 1955, 51, 236-241.

59. SASLOW, G., MATARAZZO, J., and GUZE, S., The stability of interaction chronograph patterns in psychiatric interviews. *J. consult. Psychol.,* 1955, 19, 417-430.

60. SHAGASS, C. and MALMO, R., Psychodynamic themes and localized muscular tension during psychotherapy. *Psychosom. Med.,* 1954, 16, 295-313.

61. SHEEHAN, J., Rorschach changes during psychotherapy in relation to the personality of the therapist. *Amer. Psychol.,* 1953, 8, 434-435.

62. SMOCK, C., Influence of psychological stress on "intolerance of ambiguity." *J. abnorm. soc. Psychol.,* 1955, 50, 177-182.

63. STEPHENSON, W., *The Study of Behavior.* Chicago: University of Chicago Press, 1953.

64. STRUPP, H., An objective comparison of Rogerian and psychoanalytic techniques, *J. consult. Psychol.,* 1955, 19, 1-7.

65. STRUPP, H., Psychotherapeutic technique, professional affiliation, and experience level. *J. consult. Psychol.,* 1955, 19, 97-102.

66. STRUPP, H., The effect of the psychotherapist's personal analysis upon his techniques. *J. consult. Psychol.,* 1955, 19, 197-204.

67. SULLIVAN, H., *The Psychiatric Interview,* New York: Norton, 1954.
68. TUMA, A. and GUSTAD, J., The effects of client and counselor personality characteristics on client learning in counseling. *J. couns. Psychol.,* 1957, 4, 136-143.
69. VERPLANCK, W., The control of the content of conversation: reinforcement of statements of opinion. *J. abnorm. soc. Psychol.,* 1955, 51, 668-676.
70. WEISS, W. and FINE, B., Opinion changes as a function of some intrapersonal attributes of the communicatees. *J. abnorm. soc. Psychol.,* 1955, 51, 246-253.
71. WILLIAMSON, E. and BORDIN, E., The evaluation of vocational and educational counseling: a critique of the methodology of experiments. *Educ. psychol. Measmt.,* 1941, 1, 5-24.
72. WILLIAMSON, E. and BORDIN E., Evaluating counseling by means of a control group experiment. *School and Society,* 1940, 52, 434-440.
73. WISPÉ, L. and LLOYD, K., Some situational and psychological determinants of the desire for structured interpersonal relations. *J. abnorm. soc. Psychol.,* 1955, 51, 57-60.

3. Some Guideposts to the Interview

Aptitude plus training for interviewing

The desire to be an interviewer is not enough. A successful interviewer must possess the essential qualifications and characteristics, and he must undergo training. No one is certain about the personal attributes which enable one person to become a skilled interviewer while another, who studies as hard or harder and perhaps knows as much or more about personality, never really attains mastery of the interview. Yet everyone who has had anything to do with the selection and particularly with the training of interviewers knows that there are some individuals who seem to "catch on" quickly while there are others, the majority, who never do, try as they may. However, all can improve with training.

It is unlikely that good interviewers are born so. Whatever it is that is involved in this aptitude, this capacity to acquire skill, seems to develop throughout the individual's formative years so that by late adolescence and early adulthood some individuals can be taught to be excellent interviewers while others must struggle simply to achieve working competence. Some of the factors involved were described in the previous chapter where the personality of the interviewer was shown to be a critical element. Research is needed in order to isolate those traits of personality which are associated with the ability to acquire excellence as an interviewer. At present people differ widely in their capacity to profit from such training.

It is not known how many people could, with training, become either skilled or even competent interviewers. Many people who do interviewing have never had the benefit of training and supervision. They simply started interviewing. With experience, some became good, some failed and gave up, and others failed but continued. Proficiency in interviewing, at least minimal proficiency, is probably within the reach of a substantial proportion of the adult population. If, as has been suggested, interviewing skill rests substantially on developing skills in human relations, then the number who could learn to be reasonably good interviewers may be quite large.

The ability to interview rests not on any single trait, but on a vast complex of them. Habits, skills, techniques, and attitudes are all involved. Competence in interviewing is acquired only after careful and diligent study, prolonged practice (preferably under supervision), and a good bit of trial and error; for interviewing is not an exact science; it is an art. Like many other arts, however, it can and must draw on science in several of its aspects.

There is always a place for individual initiative, for imaginative innovations, and for new combinations of old approaches. The skilled interviewer cannot be bound by a set of rules. Likewise, there is no set of rules which can guarantee to the novice that his interviewing will be successful. There are, however, some accepted, general guideposts which may help the beginner to avoid mistakes, learn how to conserve his efforts, and establish effective working relationships with interviewees; to accomplish, in short, what he sets out to do.

The nature, or at least the emphasis, of the interview will vary somewhat with its purpose, with the use to which it is put. Fundamentally, there are three uses of the interview; fact finding, informing, and altering opinions, feelings, and behavior. In other words, one interviews another to find out something from him, to tell him something, or to effect some changes in him. It is quite possible— even usual—for there to be more than one purpose in any given interview, but ordinarily one purpose will predominate. If the main purpose of the interview is to obtain information, it is frequently necessary to inform the interviewee about the purpose of the questions, to create positive, cooperative attitudes in him so that he will willingly and accurately reveal the information sought. When attitude or feeling change is the major goal, it is usually necessary to ascertain certain facts about the individual or the situation and to inform him of the roles he and the interviewer will play, of the ground rules to be followed, and of the goals to be sought. The point is that, while all three purposes may be of concern, one usually is the major concern or focus of the interview.

Our present concern is with the fact-finding interview. In some ways, this is the easiest. It is also the kind which is most often used. We deal with the other kinds of interviews in later chapters; additional discussion will also be devoted later to special uses of the fact-finding interview.

Although it may appear to be a relatively simple process, the fact-finding interview presents numerous difficult problems. Principal among these is the fact that the interview is an interaction between two persons. Some of the issues involved in this kind of interaction have been dealt with in the preceding chapter. With respect to the fact-finding interview, it must be recognized that the interviewee may be unwilling to reveal information in his possession. He may distort, either intentionally or otherwise, the information he does present. He may, finally, not remember the facts of concern. Here, we face problems of the dynamics of personality, especially repression, which were discussed earlier. On his side, the interviewer may have certain biases or prejudices, may not really want the truth, or may not recognize it if it is given him. He may be unable to recognize the full import or implications of facts told to him, as when he in interviewing someone whose technical knowledge or socio-cultural background creates language barriers. He may have certain personality characteristics which prevent him from dealing calmly with certain areas of discourse. These and many others represent difficulties which the interviewer must recognize and deal with if he is to be successful.

Some general principles and techniques apply to virtually all kinds of interviewing. These will necessarily be altered somewhat by the major objectives of the interview. We summarize these in a series of statements, admonitions, and precautions, first those dealing with the interview generally and then those dealing with fact-finding interviews. Additional discussion of special aspects of various kinds of interviews will be presented in later chapters.

GENERAL SUGGESTIONS

PREPARING FOR THE INTERVIEW

1. *Decide what is to be accomplished.* The interviewee will ordinarily come to the interview with his own expectations, his own objectives. However, it is important that the interviewer should know

clearly what it is that he wishes and feels able to accomplish. It may be desirable, especially for beginners, to write down these objectives, spell out possible problems and possible modifications.

2. *Know the interviewee.* If at all possible, as it usually is, learn as much as you can about the person to be interviewed. Consult school and plant records, test profiles, cumulative records, social service reports, others with whom he has dealt, friends, and employers. Precisely what needs to be known will vary with the situation, but the general principle, knowing the interviewee, holds in all.

3. *Make appointments.* By making an appointment in advance, time is saved in seeing the interviewee promptly and in shortening preliminary explanations. You also know that the hour is satisfactory to him.

4. *Provide for privacy.* The critical problem in an interview is the establishment of sound working relationships. With two people, the interviewer and the interviewee, this is difficult enough; with more, it becomes much more difficult. Where the interview is to deal with matters which are confidential or embarrassing, having others present or within earshot may result in the interviewee's withholding facts. Self-consciousness is usually heightened. Group interviewing is widely used, but its methods and results are qualitatively different from interviewing done with only the interviewer and interviewee present.

5. *Practice taking the interviewee's point of view.* In planning the interview, put yourself in the other person's place. Try to imagine what he will think of you, how he will react to you, to your approach, to the whole interview situation. Continue this throughout the interview, however many sessions are involved. This ability to see problems as another sees them, to feel toward them as he does, is known as *empathy.* Some individuals seem to have it; others do not. A substantial amount of empathic ability is essential for successful interviewing. Within limits, it can be acquired or at least increased.

6. *Know your own personality.* Few people realize the extent to which everyone is committed in advance to certain opinions, convictions, attitudes, and preconceptions. Everyone has some prejudices, whether he realizes this or not; everyone carries with him certain stereotypes, preconceived notions about individuals and groups. There is probably no such thing as a truly open mind, one totally unencumbered by preconceptions, totally receptive to new ideas.

This does not mean, however, that such preconceptions cannot be reduced in number and effect, or that they should not be faced and either eliminated or discounted. People preparing for careers as psychoanalysts are required to undergo analysis themselves; many psychiatrists, psychologists, social workers, and others do likewise. It has not been conclusively demonstrated that such analysis is either essential or actually achieves all that it is supposed to, but some sort of study of self is highly desirable in order to bring to light not only prejudices but, more important, areas of tension, conflict, and defenses which could interfere with successful interviewing.

INTERVIEWING

7. *Establish a relationship of confidence.* The ideal relationship for the interview is one of mutual confidence. Rogers (7) in particular has called attention to the notion that this confidence must not be just one-sided, that it must rest on genuine and deeply felt respect on the part of each for the other person. To try to pretend, to put on a front of cordiality and friendship is extremely unwise, for the interviewer will almost certainly convey, by subtle means, his real attitudes and feelings. It is the interviewer's responsibility to take the lead in establishing the relationship of mutual confidence. Techniques as such are probably less important than a proper attitude. If, as Fiedler has suggested (see previous chapter) the interview relationship is a special case of good interpersonal relationships, then it may follow that people who are capable of forming good social relationships should also be better able to establish good relationships in the interview situation.

8. *Establish pleasant associations.* This may not always be possible, may not always be desirable, but it is a good, general rule. In public opinion interviewing, it may not be possible to take the time to establish pleasant relationships. In some kinds of counseling and therapeutic interviewing it may be better to let the interviewee express angry, hurt feelings which are unpleasant. However, in general, the interview should be seen as a relaxed, pleasant affair.

9. *Help the interviewee to feel at ease and ready to talk.* One of the best ways to do this is to be at ease yourself. If you are, it will probably be evident; if you are not, it will almost certainly be apparent to the interviewee. Allow the interviewee a little time to get accustomed to you and to the situation. Remember that being inter-

viewed is a new experience for many people. Help the interviewee to feel that his ideas are important, that you are interested in hearing them, in discussing them with him as an equal.

Begin with topics for discussion which are easy to talk about and non-threatening. This interchange can be like the conversation of people when they are waiting for a bus, at the ball game, or discussing the weather. However, do not prolong this warm-up too long, since the interviewee knows as well as you that these are not the things he came to discuss. Delaying too long in getting down to business may suggest to him that you are reluctant to deal with the topic.

Once you get onto the main topics, do all that you can to get the interviewee to talk freely with as little prodding from you as possible. This will probably require that you give him some idea of the area, and of ways of looking at it. Avoid, however, prejudicing or coloring his remarks by what you say; especially, do not in any way indicate that there are certain things you want to hear, others which you do not want to hear. It is essential that he feel free to express his own ideas, unhampered by your ideas, your values and preconceptions.

Do not appear to dominate the interview, nor have even the suggestion of a patronizing attitude. Ask some questions which will enable the interviewee to take pride in his knowledge. Take the attitude that the interviewee sincerely wants to realize the joint purpose of the interview. This implies a warm, permissive atmosphere that is most important in all interviews.

10. *Listen.* This is one of the most important single techniques, perhaps the one which creates the most trouble. Some people find it hard to sit and listen. They have opinions and feel a strong urge to express them. Remember that the goal of the interview is to get to know the interviewee. When you talk, he gets to know you, but you learn little about him.

Listening is a skill which must be learned and practiced. Not only must you listen to what he actually says, but you must, as Reik describes it (6), listen with the "third ear." That is, you must try to see behind the words to the hidden feelings, the half-expressed or unexpressed ideas and reactions. You must look, in other words, for the "hidden agendum" which underlies all such interviews.

11. *Allow time enough.* The amount of time allotted will vary with the type and purpose of the interview. In counseling and psycho-

therapy of various sorts, the fifty minute interview—allowing the interviewer ten minutes afterwards to write his notes and collect his thoughts—is virtually standard. One advantage of this is that these limits are things to which the interviewee must learn to adjust, a reality demand upon him. In other instances, especially where there will only be one interview, it may be desirable or necessary to let the interview go on longer, perhaps to two hours or more. Remember, however, that fatigue may become an important factor. It is therefore generally best, if there is much to be covered, to schedule another interview if this is possible. If not, you have no alternative but to continue until at least an intermediate closure is attained.

At the other end, interviewers are often under pressure to cut their interviews short. This is sometimes necessary but should be resisted. The interviewee requires some time to get accustomed to the situation, to learn to feel at ease, to get ready to talk. Talking usually brings up new materials and ideas which have to be explored if the picture is to be completed. The perfunctory, hasty interview in which the interviewee feels the pressure of time is perhaps worse than no interview at all. For example, exit interviews are potentially good sources of information about employee grievances. An employee who is leaving may be willing to be quite frank. If he is made to feel, however, that the company, as represented by the interviewer, is not basically interested enough in what he has to say to allow him time to say it, he may not only withhold information but may leave the company feeling quite unfriendly toward it.

12. *Do not dawdle.* While pushing ahead too rapidly can damage the relationship, holding back, dawdling is an imposition on the interviewee. Often, especially in public opinion or market research interviewing, the interviewee is a busy person who is taking time out from his work to take part in the interview. He will rightfully resent having his time wasted. In other kinds of interviewing, the interviewer who dawdles runs the risk of letting the interview lose direction, or fall apart. If the interviewee becomes confused, if he cannot see any goal, his anxieties may be aroused unduly to the detriment of the process. An interview is a social interaction but not a social visit.

13. *Keep control of the interview.* One way in which interviewees may seek to avoid painful or disturbing topics is to go off on extended tangents. Sometimes, it is necessary to let them do so, but ordinarily, their own feelings will be improved if you gently but firmly bring

them back to the topic. The reason for this is that they may feel that, if they are allowed to wander endlessly, you really do not know what you are doing, are yourself either in doubt or afraid of the problems at issue.

14. *At the close of the interview, watch for additional information or new leads in the casual remarks of the interviewee.* Be alert to catch the chance expressions which may drop after the interview is ostensibly ended. When the tension has been released and he is off guard, revealing things are sometimes let slip, things which he may have wanted to say earlier but which seemed to him irrelevant or too trivial for mention. Remember that the interview is not yet closed even when you have asked all your questions and held out your hand to say good-by.

INTERVIEWS FOR FACT FINDING

DECIDING WHEN TO USE THE INTERVIEW

15. *Use interviews discriminatingly.* Before depending on interviews, determine whether more reliable procedures or sources of information are available. When answers to questions can be obtained from records or documents, or by observation of situations, these answers are more reliable, and usually are obtainable more economically than by interviewing.

16. *Make sure your problem is significant.* Successful interviews center about worth-while problems that can be made reasonably significant to the persons interviewed. If your problem does not clearly stand the test of close relevance to the interest of the interviewee, consider it carefully before deciding to use the interview method in investigating it. People do not like to give time to answering questions which lead them to think of the interviewer as a snooper, nonproducer, academic person, or unpractical busybody.

17. *Use interviews to gain access to objective data.* The interview is often useful in obtaining a clue to more dependable sources of information, such as statistical data, historical records, and personal documents.

18. *Use interviews to obtain opportunity for observation.* The interview affords an excellent situation in which to observe the appearance, behavior, and symptoms of habit patterns of the interviewee, as in the counseling or the employment interview.

19. *Use interviews to determine facts which vary with particular persons in particular circumstances.* The interview procedure has been successfully employed to obtain data on actual wages received by each worker, and the amount each paid for rent and other living expenses. Census data are of this sort.

20. *Use interviews to determine opinions, attitudes, or trends of belief.* The interview is most feasible for fact finding where the answer wanted is the trend of opinion or the percentage of persons holding each kind of attitude or belief. Interviews have accurately disclosed the opinion held by workers with reference to a labor policy, such as an employment guarantee. They have revealed with reasonable reliability the proportional division of opinion among workers in regard to the justification of a strike, attitudes toward arbitration, and judgments of the fairness of police officials toward strikers. With reference to such questions, objective data are most difficult to obtain. The interview is here the most feasible procedure for fact finding.

21. *Avoid use of the interview for compiling data of uncertain value.* The interview will not serve in questions of fact which cannot be answered by one person or group of persons better than by anyone else. A composite of mere opinions or of erroneous answers in matters of fact is not necessarily more reliable than the answer of a single interviewee or the guess of the investigator himself.

22. *Avoid use of the interview for getting general information or common facts.* The interview is least useful and reliable in securing facts which apparently might be known by all persons exposed to them but which these persons have no special reason or incentive for knowing or remembering. For instance, oral statements made in an interview should be used with special caution in determining dates, the number or percentage of individuals engaged in an activity, or other such numerical facts. They should never be relied upon for such purposes if there are written documents, minutes, records, or other objective sources of information.

PREPARING FOR THE FACT-FINDING INTERVIEW

23. *Formulate your problem.* Having determined that your problem is such that interviews are feasible aids in its solution, formulate it with the interview procedure in mind. Ask yourself just what information you want to obtain. This does not mean that you must

shape definite questions to be asked in a certain way. It means that you should have the general questions clearly in mind in organized form so that when answers are given, or an opportunity comes to lead the conversation toward an answer, you will recognize it immediately and classify it under the proper heading on your outline.

24. *Prepare a schedule or list of questions.* Even though you may not hold your interview to certain predetermined questions asked in a stereotyped form, it helps you to think of the right kind of questions and topics for informal conversation if you work out an ideal list of questions before you begin. These may be of two sorts: first, the general questions which you hope to be able to answer after the interview—that is, an outline in question form of the information you want to secure; second, a list of specific questions which appear feasible and conceivably might be asked, either directly or indirectly and incidentally.

25. *Know your field.* Reading about the subject of investigation helps in formulating important questions for inquiry. To know what has been written on the topic also makes it easier to discuss it intelligently.

26. *Secure letters of recommendation and authority.* When interviewing workers in a factory, it is well to have evidence of permission from the manager or other official. Before interviewing members of a union on any questions of significance to the organization, see the union leaders. It is only fair to the officials in authority, to the members, and to the organization as a whole. A letter or card from a responsilble person secures a hearing and shortens the process of explaining that you have a legitimate reason for seeking the information.

27. *Choose your interviewees with care.* Persons should be selected for interview who are in a position to have the information wanted. Experts on one subject will often talk freely on other subjects about which they know very little, but volubility is no test of accuracy, nor is renown a guarantee of knowledge in all fields. Many people often obligingly attempt to give information even when they do not have it to give. Nearly everyone has received incorrect street directions from a person who hesitated to admit ignorance, preferring to hazard an inaccurate statement. Guard against hearsay evidence. Care, therefore, should be exercised in selection of the persons to be interviewed, for here is one of the greatest possible sources of error.

28. *Secure enough interviewees.* Up to certain limits, the reliability of information obtained increases with the number of persons interviewed. The smaller the number of interviewees, the greater the increase of reliability with the addition of others. The number of interviews needed depends upon the variability of the information obtained. The more the interviewees differ in their statements, the more persons it is necessary to interview. In general, for fact finding in one particular situation, locality, or set of circumstances, regarding a problem of industrial relations where views differ widely, not less than thirty interviews will be needed to indicate clearly the trend of attitudes; while between eighty and a hundred are needed to give the true picture with a high degree of reliability. An estimate of the number needed for reliability may help the investigator to decide whether or not interviews are feasible for fact finding on a particular question.

29. *Sample the entire group.* For a true picture of knowledge, attitudes, or opinions of a large group, all subdivisions or factions should be proportionately represented among those interviewed. Unless such fair representation or sampling is definitely provided for, various circumstances or unrecognized factors may cause interviewers to get a distorted picture.

INTERVIEWING FOR FACTS

30. *Do not ask questions directly until you think the interviewee is ready to give the desired information and to give it accurately.* The ideal interview is one in which you have found a person who is able to give the information wanted, and have led him to have the same interest in giving this information that you have in obtaining it. Then you can have his co-operation in getting precise answers to definite, direct questions. But even then, direct questions may inhibit his free and full narrative account of the information he has to give. Statements he makes spontaneously are generally far more accurate. In many cases, it is better to encourage him to talk, no matter how irrelevantly. Much of the desired information will then emerge without resort to direct personal questions which sometimes cause resentment or misunderstanding. You can guide the conversation by relevant statements of your own. Moreover, if you find it necessary to ask questions to bring out certain points, introduce them in such a way that he will understand them as expressive of interest in what he is saying.

31. *Let the interviewee tell his story; then help him to supplement*

it. Although the free narrative report is less complete, it is more accurate than the constrained inventory. After the interviewee has had a chance to give the main story unbiased by questions, you may safely, by questioning, help him to complete the parts omitted.

32. *Ask questions at first that are not likely to cause refusal to answer or to provoke any form of negativism.* Begin with questions that the interviewee can and is willing to answer. Cooperation is ensured partly by establishing the habit and attitude of answering. Risk questions that may arouse resentment only as a last resort after related questions have failed to encourage him to volunteer the information.

33. *Ask only one question at a time.* Do not confuse the interviewee by asking two or three different questions at once. Even though he should be able to think of each and its answer separately, he may not be able to organize his statements so that you can segregate the answers.

34. *Keep on the subject.* People cannot ordinarily talk straight to the point. When necessary, ask a question or make a suggestion which will lead back to the general subject of the interview. Formulate in advance some questions or remarks which can be used for this purpose. Several restatements of the main topic of inquiry, in different phraseology, are useful to this end.

35. *Avoid the rôle of teacher.* Most persons do not appreciate having an outsider, often a novice in their special field, tell them how to do their work or run their business. Let the interviewee be the teacher. Do not yourself attempt to harangue or moralize for his benefit but let him criticize or moralize all he wants to. The only occasion for differing with him is to get him to state his opinions or release his feelings.

36. *Be straightforward and frank rather than shrewd or clever.* Do not try to adopt astute methods. A person whose statements are worth securing is seldom deceived by cleverness; the interviewer only invites deceit and gets fooled himself. When you undertake to be subtle and shrewd, you make it difficult to assume the best in the person you are questioning, and thus to secure the best. Then, too, if you try to deceive or trick the interviewee, it becomes more difficult for you to discriminate between truth and deviations from it, and to remain loyal to accuracy in your report.

37. *Take pains to phrase your questions so that they are easily understood.* Wrong or inaccurate information is sometimes given

merely because the question is not interpreted as you expected it to be. Therefore scrutinize your wording critically and try to avoid ambiguity.

38. *Avoid implying the answer to your own question.* The interviewer who wants a straightforward, unbiased answer scrupulously avoids asking leading questions, since a leading question assumes a fact and by its very form suggests an answer which may or may not be the true one. For instance, the question, "You would like to earn more by piece rate than by day rate?" not only implies that the workman would prefer the piece rate, but also suggests that he would earn more by it, neither of these assumptions being necessarily true. If he wants to please you, he will simply accede to the suggestion. If he is not interested in giving you a correct answer, he may still acquiesce in order to end the interview as soon as possible.

The definite article "the," as in the question, "Did you see the broken belt?" strongly implies that there was a broken belt, whereas the indefinite article "a," as in the question, "Did you see a broken belt?" does not definitely imply that there was any broken belt to be seen. The latter type of question, then, is less likely to suggest an inaccurate answer.

39. *Help the interviewee to realize his responsibility for the facts.* This may be done by conveying the impression that the facts will be checked. A better method, however, is to work toward the establishment of a sound interview relationship in which the interviewee comes to share the same goals as the interviewer. When this is accomplished, he will exert himself to the utmost to provide accurate information.

40. *Avoid impertinence.* If you find it necessary to ask questions which might cause a man to be reserved and give evasive replies, lead him to talk about something more or less related to it and then interject your question as an interested listener, with no emphasis on its special significance. If any of your necessary questions prove, on experience, to be frequently resented, you should think out a way of getting the information indirectly—a woman's age, for instance. To avoid being refused an answer, it may be necessary to ask a series of questions in which the interviewee can see some point relevant to the conversation, instead of asking a single question which to him means pure impertinence.

41. *Keep the important questions in mind until adequate information is obtained on each one; but as soon as a question is definitely answered, dismiss it in order that you may concentrate on the next*

one. By putting out of mind a question already answered, you gain two advantages. You are better able to think about other questions and direct the conversation toward an answer; and you avoid talking too much on one subject, which may wear out the interest of the interviewee.

42. *Get the full meaning of each statement.* Scrutinize each answer carefully for suggestions or leads to further questions.

43. *Give the interviewee opportunity to qualify his answers.* He should have opportunity to tell the real truth and the whole truth. Sometimes this cannot be done in one categorical answer. Often it is not only unfair but also conducive to unreliability to frame questions so that a "yes" or "no," or some circumscribed answer or definite classification, is called for. When such an answer is implied, encourage the interviewee to qualify or explain his answer. For instance, when certain strikers were asked whether they were in favor of arbitration, they would say "yes" or "no," but when encouraged to say more they would add, "We favor arbitration as a general principle, and we wanted it at first, but we are no longer willing to let them arbitrate. It's too late."

44. *Check answers whenever possible.* Probably the simplest way to check your understanding of the answer is to repeat it in your own words and ask whether that is what is meant. If the answer can be stated in relation to other facts, giving it a new or added significance, that should be done. That is, after the interviewee has given his answer, let him know how you understand it.

45. *Record all data at once, or at the very earliest opportunity.* If the interview was not electrically recorded, reduce all facts to writing as soon as possible. Restatement or recall at a later time, unassisted by written notes, is full of omissions and of incorrect additions. Forgetting is exceedingly rapid during the first few minutes. Inaccuracies enter early. Careful interviewers who have checked the accuracy and completeness of their own subsequent recall of facts have been appalled by the losses and the errors. Reports rapidly diminish in value with lapse of time between the interview and the writing. If you cannot arrange to use a blank form or notebook during the interview, note down the facts immediately afterwards.

46. *Practice separating facts from inferences.* This is a difficult but indispensable procedure in all investigations. In preparing your account of an interview, distinguish carefully and report separately (a)

observed facts, (b) statements made by the interviewee, and (c) inferences from the observed facts or from the interviewee's statements.

47. *Check percentages and fractions of quantities by translating them at once into numbers.* When the interviewee's answers contain statements of percentages, restate them to him in terms of gross numbers. Many persons have vague ideas of quantities when expressed in the form of percentages or fractions of the whole. There is a tendency to exaggerate in terms of fractions or percentages. To illustrate: if a worker states that three-quarters of the employees in his mill are members of the union, and you know that twelve hundred work there you should then ask whether nine hundred of the millworkers are members. The interviewee is quite likely to answer that there may not be quite as many as that, but possibly seven hundred.

48. *Be on the alert for constant errors.* There is, for example, a common tendency to underestimate long distances and long periods of time, and a tendency to overestimate short distances and short periods of time. If the long period is filled partly with uninteresting or monotonous events, there is a tendency for the uneventful lapses of time to drop out of mind and the novel or important events to come together in memory so that they seem to be nearer in sequence than they really were, foreshortening the estimated period of elapsed time. All such constant tendencies to error should be watched for and discounted or corrected.

49. *Do not assume that agreement among interviewees' statements assures their truth.* Agreement may be due to the same constant error arising from preconceptions or general mental set.

50. *Get all the facts.* It is the responsibility of the interviewer to get reliable information and to get all of it that is needed. He must take the initiative in exhausting the resources of data that can be brought to light. Some of these come easily in the form of specific statements of fact, but many are merely clues or signs which must be carefully interpreted and skillfully verified.

51. *Secure a confirmatory written summary after an important interview.* A written report agreed upon by both interviewer and interviewee, after time has been allowed for digestion of facts brought out in the oral interview, takes advantage of afterthoughts and provides for corrections, additions, and clarification of misunderstandings.

52. *Check results statistically against reliable criteria.* Only accur-

ate results justify the use of interviews. Subjective judgments and the methods of arriving at them should be tested by objective data whenever these are available. This is especially true in regard to employment interviews in which judgments based on interview should be checked against past performance and also against later success of the persons selected. Such comparisons and tests reveal how skillfully you have followed the essential principles of interviewing which underlie the foregoing suggestions.

This chapter, frankly elementary and didactic, has viewed the subject broadly from the point of view of the interviewer who wants to appropriate as rapidly as possible a distillation of the experience of those who have engaged extensively in interviewing for various purposes, and have thought how these ends are best accomplished.

The study of typical interviews as recorded in the literature likewise helps in appraising the interview method as a whole, and in selecting particular items of technique for emphasis and practice. It also prevents one from falling into routine, and encourages the elastic approach needed for adaptation to changing conditions and to different personalities.

To learn how to interview well, actual practice is indispensable. But this is a slow and wasteful process unless the learner thinks constructively about what he is doing and systematizes his experience. Thus it pays, after an interview, to review it critically, to note its excellent features so that they may be readily used again as occasion requires, and to select weak spots to be corrected. This can be done much more effectively if the interview was electrically recorded. In the early stages of learning, the interviewer should get much help from reviewing his recorded interview under the supervision of an experienced interviewer.

In the review of an interview, some of the questions to be considered are: Was time wasted in preliminaries? If so, plan your next approach with care, and get down to business more promptly. Did the interview get out of hand? Think of ways in which to hold the next one to the line without loss of necessary spontaneity. Was your interviewee uncertain as to just what some of your questions meant, or did they seem to strike him as trivial or pedantic? Then concentrate on improving the phraseology of your questions so that they will be clearly expressed within the range of his familiar vocabulary. Be specific in your self-criticism, and pick out for further practice and improvement one point at a time on which to concentrate. Before each new interview it is well to think out some one way in which to improve on earlier performance.

Detailed comparison of your own more successful and less successful interviews discloses the particular features most needing attention. Comparison of your procedures with those of others engaged in similar work also serves to indicate the direction of an increasingly effective method.

Success in interviewing is attained by discovering, mastering, and integrating the many specific habits, skills, and techniques required in order to formulate clearly the purpose of the particular interview, to plan its course intelligently, and to carry through its successive steps, from first approach to final write-up, expeditiously and well.

In succeeding chapters the reader will readily see how far the principles and concrete suggestions here compiled need qualification and extension, as the process of interviewing is adapted to meet different situations such as those arising in the clinic, the courtroom, the employment office, the school, the social agency, or the commercial survey.

References

1. ANON., *Interviews, Interviewers, and Interviewing in Social Case Work*. New York: Family Welfare Association of America, 1931.
2. ACHILLES, P., Methods of conducting and recording vocational interviews. *Occupations*, 1931, 9, 303-308.
3. ANDRUS, E., Counselor's interview to assist in the choice of subjects and occupations. *Occupations*, 1934, 12, 78-84.
4. BOGARDUS, E., *The New Social Research*. Los Angeles: J. R. Miller, 1926.
5. ROETHLISBERGER, F. and DICKSON, W., *Management and the Worker*. Cambridge: Harvard University Press, 1939.
6. REIK, T., *Listening With the Third Ear*. New York: Farrar, Straus, 1949.
7. ROGERS, C., *Client Centered Therapy*. New York: Houghton-Mifflin, 1951.
8. STRANG, R., *Counseling Techniques*. New York: Harper, 1949.
9. WARREN, C., *News Reporting*. New York: Harper, 1939.
10. WEBB, E. and MORGAN, J., *Strategy in Handling People*. New York: Garden City, 1930.
11. YOUNG, P., *Interviewing in Social Work*. New York: McGraw-Hill, 1935.

4. Selection and Training of Interviewers

WE HAVE already implied the need to consider the problems of the selection and training of interviewers. If there are indeed skills, techniques, and areas of knowledge which the skilled interviewer must possess, these must be learned in a training program designed to teach them. If the characteristics of the interviewer are important in determining ability to profit from training, a selection program must take these into account. Since not everyone can learn to become a competent interviewer and since training facilities are already overcrowded, only those who can profit optimally from training should be admitted. Because so much is at stake in terms of human welfare, only those persons who can show that they are competent should be employed as interviewers.

Both selection and training need constant evaluation if they are to improve, if they are to keep up with changing requirements and needs. Evaluation of these processes, however, requires a criterion against which they can be measured. Before turning to selection and training as such, therefore, we will discuss briefly some of the problems encountered in finding, developing, and using a criterion.

The Criterion

A criterion is an independent measure of the event or process being studied. If we are building a test of mechanical ability, we need some other, independent measure of skill as a mechanic against which to measure the scores obtained on the test. If the test scores do not correlate with competency at the task, we must face the possibility that the test is not in fact measuring what it is supposed to.

A good criterion must possess certain characteristics of its own. Thorndike (15), Toops (16), Brogden and Taylor (3), and Cureton (4) have all written very useful and penetrating discussions about the criterion which are recommended to those wishing to pursue this important topic further. Thorndike has distinguished among three kinds of criteria: immediate, intermediate, and ultimate.

The ultimate criterion is the one of most interest to the investigator, but it is also the one which is typically the least available. For instance, the ultimate criterion for a psychotherapeutic interviewer is his ability to help patients overcome their disturbing conflicts. This, however, presents many difficult problems. We must decide what is meant by a cure, and this is by no means easy. We must also decide which patients are cured or to what extent they are cured. We must decide on time limits. That is, must the patient remain cured for a month, six months, a year, or longer? There are more problems involved in this ultimate criterion, but these suggest some of the difficulties.

The intermediate criterion, on the other hand, is somewhat more available but may be proportionately less crucial. For example, the intermediate criterion for a therapeutic interviewer might be his ability to complete a course of training such as the Ph.D. program in psychology. This has some reality in that more and more licensing and certification laws and ethical codes require this level of training for practice. However, it must be admitted that not everyone who completes a Ph.D. program in clinical or counseling psychology is equally good at therapeutic interviewing. To this extent, the intermediate criterion is deficient. On the other hand, obtaining reliable information about this intermediate criterion is easier than in the case of the ultimate criterion.

Finally, we might use what Thorndike has called the immediate criterion. This, for our purposes, might be the completion of a single course in the theory and practice of clinical interviewing. This information is relatively easy to get, and a case for its relevance might be made. That is, unless a student can complete this course, he cannot complete the Ph.D. program in clinical psychology. Unless he can complete this program, he is unlikely to be permitted to practice. However, just as all those who complete the Ph.D. program are not equal in skill in therapeutic interviewing, so those who complete the single course are not equal in ultimate interviewing skill.

These three kinds of criteria point to one of the characteristics which a good criterion must have: *relevance*. To be completely useful, a criterion must be made up of the same elements, combined in the same proportions, as the behavior in which we are ultimately interested. The immediate criterion is thus probably the least relevant while the ultimate criterion is ordinarily the most relevant. This is not automatically so, but it is more often true than not. However, the difficulties in obtaining accurate and complete information about the ultimate criterion often push investigators back to the intermediate or even to the immediate criterion. Research and evaluation done with these can be quite useful, but the results of such studies must always be viewed with an eye to possible distortions and deficiencies.

The other general characteristic which a criterion must possess is *reliability*. By reliability is meant freedom from error. Because error, as discussed in connection with reliability, is random, this means that its presence reduces our ability to predict since we cannot predict a random occurrence. It is like conducting a study of the effects of nutrition on height where height measures are taken with a rubber yardstick.

There are two ways to obtain a criterion: find one which already exists or develop one. Most often, investigators search for criteria which already exist. School grade averages, sales records, production records, recidivism rates, turnover data, and accident rates are examples of these. This information has already been collected in most cases although usually for other than research purposes. Nevertheless, such indices have been widely used as criteria.

Developing a criterion is more difficult, but the trouble is often rewarded. Rating systems of many kinds are probably the commonest criteria thus far developed. Some of these have been good, others not worth much. Ratings require great care if they are to avoid a number of serious deficiencies. Properly done, however, ratings can be good as criteria.

Performance tests are another example of developed criteria. Most commonly, the investigator sets up a miniature of the work situation. For example, the airlines have spent a great deal of money in building airplane cockpits complete with all of the instruments found in real airplanes. These simulators are so constructed that the instruments can be made to duplicate a wide variety of situations which the pilot might encounter in the air. The simulator can be used to evaluate ground training programs and to see whether students have in fact learned how to apply their lessons without at the same time risking lives and costly aircraft in actual flight.

Still another kind of developed criterion is the psychometric. Here, tests are employed. These tests are often the final evaluation on the one hand and a selection device on the other. Tests used for Certified Public Accountants, Certified Life Underwriters, lawyers applying for bar admission, psychologists seeking diplomas awarded by the American Board of Examiners in Professional Psychology, and physicians seeking board status, are examples. These tests provide criterion information relevant to the training program and to the selection for that program; they may also serve as selection devices for further progress in the occupation. They are typically intermediate criteria but are nevertheless useful.

Developing a criterion is a difficult task but one which is being attacked more and more frequently. It is first necessary to describe the activity involved. The commonest technique in use is the job analysis. Here, a thorough study of a sample of employed workers is made. This sample may be made up of individuals who are presumably successful or it may include individuals who are merely employed on the job.

All activities of the job must be carefully recorded. This is time consuming but essential. It may be necessary or desirable to go beyond the actual job duties to such things as interpersonal relationships. For instance, a man might be technically quite competent to perform the actual duties of the job but be personally unacceptable to his co-workers. This unacceptability might not affect his actual performance but might lead to his leaving for another position. If turnover is a matter of concern, information about social relationships must be gathered.

Once the job has been analyzed, the information collected still needs to be studied further. A job may be made up of many different activities but these might, on analysis, be found to cluster into a smaller number of job elements. Identifying these elements will enable the investigator to simplify his task considerably.

A variant on the usual techniques of job analysis is the Critical Incidents method developed by Flanagan (7). Flanagan's assumption, in developing this approach, was that the identification of crucial behavior items—very fine or very poor performances—would give a better picture of a job than would a more conventional job analysis which covered the entire range from good to bad. In the Critical Incidents approach, competent observers such as foremen, supervisors, commanding officers, and others in a position to know and observe the job, are asked to tell about incidents they have seen in which men did either extremely well or extremely poorly. These incidents are then collected and analyzed for clusters.

However it is done, whether by selecting one of several already available criteria or by developing a criterion to fit the special case, it is essential that such an independent measure be available against which to evaluate both training and selection programs. Without such a criterion, there is no way of resolving divergent points of view based on purely theoretical considerations, hunches, or biases.

Selection

The basic goal in selection is prediction. If one is able to predict future performance with reasonable accuracy, then it is possible to choose those whose predicted performances are good and to reject those whose predicted performances are poor. The problem of selection, therefore, is to find those measures of present status which will predict future status.

The prediction of performance in college has been widely studied and is a good example. Many colleges cannot or do not wish to accept all students who apply for admission. They wish, on the other hand, to accept only those who are capable of progressing satisfactorily toward completion of the program of study. In order to perform this selection, college officials must find those characteristics of high school seniors which will forecast their performances as college students.

This is accomplished by collecting information—including school records, test scores, biographical information, and teacher ratings— on all applicants. Nothing is done with this information until the criterion, typically grade point average for the freshman year, is available. The predictive information is then correlated with the criterion; commonly, these correlations are combined into a multiple correlation.

In theory, this is simple. In practice, it is often difficult. Consider the matter of selecting interviewers. Here, a criterion such as freshman year grades is meaningless. Interview training ordinarily begins much later, increasingly only at the graduate level. Although grades are available, there is a serious problem involved in a restricted range. As a college class progresses through the four-year program, the weaker students tend to drop out. This reduces the range of talent. Also, the range of grades among seniors is smaller than among freshmen. These restricted ranges tend, for reasons involved in the correlational technique, to lower the correlations and to make prediction harder.

Even more important, grades themselves are probably a less adequate measure of performance at the senior and graduate level than they are among beginning students. It is true, of course, that more and more training of interviewers is being done at the graduate level. This in turn means that course grades as indicators of progress toward degree requirements retain their importance for some time. It is also true that training in psychiatry, psychology, social work, law, and guidance is usually required at the graduate level before the individual is permitted to engage in interviewing in these fields. Therefore, the intermediate criterion of ability to complete such a training program is useful and, to some extent, critical.

However, there is still an urgent need for an ultimate criterion. Without such a criterion, improvements in training programs must be made in substantial and debilitating ignorance.

Perhaps the largest scale attempt to study the selection problem as it relates to the training of interviewers (specifically, clinical psychologists) is the one reported by Kelly and Fiske (9). A variety of techniques were applied. These varied from the standard psychometric devices measuring abilities, interests, and personality through interviews to situational tests and biographical data analyses. Unfortunately, the results were discouraging, and the study has been criticized for important flaws.

Perhaps the commonest selection device in use at the present is the preclinical training program. In psychology, this means that many departments make little or no differentiation among students during the first graduate year, preferring to wait until grade records are available so that a decision can be made about the likelihood of the student's being able to complete the degree requirements. In psychiatry, students are not admitted to residency programs until they have completed the requirements for the M.D.

This practice rests on a somewhat tenuous assumption, one which cannot be adequately tested in the absence of an ultimate criterion. The assumption is that training in so-called basic psychology (experimental, statistics, theoretical psychology etc.), in medical science, or in social work theory is an essential prerequisite for training as an interviewer. There are arguments both pro and con, and we cannot even summarize them here. To date, the professional associations concerned seem inclined to support this assumption.

This means, then, that the selection of many interviewers is a multistage process. Selection is initially concerned with the applicant's promise a medical student, a graduate student in psychology or guidance, a student in social work, or in personnel administration. Because these graduate and professional programs stress certain kinds of verbal-symbolic abilities, it is no wonder that a favorite selection device is the test of intellectual ability. The Miller Analogies Test is widely used. The Medical College Admission Test, which is largely a scholastic aptitude test, is required by most medical schools. Sometimes interviews are required; occasionally measures of vocational interest are obtained; less frequently, personality appraisals are sought and even studied. In the vast majority of cases, however, letters of recommendation, undergraduate grade records, and measures of intellectual ability are the bases for selection.

How well these variables predict the student's ability to learn to interview is difficult to say. The fact of the matter is that, unless he can complete a training program, his chances are slight of demonstrating his interviewing ability. It has been widely observed by those in charge of the training of counseling and clinical psychologists, psychiatrists, lawyers, and social workers that many students who are able to complete the formal training make poor interviewers while others, unable to pass courses in the basic sciences, show considerable promise in the interview situation.

Many training institutions are attempting, however, to add to the present selection programs measures designed to identify potentially able practitioners. This is often done during the first year in residence or even later. Frequently, it is accomplished by the use of try-outs. Here, the students are put into either actual interview or role-playing situations and carefully observed. On the basis of their performances in these try-outs, faculty members decide which students shall be permitted to continue in the training program for interviewers. In other words, early parts of the training program are used as entries in the selection system.

The use of the training as a major aspect of the selection program is an example of the situational test or job try-out procedure. This method has the obvious advantage that it most closely resembles the actual work situation and therefore may be presumed to share many or most of the same characteristics. In many cases, the training program passes through steady stages directly to the work situation.

The principal disadvantage of this approach to selection lies in the fact that its application often comes quite late in the process. For example, in psychiatry, the resident begins therapeutic interview work only after he has completed medical training, including the internship. In psychology, little is done until the second or often the third graduate year when the student is at or beyond the master's degree. Students judged unable to master interviewing (as well as other required) techniques often face serious difficulties in adjusting their occupational goals to the fact of rejection.

Another important disadvantage of the job try-out method of selection is its cost. Developing and maintaining facilities in which students can receive closely supervised experience in interviewing is quite expensive. Electrical recording equipment and one-way mirror observation rooms are expensive. Staff time required to perform enough observation for adequate reliability is even more expensive. The Education and Training Board of the American Psychological Association has recommended that practicum facilities (in which try-outs are often given) have as many fully qualified staff members as trainees. Although this seems to be a wise recommendation, it does indicate one source of cost in the try-out method of selection.

A possibility for the improvement of selection programs lies in the use of the try-out period as a criterion with which to develop better psychometric techniques. Much of the attention to date has been directed toward predicting ability to succeed in formal, classroom activities. This is important, particularly since those in charge of training insist that students complete this training satisfactorily before they become interviewers. Yet the try-out, or practicum period of training, has not yet been exploited as another intermediate criterion.

Because, as we indicated in Chapter Two, the personality of the interviewer, especially as it operates in interaction with a variety of clients, is so crucial to the outcome of the interview, the practicum period, as a criterion, provides investigators with an opportunity to develop selection procedures which take into account those personality characteristics of applicants which may be shown, by careful research, to be related to success as an interviewer.

Training

Suggestions and recommendations for the training of interviewers are available in great quantity. Unfortunately, few of these have been subjected to the kinds of evaluative analyses which could tell those concerned whether the methods are really good or not. Most stem from some theoretical position and due to this are presumed to have a kind of validity of their own.

Whether, in fact, different theoretical approaches actually make any difference in the behavior of the interviewers is a moot point. Fiedler's work (6) in particular suggests that people trained to a high level in a variety of "schools" actually became quite similar in their interview behavior as they acquire skill from experience.

An interesting, if not scientifically compelling, demonstration of this took place at a meeting of the American Personnel and Guidance Association in 1954. Here, three experienced counselors of quite different theoretical approaches to counseling all conducted interviews with the same "client." The client, actually a Ph.D. in clinical psychology who had developed a careful and elaborate case history to role play, was interviewed for about twenty minutes by each of the three psychologists. Admittedly, this is a brief time for differences to show up. What differences there were were contrary to expectations. The counselor who was trained in the client centered approach was the *only one* who discussed test scores with the client. The counselor trained in the Minnesota approach was, according to several observers, the most "non-directive" in his interview.

The absence of a really adequate criterion, a problem discussed in the sections immediately preceding, precludes really definitive research on the effects of different systematic approaches on the training of interviewers. Most persons concerned with training still feel that the theoretical approach does make a difference, but the evidence is so scattered, so fragmentary, and so conflicting that no sound generalizations seem possible at this time. Those who become seriously involved in interviewing as a career will certainly need to review the theoretical and research literature on this point.

Leaving considerations of theoretical position aside, there are two major aspects to the training of interviewers: didactic and practicum. In addition, it should be noted that interview training as such is rare. Most interviewers are trained as professional workers with a wide variety of duties. Clinical and counseling psychologists must acquire skills in psychometric procedures as well as interviewing; market research and public opinion pollers must learn techniques of sampling; psychiatrists must acquire many other therapeutic skills besides interviewing, such as chemotherapy; social workers have to master such essentials as knowledge of community resources; personnel interviewers frequently must know other aspects of the selection, training and, labor relations programs. Training in the techniques of the interview, therefore, constitutes but a part of the total training for these professions.

There is considerable disagreement over the question as to whether the didactic training should precede, follow, or be intermingled with the practicum work. There are arguments and precedents on all sides. Some experts are quite sure that training in the basic science, especially in psychology, in personality theory, in experimental methods, and in the theory of interviewing, must precede experience in interviewing as such. Those who hold this position insist that such training in the basic science is essential if the trainee is to be ready to observe what goes on in the interview, to interpret what he sees and hears properly, and to understand the professional setting and its requirements. Part of the training of a scientist is learning what to observe. Proponents of this point of view insist that, since the interview is such an extremely complex situation, trainees must have some preconceptions about what will happen and why before they can approach the interview intelligently. They also insist that interviewer behavior must be based on an understanding of the dynamics of behavior, an understanding which can and should be developed in advance of actual experience.

On the other hand, there are those who feel that experience in the interview situation should *precede* much or most theoretical training. This view rests on the belief that the student should first encounter the phenomenon, should be puzzled by it, and should therefore raise questions which then give his study of the basic science more meaning and direction. They feel that too many students approach the interview so full of preconceptions that they are in fact unable to observe clearly what actually happens. Rice's classical study is pertinent here in that it is known that people often see what they are looking for. Thus, an interviewer with a Freudian bent might "see" substantially different things in an interview than would one with a Rankian point of view. Each would be looking for different things and each would interpret what he saw differently. Those who believe that the student should first experience the phenomenon and then study the theoretical materials relevant to it insist that the naive observations of an intelligent, well-adjusted individual provide him with questions which will give his later study more meaning and direction. This approach, of course, means that the interviewees selected for the trainees to see must be chosen with great care. The trainee is in no position really to help them much, and safeguards must be set up to preclude the possibility of harm to the interviewee. These safeguards can ordinarily be provided however, if those in charge of the training arrange conditions carefully. Therefore, such risks with a trainee should not be taken as a crucial objection to the point of view.

The third alternative with respect to timing is to intermingle the two kinds of experiences. Here, practicum work and didactic study run along simultaneously. As the classroom training proceeds from general to specific, practicum experience proceeds from relatively simple exercises to the handling of increasingly difficult cases. An example of this approach, which is probably the one favored by most training personnel, may be seen in the practicum program in the Department of Psychology at the University of Maryland. This program covers, typically, four years and leads to specialization in counseling psychology at the Ph.D. level.

During the first and second years (at the end of which the student normally completes the master's degree), the emphasis is on the core curriculum which includes training in experimental psychology, personality and motivation, advanced statistical methods, history and systems of psychology, and related courses. Courses in testing, theory of counseling, abnormal psychology, diagnostic procedures, and the like begin in the first year as a minor part of the classroom program, gradually increase in proportion until they make up the bulk of the work during the last years.

Through the four years, students are required to be active in practicum training under close supervision of the faculty. In the first year, the practicum deals with such things as studies of the setting (personnel agencies, clinics, job placement facilities, and similar activities), with supervised practice in test administration and scoring, with discussions of professional roles and responsibilities, with role playing in interview situations, and, finally, with opportunities to conduct intake or initial interviews while being observed and recorded. In the second year, students normally carry one or two cases, carefully selected by senior staff members, and under close supervision (through direct observation and tape recording). They participate in group discussions which resemble staff conferences and which deal with cases under way. In the third and fourth years, they carry progressively more and more complex cases, still under supervision but with greater latitude for independent judgment. They also see a wider variety of cases including rehabilitation problems, hospitalized patients, and adults.

The assumption underlying this approach is that early exposure to the interview situation is desirable in that it makes the student aware of many problems and questions for which his graduate work is intended. At the same time, he is not given the opportunity, by being allowed to do a great deal of interviewing, to practice his mistakes.

It is recognized that this program does not fully qualify an individual as a counseling psychologist. Further training under supervision is necessary even after the Ph.D. requirements have been completed. He is, hopefully, prepared to engage in a wide variety of activities which will, over time, give him the background necessary to assume full responsibility for his work.

Techniques of Supervision

The supervision of trainees (and, for that matter, all interviewers who need or wish objective appraisal of their work) is often done with the aid of observation and electrical recording. The tape recorder is becoming almost universally used in training. First used extensively by Rogers and his students (see Chapter Two), it is now standard equipment in most training centers. Almost an answer to the poet Burns' plea for the power to see ourselves as others see us, the tape recorder provides a permanent record of an interview which the supervisor and the trainee can study at their leisure. It comes as a shock to most persons to hear how and what they said in the course of an interview. It is an enlightening experience and often an embarrassing one for even the most experienced interviewer.

When tape recording first came into widespread use, there were many discussions about the ethical problems involved. Some felt that its use violated the confidentiality of the interview. Many insisted that the recording be done without the client's knowledge, and myriad techniques were developed for concealing the microphone. Now, however, the consensus of opinion is that, if the recording is played and discussed only under proper circumstances (as in supervision conferences), it is no more a violation of confidence than test protocols and interview notes. Moreover, most interviewers now feel that secrecy is undesirable; they set the microphone in plain view, tell the client that the interview is being recorded, and indicate that, if he wishes, he can turn off the recorder by pressing a switch which is before him. This almost never happens, and very few clients have any objection if they know what is happening and why.

Another technique which is becoming increasingly popular is the use of direct observation. Sometimes, the supervisor sits in the interview office and observes the proceedings. This seems to create more uneasiness on the part of the interviewer, particularly if he is new at the business, than it does in the client. Consequently, one-way vision screens are now being used widely. These are partially silvered mirrors. From the interview room, they look like mirrors. An observer on the other side, however, can see through the screen quite well. A microphone to carry the conversation completes the apparatus.

As with recordings, there was an initial attempt to disguise the mirror and its use. Now, however, the interviewee is ordinarily informed that the interview is being observed through the screen. In a few minutes, both the interviewer and the interviewee usually forget about the screen and the microphone and proceed as if these were not present. Of course, such observations must be restricted to those who have legitimate reasons for making them. Supervisors and other trainees are the only ones who normally should be allowed in the observation room. Sometimes, in work with children, parents are permitted to observe so that they can see how the child reacts without the parent affecting his behavior.

Another technique which is gaining increased attention as a training device is the use of role playing. First associated principally with the work of Moreno (11), role playing technique has been studied and modified by many others. It involves, fundamentally, a kind of acting out of roles. For example, one person, perhaps the supervisor, might play the role of a client while the trainee could assume the interviewer's role. These roles might later be reversed. It is often quite impressive to observe the insights which people can develop from seeing both sides of the situation in this manner.

Sometimes, the roles are prepared with extensive directions. At other times, the process can be spontaneous and informal with, for example, the supervisor interrupting a case discussion and saying,

"Now, let's see what is involved here. You take the part of your client, and I will be the interviewer. We can start from where you said . . ."

Many wonder whether, in role playing, the individuals can become as emotionally involved as they are in the actual interview itself. There is no definitive answer to this, but most of those who have employed this technique feel that the roles acquire considerable reality to the participants. Role playing is also widely used in management and in training supervisors in methods for dealing with employees.

One major advantage of role playing is that a real client, with real and perhaps pressing problems, need not be involved. Thus, new trainees can get some valuable experience without running the risk of injuring a client or patient. It is also less expensive than either recording or the use of the one-way screen, because no equipment is required. There should be no tendency to think of role playing as a complete substitute for other training methods, but it is a valuable technique with possibilities which are just beginning to be discovered and exploited.

No matter what training aids are used, there is no substitute in interviewer training for an opportunity to take part in a great many interviews. Only with continued practice can the individual gain the poise he needs, the perspective, and the insight into his own reactions and relations with clients. As we mentioned earlier, providing this experience for trainees is time-consuming and expensive. A training facility, such as a counseling center, an outpatient clinic, or a personnel office, must be maintained and prepared to accept clients. There must be experienced interviewers on hand who are willing and able to devote a great deal of time to supervision. Just assigning the trainee a heavy load of cases is not enough. This often leads to his practicing his mistakes and to his developing a mistaken and misleading confidence in his abilities. The experience provided *must* be under close and regular supervision. The need for such supervision never, in the opinion of most leaders in the field, comes to an end. No matter how much one has learned about the interview, there always remains more to be learned.

One final issue in training for interviewing needs to be mentioned. There are some, notably the psychoanalysts, but also many psychiatrists, psychologists, and social workers, who believe, even insist, that the trainee should himself undergo a didactic analysis or therapeutic experience. To become a psychoanalyst, one must undergo psychoanalysis. The assumption underlying this point of view is that, to be a good psychoanalytic interviewer, one must be aware of one's own conflicts and problems, and must have as many of these as possible removed so that they will not later interfere with the interview relationship.

The other point of view is that, if selection takes into account the adjustment level of the trainee and a check of the personality reveals no serious problems, intensive therapy in the form of formal analysis does not seem necessary. The proponents of this view feel that the psychoanalysts may have made too much of the alleged advantages of having been analyzed, that most people who are intelligent enough and who possess the other necessary characteristics can become perfectly good interviewers, even in the therapeutic situation.

There is some evidence (see Chapter Two) that having been analyzed does have some effects on interview behavior. A great deal more research needs to be done employing a criterion of client improvement before a final answer can be reached. Some training centers in psychiatry, psychology, and social work strongly recommend that trainees undergo analysis, but few of them actually require it. Opinion is divided, and individuals will have to consider the issue on its merits and make their own decisions.

REFERENCES

1. AMERICAN PSYCHOLOGICAL ASSOCIATION COUNSELOR TRAINING COMMITTEE. Recommended standards for training counseling psychologists at the doctoral level: report of the conference on training of counseling psychologists, Northwestern University, August 29-30, 1951. *Amer. Psychol.*, 1952, 7, 175-181.

2. AMERICAN PSYCHOLOGICAL ASSOCIATION COMMITTEE ON TRAINING IN CLINICAL PSYCHOLOGY. Recommended graduate training program in clinical psychology. *Amer. Psychol.*, 1947, 2, 539-558.

3. BROGDEN, H. and TAYLOR, E., The theory and classification of criterion bias. *Educ. psychol. Measmt.*, 1950, 10, 159-186.

4. CURETON, E., Validity. In Lindquist, E. (Ed.) *Educational Measmt.*, Washington: American Council on Education, 1951.

5. CUTTS, N. (Ed.), *School Psychologists at Mid-Century*. Washington: American Psychological Association, 1955.

6. FIEDLER, F., Comparison of therapeutic relationships in psycho-

analytic, non-directive, and Adlerian therapy. *J. consult. Psychol.*, 1950, 14, 436-445.

7. FLANAGAN, J., Critical requirements. In Dennis, W. (Ed.) *Current Trends in Industrial Psychology.* Pittsburgh: University of Pittsburgh Press, 1949.

8. GUSTAD, J., *et al.*, Analysis of practices in counselor trainee selection. *J. couns. Psychol.*, 1954, 1, 174-179.

9. KELLY, E. and FISKE, D., *The Prediction of Performance in Clinical Psychology.* Ann Arbor: University of Michigan Press, 1951.

10. MAIER, N., SOLEM, A. and MAIER, A., *Supervisory and Executive Development.* New York: Wiley, 1957.

11. MORENO, J., *Who Shall Survive?* Beacon, N.Y.: Beacon House, 1934.

12. RAIMY, V. (Ed.), *Training in Clinical Psychology.* New York: Prentice-Hall, 1950.

13. SHARTLE, C., *Occupational Information.* (Second Edition) New York: Prentice-Hall, 1952.

14. STROTHER, C. (Ed.), *Psychology and Mental Health.* Washington: American Psychological Association, 1956.

15. THORNDIKE, R., *Personnel Selection.* New York: Wiley, 1949.

16. TOOPS, H., The criterion. *Educ. psychol. Measmt.*, 1944, 4, 271-297.

17. *Training of Psychological Counselors. Report of a conference held at Ann Arbor July 27 and 28, 1949 and January 6 and 7, 1950.* Ann Arbor: University of Michigan Press, 1950.

Part II

The Interview for Selection and Placement

5. Interviewing Applicants for Employment

THE employment interview exemplifies three distinct functions to which attention has already been drawn: securing information, giving information, and establishing a friendly relationship. The interview is, first of all, a means of obtaining from the applicant the facts about his experience and qualifications on which selection and placement are based. It serves, in the second place, to give him a picture of the position he is to fill and of the firm with which he will be connected, disadvantages and exactions as well as opportunities being fairly presented. The third function is to make a friend of the applicant, whether he is hired or not. The interviewer needs to keep all three of these functions in mind when reviewing his methods and techniques.

In actual practice these functions are often only imperfectly performed. An overworked interviewer may have too little time in which to get from the applicant the necessary information on which to base a sound judgment as to his suitability, to describe the work well enough to enable him to decide whether he really wants it, and to leave him with a well-founded impression of the interviewer's purpose to be genuinely helpful. Brandenburg (6) visited twenty-one employment offices, and then described the best and the worst interviews. One of them ended in two minutes and forty-five seconds, even though the applicant had come ten miles and had waited two and a half hours.

Time Limits on Interviews

Some of the practical considerations which place limits on the procedures to be followed in the employment interview are not always appreciated. Often the interview must be extremely brief—one to five minutes in length. Such are the interviews with applicants for specific jobs, whether they are routine office positions, unskilled labor, assembly work, machine tending, or employment in a skilled trade. Many selling positions also are filled after relatively short interviews. A longer time is usually taken in considering candidates for supervisory, executive, engineering, or other technical positions, or for trade or technical apprenticeships where ability to learn and to develop as well as to do the work immediately in hand has to be predicted. When applicant or employer is in doubt as to which of two or more opportunities best suits the candidate's abilities and interests, the interview is necessarily longer than when the only point to consider is his suitability for one particular opening.

During periods of expansion of the labor force, the employment interviewer has to work rapidly and to organize his interviewing with a view to maximum accomplishment within the time available. Such conditions prevailed, for example, in one company when the number of employees rose from about 12,400 to 20,400. To provide for this growth, and also to take care of labor turnover, which is necessarily high during periods of rapid expansion, about 22,000 employees were hired. These were selected from among 176,000 applicants. The number added to the payroll compared with the number who applied was in the ratio of 1 to 8.

There were ten interviewers. The most experienced and capable of these were entrusted with the preliminary interviewing which precedes the filling out of the application blank. These first interviews were necessarily very brief—one minute or less—especially when held during the hours from eight to eleven in the forenoon while the rows of benches in the waiting room of the employment office were particularly crowded. By means of this preliminary interview, roughly 40 per cent of the applicants were selected for further consideration, the others being weeded out because of obvious unsuitability or because there were at the time no openings in the special field of work in which they were interested.

Only after the preliminary interview was an application blank given to the candidate. At this time an appointment was made for further interview after the form calling for full personal history data had been filled out. During the stress of rush hours, many of these appointments had to be deferred until the afternoon.

The time devoted to the main interview varied greatly. The average was about five minutes, during which the information on the application form was reviewed and any significant omissions supplied. The interviewer also explained, when necessary, the nature of the job, the rate of pay, and other facts essential to a decision. After doubtful points had been cleared up, the interviewer noted his comments and conclusions on the application form. If the applicant was tentatively accepted, the next step in the case of many of the candidates was a visit to the office of the vocational service, for aptitude testing. To administer the employment tests required from fifteen to forty minutes, depending on the type of work for which the candidate was being considered.

With the results of these examinations before him the interviewer talked again with the candidate, sometimes raising a question as to the desirability of placement in a kind of work different from that originally intended.

After a definite decision regarding initial placement had been reached, the applicant was next taken to the medical department for physical examination. This examination occasionally led to rejection, or to conditional acceptance with the proviso that minor health defects be corrected or that employment be limited to specified types of work.

One other step in the procedure involved a visit of the applicant to the department where he was to work, in order to give him a chance to meet his prospective supervisor and to see the working conditions. While it was within the province of the supervisor to reject the candidate at this time if his impression was an unfavorable one, only in rare instances was this done.

In all cases of unfavorable report by either supervisor or medical department, the interviewer once more discussed the situation with the candidate to determine whether there might not be work elsewhere in the plant which he could do, or to suggest some other possible solution of the problem presented. If, as was most frequently the case, the interviewer's judgment was confirmed by the supervisor and the medical officer, the applicant was given his employee's manual, pass, and instructions to report for work.

If the reader imagines that the process here described is unique or far from representative of what transpires in well-manned employment departments, let him visit other large firms. This same year the employment office of a large department store as it happens, also interviewed 176,000 applicants. Of this number, about 13,000 were employed, roughly one out of thirteen of those who applied. Confronted by such a task, the employment department naturally had to make short shrift of many obviously unsuitable candidates, interviewing them briefly at the rail and selecting for serious consideration only about a third of those who sought employment. About one minute on the average was devoted to this preliminary interview. The time available for the second interview was five or six minutes.

The following year, to secure more time for the employment interview without adding to the staff of the department, an inquiry was undertaken to discover which of the interviewers were particularly keen and accurate in their first impressions. A study was made of the work of all the interviewers, and of the relationship between their initial estimate of applicants and the later success of the employees chosen. Interviewers selected in this way were given special training for the exacting duty of making the first rough selection among the candidates. A booth now provided privacy for the preliminary interview. The time allotted to it was from one and a half to three minutes. In this time a better sifting of the applicants was made and a smaller proportion of them chosen for further examination, so more time was available to devote to the employment interview proper— the office interview, as it is called. Here those applicants who are seriously considered for employment now receive a searching interview from 20 to 25 minutes in length. In cases of rejection, however, the examination is often of much shorter duration. From 20 to 65 minutes, depending on the type of position for which the applicant is being considered, is ordinarily devoted to employment tests, although a few require as long as an hour and a half, but 50 per cent of the cases used less than 40 minutes. The medical examination takes six minutes on the average.

The benefits of increased emphasis on the preliminary interview were striking. By painstaking selection in these interviews it was necessary to give office interviews to only 35,057 applicants in order to secure the 11,380 new employees required to maintain the same-sized working force. The number of applicants given psychological examinations during that year was 14,500.

Another type of interview in this firm deals with those employees who are referred for transfer or promotion, or who are maladjustments or problem cases. When transfer of an employee to an executive position is under consideration, the interview sometimes lasts as long as three hours. When it is a matter of personality adjustment about 30 minutes is usually devoted to each interview.

A Chicago factory with 30,000 employees devotes five minutes on the average to each employment interview; but during emergency periods of expansion this time has been shortened to three minutes. In interviewing candidates for supervisory and executive positions, a much longer period of time is customary, partly because the informing and motivating as well as the fact-finding functions of the interview are more obviously necessary. The most desirable candidates have to be wooed and won as well as chosen.

It must not be forgotten, then, that a vast proportion of employment interviews are necessarily short. No satisfactory appraisal of the candidate is possible in so brief a period if the interviewer does not have before him full details of the interviewee's experience and personal history as recorded on a well-devised application blank. Also, the interviewer needs to be thoroughly familiar with each of the several jobs for which he is hiring; there is scarcely time for him to stop and refresh his memory by referring to his file of job specifications, much less to visit the department to see for himself the nature and requirements of the job. The interviews have to be crisp and to the point, as only an interviewer can make them who knows intimately the different sorts of work for which he is hiring, and who has mastered the techniques of drawing out from the applicant the salient information about his real qualifications.

Smaller firms cannot always maintain as complete an equipment for their employment work as do large offices, but they must somehow or other take most of the different steps here considered essential. If no standardized employment tests are used, they must fall back on the traditional unstandardized test of seeing what the applicant can actually do on the job. In the absence of a medical examiner, the employment interviewer and the foreman or supervisor must be alert to note defects of strength or health which may disqualify an applicant for certain exacting employments. And if no thorough job analyses have been made as bases for personnel specifications, much of the responsibility for selection has to be carried by the superintendent or foreman who knows most thoroughly the demands of the several positions to be filled. In any event, it is essential to bear in mind the total process of selection and placement within which the employment interview finds its setting.

Securing Valid Information for Selection

Of the three functions of the employment interview, that of securing correct information from the candidate is the one which has received most attention and study. It is necessary to obtain not only items of the applicant's personal history but also data regarding his abilities, interests, and personality traits which may predict his success. The value of maintaining good records of employee accomplishments and of statistically analyzing the accumulated experience, in order to find out just which items of information obtainable by interview are really significant indicators of success on the job in question, has been well illustrated by Kenagy and Yoakum in their book, *The Selection and Training of Salesmen* (12). The measurable criteria of success in different kinds of work, and the ways of using such data to ascertain how much weight is to be given to the different items of fact regarding an applicant, are outlined in Bingham and Freyd's *Procedures in Employment Psychology* (5), and Bellows' *Psychology of Personnel in Business and Industry* (2).

The practice of sorting applicants by means of a preliminary interview is common, as we have seen. Many employers, particularly of salesmen, make an earlier sifting based on letters of application. Only those not eliminated by this rough sieve are asked to fill out a comprehensive application blank or personal history sheet. The information here recorded then serves as a point of departure for the main interview. Although the interviewer may not open the conversation by pointed questions about personal history, the record frequently gives him a lead; and often one aim of the interview is to check over and supplement the information already recorded by the applicant. In this connection, the application form serves as a reminder or check list of essential items to be considered.

The value of the application blank as used in employment offices varies partly with the nature of the information sought. The worthwhileness of each item depends partly on the possibility of obtaining it accurately, partly on the closeness of its correlation with success in the position to be filled. Time is wasted in considering information not definitely known to be related to success in the particular job. It should be remembered that some items on the blank are included not because they have any connection with probable success, but because they are required for other purposes as matters of record. Seldom does a man's place of birth, for instance, indicate his probable success.

Extensive statistical investigations have been made to determine the predictive significance of different items of personal history commonly appearing on employment blanks. The most notable of these aimed to discover the relationship of certain items to success in selling life insurance. It was found, for instance, that applicants were more likely to be successful if at the time of hiring they had an age of approximately 35 to 40 years, had two or more dependents, had membership in social organizations or clubs, carried life insurance, and already had experience in selling life insurance. Kurtz (14) describes excellent methods and results of selecting salesmen by personal history items. Stead, Shartle, and Associates (16) report that such personal data, together with certain interest and personality items, are among the valid predictors of success in department store selling.

Some years ago, one of the authors made a statistical study of success and failure of women employed on a well-paid machine-tending job which required strength, stolidity, indifference to noise, and coolness under conditions of surprise when as often happened, something went wrong with the machine. Forty-three per cent of the 228 employees studied were successful in the sense that they had the ability and the willingness to continue at this work for at least six months. But marked differences in this respect were found to be associated with differences of racial stock as inferred from data on the application blank. Under the conditions prevailing in that community, girls of native American stock (those whose fathers were born in this country) did not nearly so often succeed in this particular work as those whose parentage was Austrian, German, Scandinavian, Czecho-Slovak, or Polish. Those of Italian parentage, and the English, Irish, and Scotch, were between these extremes, as shown in Table 2. The

TABLE 2

Showing the Significance of an Item on the Application Blank.
Percentage of Employees, From Different Racial Groups,
Who Proved Successful in a Certain Machine-Tending Job.

Racial Groups	Number employed	Per cent successful
I. Austrian, German, Scandinavian	22	63
II. Czecho-Slovak and Polish	136	50
III. Italian	14	43
IV. English, Irish, and Scotch	19	26
V. American	31	19
Scattering	6	33
Total	228	43

employment interviewers had in a general way been aware of these differences, but were surprised to find them so marked. It must not be inferred that these data provide evidence of racial differences as such. Rather they reflect differences in socio-economic status and cultural backgrounds characteristic of the samplings of these various racial groups who at the time were seeking factory employment in this community. This same study brought to attention the previously unsuspected fact that exceptionally keen eyesight was much more frequently found among those who made the highest earnings on this particular machine-tending job. It illustrates the value of quantitative studies, in acquainting the interviewer with the relative significance of items to be considered in selecting and placing employees where they will be most productive and contented.

One source of unreliability in the interview lies in giving consideration to so-called facts which are supposed to have been secured with accuracy but which really cannot be obtained at all. Burtt (7) has pointed to a number of factors which contribute to this unreliability. He observes, first, a proneness to make unwarranted inferences from personal appearance and physiognomy. If the interviewer has, for instance, had an unpleasant experience with some person with a long nose or red hair, he may more or less unconsciously develop a tendency to impute the same unpleasant characteristics to an applicant with similar features. Most persons unwittingly make some such generalizations which influence judgments about people they observe. To be sure, these generalizations may occasionally be correct, but it is impossible to ascertain whether or not this is so without recourse to statistical methods. The interviewer, therefore, should guard against judgments based on his personal opinions, unless he actually knows that his predilections have statistical foundation.

The frequent assumption that habits are general rather than specific is a second factor making for unreliability of the interview. It is often assumed that a habit formed in one field with reference to one kind of situation will operate equally in other fields. A common supposition is that the applicant who is neat in dress will likewise be neat in work, or that a person who talks rapidly and seems very much alive will also be a rapid worker, or that one with awkward physical posture will be inaccurate and clumsy in manual work. As a matter of fact, habits are not usually generalized to this extent, but are more frequently specific in character.

The applicant's nervousness is a third factor which Burtt mentions as sometimes contributing to the unreliability of the interview. Many a candidate, in the excitement of what is for him a crucial situation, behaves in a distinctly unusual way. He is not really himself.

Yet the applicant's reactions are often symptoms of certain habit patterns which make him fit or unfit for the particular position for which he is being considered. Even after allowance is made for the strain on the applicant, a candidate who shows excessive nervousness is not suitable for certain vocations. Personal appearance is important where success is affected by the impression made on other people. Many men and women do not feel confident in buying clothing from a strange salesperson who is not well groomed and appropriately dressed.

The public does not seek the window where they are waited on by a man with disfigured face or dirty fingernails. The interviewer gives attention to physiognomy for the purpose, not of reading character, but of deciding how the applicant's appearance will impress the people with whom he is to deal.

Some experiments in interviewing have undertaken to measure the reliability of judgments based on personal interviews. There have been practical tests, for instance, of the ability of sales managers to interview aplicants for selling positions. One of the earliest of these was reported by Scott, Bingham, and Whipple (15) in 1916. Because this pioneer study gave clear-cut and somewhat startling results, the essential parts are here reproduced.

The interviewers included twenty sales managers and three investigators of problems in selecting salesmen. The men interviewed were real applicants, some of whom were to be employed.

Each applicant had been given the following instructions:

In Room A is a merchant who is to be regarded as a "buyer." You are to enter Room A, introduce yourself to Merchant A, and try to sell him some kind of merchandise. You will spend five minutes with Mr. A, then pass on to Room B and repeat your selling talk to Merchant B. You will keep this up until you have called on all the "buyers."

You may sell any line of merchandise. The following are examples: automobiles, breakfast food, clothing, fountain pens, life insurance, office supplies, real estate, rubber goods, sporting goods, tobacco, typewriters, etc.

You may make the same talk to each "buyer." If you decide to sell an automobile, then you may assume that each of the merchants is an automobile dealer. If you decide to sell a breakfast food, then assume that each "buyer" is a grocer, etc.

Present your merchandise for five minutes in such a way that the "buyer" will actually want to purchase your line. Sell as you would if the "buyer" were a real prospect.

Prepare your line of talk in advance!

A summary of the verbal instructions given the interviewers is as follows:

Each of you twenty-three gentlemen is to be assigned to a room on this floor of the hotel. You are responsible for what happens in that room. Each of the twenty-four applicants will call on you for five minutes. You are to assume that you alone stand between the applicant and the payroll of the company. Give each applicant a grade so the company will know which man you recommend as best, or second best, etc. If, after you have interviewed them all, you still desire a further conference with any or all of the applicants, you will find them waiting in Room 1336. The applicants have all prepared a sales talk or sales demonstration; but if you so dictate, the sales talk will not be given you, but you may pursue any method which you believe will enable you to judge wisely of the probable efficiency of the applicants.

Table 3 presents the judgments of the twenty-three interviewers on each of the twenty-four applicants. The capital letters are code symbols for the names of the applicants; the small letters stand for the names of the interviewers. The figures in the body of the table indicate the rank order of the applicants. Thus applicant "A" was judged by interviewer "a" to be the thirteenth best of the group of twenty-four; he was judged to be the best of the group by interviewers "i" and "u." The last column indicates the extreme range of rankings received by each applicant. Applicant "A" was judged to be the best and also the twenty-second best of the group. The next to the last column gives the consensus of opinion of the twenty-three interviewers. The two-place figures at the bottom of the table express the agreement of each interviewer with the consensus of opinion of all the interviewers. Thus the agreement of interviewer "c" with the consensus is expressed as .70. This is the correlation between the rankings assigned by the individual interviewer and the rankings by the consensus of the twenty-three.

A study of this table reveals not merely a wide range of opinion

TABLE 3

SHOWING RANKS ASSIGNED TO TWENTY-FOUR CANDIDATES FOR SELLING POSITIONS BY EACH OF TWENTY-THREE INTERVIEWERS

APPLICANTS	a	b	c	d	e	f	g	h	i	j	k	l	m	n	o	p	q	r	s	t	u	v	w	Av.	Range
A	13	14	12	11	18	7	3	19	1	4	4	8	5	5	18	5	16	22	10	11	1	5	19	10	1-22
B	2	8	7	7	12	7	3	·	6	1	2	2	3	3	7	1	3	2	10	11	4	12	4	2	1-12
C	23	22	17	2	11	20	20	13	12	7	15	12	11	24	23	12	19	11	10	5	24	11	7	15	2-24
D	18	21	8	8	9	9	14	·	18	2	15	14	17	7	19	15	15	6	5	24	7	10	17	13	2-24
E	22	19	16	24	24	17	23	22	18	22	23	19	20	17	18	19	23	18	23	17	22	15	23	24	15-24
F	20	23	15	23	14	15	9	22	21	24	15	19	23	20	14	21	22	23	16	21	15	20	20	21	9-24
G	11	15	13	16	13	12	18	16	24	12	15	23	22	22	12	22	17	17	16	11	20	18	21	19	10-24
H	15	24	24	20	23	23	23	22	23	23	15	19	24	7	23	10	24	24	10	23	14	24	22	23	7-24
I	16	11	6	18	15	20	23	11	20	·	23	15	13	18	7	20	20	20	16	17	13	19	14	17	6-23
J	12	17	21	19	19	17	23	22	16	15	15	23	24	15	18	24	21	24	·	17	20	23	22	20	7-24
K	10	11	6	11	15	20	14	11	16	·	15	5	13	15	3	24	24	20	·	15	14	14	9	14	6-23
L	7	9	2	3	10	14	3	3	8	15	15	5	9	9	3	19	21	3	23	17	13	9	13	6	3-23
M	14	5	23	9	16	24	18	19	3	12	15	12	8	3	18	3	9	8	10	16	2	16	5	12	2-19
N	24	6	1	22	3	4	20	16	·	15	23	19	14	9	23	9	13	7	21	10	11	7	24	3	2-21
O	8	2	18	6	16	19	3	12	21	4	3	3	18	9	23	12	9	8	18	7	3	21	11	16	12-24
P	21	13	3	17	3	1	14	1	14	12	15	19	4	16	11	2	14	10	15	·	6	5	10	5	1-16
Q	9	18	11	4	5	6	3	9	15	2	7	2	10	7	12	10	2	1	19	1	4	17	8	18	8-21
R	5	16	4	14	7	3	9	7	9	15	7	19	18	10	7	15	9	14	16	14	3	5	3	7	1-22
S	4	4	1	10	21	10	9	16	9	20	2	8	19	13	18	10	1	9	19	21	22	1	6	18	1-19
T	17	20	22	15	6	5	14	2	12	7	15	19	16	6	3	3	14	9	5	11	20	17	2	2	6-22
U	3	1	10	5	1	2	3	5	17	9	5	5	6	13	10	4	9	16	9	7	8	2	1	4	1-20
V	5	2	5	1	2	12	9	4	7	18	15	8	1	10	3	8	1	9	5	4	17	3	12	9	1-16
W	1	3	19	13	8	17	14	4	4	20	7	8	9	7	9	·	·	16	2	·	8	8	16	11	1-18
X	19	10	14	·	·	17	7	7	10	20	7	8	9	7	9	·	·	13	5	·	8	13	11	11	2-20
	77	69	70	82	76	78	81	76	76	59	69	83	72	55	69	74	81	67	63	69	55	85	69		

regarding almost every applicant; it shows that in spite of these variations there was a fairly definite agreement among a majority of the interviewers on many of the applicants.

Another fact that stands out is that successful sales managers differ widely in their ability to judge men in a brief personal interview. The range of correspondence with the consensus runs from .55 to .85. In earlier tests of a similar sort, sales managers were found whose judgment of applicants went as low as .14, indicating practically no similarity to the consensus of judgments of executives whose ratings of the applicants were taken as expressive of the standard of the firm.

The important practical question, then, is how to improve the reliability of the interview for employment. The first step is to distinguish what can be learned by interview from what cannot be obtained in this way. Charters (8) has stated some of the facts which the interviewer can and cannot determine. He can form opinions on the appearance and manners of the prospect, his likeableness, his attitude toward the organization's kind of work, his outside interests and hobbies, his forcefulness, his brightness in conversation, and any disagreeable mannerisms. He cannot, however, tell how dependable, honest, persistent, or loyal a person is. Traits which do not actually function or enter specifically into the behavior of the interviewee *during the interview* cannot be judged with any accuracy. In other words, the interviewer can get useful impressions of only a limited range of personality traits; namely, those traits which are significant in so far as people are impressed by them.

Assessment of Personality Traits

In much important work of the world, certain personality traits and predisposed patterns of behavior are as much or more essential than the knowledge or skill involved. The knowledge and skills can usually be measured by achievement or proficiency tests, or the ability to acquire them predicted by aptitude tests. The assessment of personality and prediction of its behavior is not yet adequately based on measurement, and many psychologists and psychiatrists believe that the task is so complex that it will always depend essentially on holistic judgment. Also, some studies have indicated little agreement between personality traits exhibited during stress conditions and those assessed in ordinary situations by methods depending on judgment questionnaires. It was thought then that ratings made of persons under stress should be more valid for predicting what they would do under similar situations. Studies, however, have revealed that observations of applicants under stress proved little or no more valid than interviews with applicants not under stress, and the interview method was still the one which revealed the most about the personality of the applicant.

The first and most extensive attempt in the United States to assess the merits of men and women by observation of behavior under more or less stressful situations was that which was undertaken during War II for the Office of Strategic Services and reported in the volume entitled *Assessment of Men* (1). The most important, although least novel, feature of the process was the individual interview. The other procedures, some of them producing stress, were designed to bring out behavior significantly symptomatic of traits desired or not desired for certain jobs to be undertaken in the war service.

The methods tried were first used by the German military psychologists, and after them by the British. In the United States the candidates assessed were studied intensively over a three-day period in an isolated setting where they lived with the staff assessing them. The recruits were observed from the time they arrived, during meals, and at other times, as well as in test situations. They were given various tasks to bring out major characteristics. For example, the ability to get along with others was revealed by six different methods: Interview; observations through a three-day period; individual task situations where the candidate was faced by the necessity of dealing with one or more persons in achieving his end; group task situations in which a team of candidates was instructed to cooperate in performing a prescribed task; projection tests; and sociometric questionnaires in which the candidates acceptance or rejection by his fellow candidates was estimated. The interview was found to be the most important single procedure in the assessment program. This is made clearer and emphasized by some quotations from the report.

It (the interview) provided the frame of reference in which all other observations were evaluated. From it came a large measure of the understanding of the person which made it possible either to recommend him or not to recommend him for his proposed assignment.

. . . .

The technique of the interview was very flexible. It was felt that any effort to force the inquiry into previously determined channels would inevitably result in loss of spontaneity and make for an artificiality of atmosphere in which no real understanding of the person could be attained. The interview was regarded not only as a source of important historical data, but also as an exceptionally revealing test situation. It was not always what the candidate produced in the way of factual information which was important in studying his reaction patterns; in many instances his behavior during the interview constituted the most significant datum. How did he handle the natural discomfort of being scrutinized and called upon to explain his life record? Was he frank, open, and sure of himself? Was he timorous, uncertain, and lacking in self-esteem? Was he friendly or withdrawn? Was he surly or did he display a degree of equanimity? Did he manifest an interest in learning about himself or was he evasive, rigid, and inclined to rationalize his personality liabilities?

Personality Ratings from Life History Interviews

A study of the use of life history interviews by persons skilled in clinical interviewing is reported from the Air Force Personnel and Training Research Center (22). The purpose of an extensive psychological assessment of a group of 100 Air Force captains was to develop a set of evaluative procedures which would identify those officers who would be most effective in their jobs. One source of data was the two-hour life history interview with each subject. There were two interviewers, and each interviewed 50 captains and rated them on personality traits. The interviewers were kept ignorant of other sources of information on the captains. One such source of information was considered "criterion" information, by which is meant information concerning each subject's on-the-job performance as an officer in the Air Force.

The interviewers attempted to learn as much as possible about each subject's life. The subject was encouraged to report freely and in his own way the main events of his life as he saw them. The scope of the interview, degree of rapport, and time available compare favorably with standard anamnesic procedures in court work or psychiatric clinic intake interviews. A structured interview schedule was followed. Thus, the interviewers obtained systematic coverage of theoretically important areas of life history by appropriate transitional questions, so that at the end of the interview information had been obtained on such matters as the subject's memory of himself as a child, his imagery of his mother and father, his relations to his siblings, his own health, the kind of childhood play he liked best, his performance in school, his sexual development through adolescence and into early manhood, his current sexual adjustment, the circumstances of courtship and marriage, his relations with his wife and with their children, his own and the family's attitude toward religion, his adjustment in his Air Force career, and his long-range plans for himself.

Ten of the variables rated were presumed to be of fundamental significance for personality functioning. A factor analysis was made of these ratings, and four factors were extracted, as follows: (1) Drive for professional achievement; (2) stability of present adjustment; (3) personal scope and capacity for achievement; and (4) character structure and mode of adjustment. Correlation of the four factor scores with Air Force criterion measures of officer effectiveness gave some indication that the factor scores may be of value in identifying officer promise. The fourth factor appears to offer the best single criterion predictor, for two of its five criterion correlations were significant at the .01 level and a third at the .05 level. The report contained the following concluding paragraph.

All in all, the correlations with the criteria produced by the interview factor scores provide support for the notion that a life-history interview is still one of the better ways of assessing an individual for performance-potential on the job. It would seem from the present results that the chief factors which should be looked for are ones directly connected in a commonsense manner with job performance: namely, motivation to succeed, and the moral fibre and interpersonal skills necessary to implement such a basically favorable motivation.

Validity Factors in the Employment Interview

Analysis of employment interviews has helped to reveal wherein they are valid and why they are valid or not valid. Daniels and Otis (9) collected a sample of sixty interviews by recording them electronically in the employment offices of eight companies. The average interview lasted ten minutes, of which the interviewer spoke 5.72 minutes, and the applicant spoke only 3.02 minutes. In only one company did the applicant speak longer than the interviewer. Other evidence has indicated that the better employment interview is one in which the interviewer listens while the applicant reveals his qualifications. The information volunteered by the applicant varies with the time the applicant speaks, the correlation being .83. This category also correlated positively with the amount of new information answers by the applicant, .40, but negatively with the number of old information questions and answers, —.29. The method of establishing rapport in an interview by asking an applicant what is already on the application blank apparently is not productive in that the applicant volunteers less than he otherwise might. The correlation of the number of volunteered information statements by the applicant and the total number of brief responses on the part of the interviewer, .85, indicates that this somewhat non-directive technique of obtaining information is an effective one.

Some of the other conclusions, relating more to the method of analysis of the interviews, may be of interest here. Interviews do not appear to be affected by the fact that they are recorded. The method of analysis described in this study makes it possible to compare interviews for widely differing jobs, and to compare the methods used by different interviewers.

Evidence that the reliability of ratings based partly on interviews can be improved, is yielded by a study of the interview method in an officer candidate evaluation program for the U.S. Coast Guard Academy. Candidates were interviewed and rated by a psychiatrist and two psychologists. For each candidate the interviewers had ability and personality test scores and personal data questionnaires at hand to assist in the interview and rating. The reliability of the ratings as measured by the correlations between the ratings by different interviewers ranged from .80 to .88. The agreement of raters was doubtless partly due to the use of the same test scores and other data, but that does not explain all the intercorrelation, for the ratings correlated only .65 with the combined test scores. Interviews for evaluation and selection are apparently much more reliable when interviewers have adequate information, are well trained, and have arrived at common criteria.

The validity of work histories obtained by interview from applicants might well be questioned, but one investigation has shown the accuracy of this information to be remarkably good. When work histories with respect to weekly wages, duration of employment, and job duties were checked with former employers, the correlations were between .90 and .98.

Rating scales and similar devices have been used with more or less success to increase the dependability of judgments based on employment interviews. The aid obtained from these scales depends first of all on whether the traits considered are such as can be rated or judged at all in an interview. It also depends on the way the particular rating scale is constructed, and on the intelligence and skill with which it is used. At its worst, the rating scale may become a substitute for good judgment, and by its superficial appearance of scientific objectivity lead to an erroneous assumption that a personality has been accurately measured. At its best, a well-constructed rating scale aids the interviewer in focusing his attention on the relevant traits, one by one, in judging these traits, and in recording his judgments with greater accuracy and consistency than otherwise would result from a general impression. An excellent description of interviewing procedures, rating scales, and employment tests, with citations to published researches on these technical subjects, is found in Chapters X-XVI of *Industrial Psychology* by Viteles (20), Chapters III-VII of *Psychology of Personnel in Business and Industry* by Bellows (2), and *Appraising Vocational Fitness by Means of Psychological Tests* by Super (17). Chapters X-XIII of *Aptitudes and Aptitude Testing* by Bingham (4) have special relevance to employment practice. *Occupational Counseling Techniques,* by Stead, Shartle, and their associates (16) tells about the methods followed by the Occupational Research Program of the United States Employment Service in developing and using standardized oral trade questions, rating forms and tests, and in validating these and other predictors of satisfactory occupational adjustment.

The rating scale as an aid to the personal interview in industry has had its ups and downs. It is now commonly recognized to be a rough tool rather than an instrument of precision, a device to focus attention on essential characteristics and ensure their careful consideration rather than a means of measuring with exactness small differences of personality. Casually assembled scales are worse than useless, leading only to an appearance of precision which does not exist. On the other hand, a scale that has been judiciously constructed and tested is often a genuine help to the interviewer in making up his mind and in recording his opinions for future reference.

Intelligent procedure in the employment interview obviously demands accurate knowledge of the job to be filled. Actual interviewing for job analysis should constitute an important part of the training of the employment interviewer. He should share not only in the preparation of hiring specifications but also where possible in the job analyses made for the light they throw on training, wage setting, or job simplification.

The Occupational Research Program of the United States Employment Service has since 1935 added many valuable resources to the equipment available to employment interviewers. Of these the *Dictionary of Occupational Titles* (19) is an indispensable source. Many volumes of *Job Descriptions*[1] supplement this dictionary, covering intensively the occupations found in job machine shops, job foundries, the retail trade, the construction industry, the laundry industry, the autombile manufacturing industry, and the cotton textile industry. Each description gives a realistic picture of the job in terms of the precise operations the worker performs; the material, machinery and tools he uses; and the education, experience, and training he needs in order to qualify for the job. Ready access to such descriptions speeds the work of the employing interviewer and also increases the likelihood that he can secure from the public employment offices those applicants who most closely match the specifications. In the Foreword of the *Dictionary* is an account of the methods followed in interviewing and observing workers in order to prepare these job analyses and occupational definitions, a truly monumental task. Such an investment in research is, however, being repaid many fold through the facilitation of correct placements in business and industry.

The follow-up interview and the interview at time of separation are of value as supplements to the employment interview. They help to reveal the elements of success and of failure in the hiring procedure. It is most illuminating to the employment interviewer when he can have the assignment of interviewing, at time of exit, the very man he originally employed.

The most important function of the exit interview, of course, is to learn why the employee is leaving. It is not difficult to draw out some form of statement from him, but it is quite a different matter to uncover the true cause for his departure. Reasons for leaving obtained in a perfunctory exit interview are not at all dependable. Often the employee, in order to end the interview as quickly as possible, will allege the reason which he believes will seem most plausible. Then, too, the real reason is seldom one specific thing, and the employee does not want to try to tell everything, even if he could. Too often he has good reason to fear that he would be misunderstood if he attempted to explain at length. Frequently the reason for leaving is an accumulation of a number of grievances, focused at a time when the employee would rather resign than submit any longer, or when he has an opportunity to leave. On the other hand, the employee often does not know or has

[1] United States Government Printing Office, Washington, D.C.

not clearly formulated his main reason for leaving. The minor but immediate or precipitating cause, which he gives, is at the moment his obvious reason. One investigator has indicated this point clearly. "The fact that he does not complain about hours and labor policy and that those very rarely appear as the reason for leaving is not, to my mind, that he won't tell the exact reason or that hours play a smaller part in his actions than earnings and treatment, but treatment is such a personal thing that his evaluation of it is vague enough to make it merely a hope that things will be better at the next place."[2]

The employee finds it difficult to analyze the total situation; if he attempts it, he may even rationalize and accept the most conventional ground for leaving. The interviewer therefore must sympathetically co-operate with the employee in isolating the fundamental reason or reasons. He should remember that the employee may commendably be seeking advancement, and may not necessarily have any complaint with the plant. The thing that is uppermost in the employee's mind is that there are more attractive opportunities elsewhere. He really is trying an adventure. If so, he cannot formulate his statement more definitely than that he dislikes to go but feels that the opportunity is too good to ignore. The problem of obtaining his real reason, then, is similar to that in other fact-finding interviews, and involves the question of the reliability of the interview for such purposes. The exit interview has, as we have seen, some difficulties inherent in that particular social situation, and so demands specific training, tact, skill, and understanding for its successful accomplishment.

Skill in the vocational counseling interview, too, has come to be recognized as a necessary part of the professional equipment of employment interviewers. When an applicant learns that the pay or the conditions of work are not what he expected or that he is obviously not suited for the position or that the vacancy has already been filled, he may have no interest in pursuing the subject further. But he may want to prolong the interview, in the hope of getting a suggestion as to where next to turn in his quest for a job. If the interviewer can then be of real assistance by taking an interest in the applicant's problem and pointing the way toward openings elsewhere or suggesting a suitable line of vocational training, he builds good will for his firm while doing a service to his interviewee.

Such counseling is an integral part of the interviewer's responsibility

[2] Personal letter from Anne Bezanson, Industrial Research Department, Wharton School of Finance and Commerce, University of Pennsylvania.

to his employer and to the public. Indeed, during the years of the great depression, when few new employees could be taken on, many prominent banks, stores, and industries followed the practice of retaining on their staffs able personnel interviewers who gave generously of their expert knowledge about occupations and abilities. In good times also it is not uncommon to find in an employment department an interviewer who specializes in vocational counseling of applicants for whom the firm has no place. The schools and colleges should, and frequently do, maintain professionally qualified counselors to advise their students and former students regarding training, placement, and progress in their careers.

The fact is that occupational adjustment of youth and of displaced older workers is a responsibility too heavy to be carried by any one kind of institution. The search for work, for the right kind of work, must not be left to the applicants aided by the schools alone, or by such assistance as public employment services and social agencies can supply. Industry has a vital contribution to make to the common enterprise. It is a privilege and a duty of employment interviewers to counsel, as well as to question and to select for hiring.

Returning now to the employment office, it is well to remember that throughout the employment interview, and in the use of all devices for the selection of employees, the task is one of diagnosis. The interviewer looks for symptoms that indicate fitness or unfitness for a job. The information he secures from an applicant helps to fill out the details of a mental picture which he is trying to complete. It is a picture which fits the applicant into the job, or which rules him out of consideration. Rejection is not necessarily because of indications of inability of the applicant to do the work, but may be because of his failure to show habit patterns, temperamental disposition, and mental health and strength, which offer a prediction of permanency, responsibility, good morale, and ambition. The study of the applicant's fitness should include, as we have seen, a preliminary interview, a psychological examination, a physical examination, and a final interview. All aids should be utilized, but the applicant should not be definitely engaged until an appraisal based on the complete record of findings has been made.

The ideal interview has been described as a conversation in which the applicant is analyzed by getting acquainted with him, by talking with him about something in which he is interested. The importance of pleasant surroundings has been emphasized. But as Weakly (21) states, the advantages of congenial physical surroundings are minor as compared with the desired pleasant atmosphere which can be brought about solely by the right personalities of those in charge of the employment office.

It is essential that the employee begin his new work as a friend of the organization, convinced that he has taken the right step. He must not, however, be overconvinced. He should have a true picture of disadvantages and responsibilities as well as of opportunities, and be allowed to build a picture for himself; if he decides that he fits into this picture, he thus sells the job to himself. Any other attitude on the part of the employment department is unfair to the applicant and leads to disappointment, loss of morale, and increase of separations. A reputation for fair dealing and faithfulness to promise is the best asset of an employment office.

While many have described the qualifications of the ideal employment interviewer, most of these analyses are in terms too vague and general to help either an employment manager who is selecting an interviewer or an interviewer who wants to increase his ability. A keen understanding of human nature, associated with sympathetic interest in the individual applicant, is most often mentioned; but a great many socially minded and personally effective people are poorly equipped for success in an employment office because they lack the necessary intimate familiarity with industrial conditions, firsthand acquaintance with the local labor market, or detailed knowledge of the nature of the work to be done and the conditions of successful development in the various positions with reference to which applicants must be appraised. Extremely valuable is the background that an interviewer commands if he himself has been a worker among the workers.

For these reasons the first step to be taken by a young man or woman who intends to become a successful employment interviewer is not to apply for a position in an employment department, but to find a job as laborer, machine operative, salesman, or clerk in the firm of his choice; and furthermore to refuse advancement to a minor supervisory post until he has had real experience of the employee's work and life. The broader he can make this foundation the better. On it he can later erect a substantial structure of supervisory experience, reading, special study, and close observation of the actual processes of industrial management, and finally bring to the employment interviewer's booth a soundness of judgment not to be gained in schools alone.

We have seen that the purpose of the employment interview is occupational adjustment, chiefly through selection and placement, and subsequently through follow-up and through replacement by transfer or promotion. It includes, first of all, an appraisal of abilities, work interests, and possibilities of growth, in relation to the requirements of the varied opportunities which the industrial situation offers. And here is its main contribution to our general study of the interview. It is the matching of job analysis and man analysis. Its successful accomplishment is in the joint interest of employee and employer.

So, too, the industrial relations interview is designed to throw light on matters of joint concern. It aims to ascertain employees' attitudes toward company policies and their satisfaction or dissatisfaction with working conditions, including management practices and supervisory relationships. The principles which govern successful employment interviewing are equally applicable to the fact-finding interview for improving industrial relations, with one outstanding difference: the interviewer in the employment office is by the very nature of the situation assured of the worker's readiness to co-operate, while the industrial relations investigator has often to win this co-operation and establish his position with the interviewee. He must then build up the employee's readiness to tell the facts, his willingness to talk frankly and sincerely. Here, as we shall see in Chapter VII, the interviewer's indispensable resources are an attitude of genuine sincerity and a substantial knowledge of the conditions and the field he is inquiring about, without which he is likely to be misled and to fall short of deserving the confidence essential to a successful interview.

But first let us make an excursion into the realm of government employment practice. We shall see that civil service agencies, continually striving to make their oral examinations at once discriminating and fair, have systematized their training of interviewers and experimented with new ways of evaluating the evidence they secure.

REFERENCES

1. ASSESSMENT STAFF. *Assessment of Men: Selection of Personnel for the Office of Strategic Services.* New York: Rinehart, 1948.

2. BELLOWS, R., *Psychology of Personnel in Business and Industry.* New York: Prentice-Hall, 1949.

3. BELLOWS, R. and ESTEP, M., *Employment Psychology: the Interview.* New York: Rinehart, 1954.

4. BINGHAM, W., *Aptitudes and Aptitude Testing.* New York: Harper, 1937.

5. BINGHAM, W., and FREYD, M., *Procedures in Employment Psychology.* Chicago and New York: Shaw, 1926.

6. BRANDENBURG, G., Developing the personal interview. *Indus. Psychol.,* 1927, 3, 229-235.

7. BURTT, H., *Principles of Employment Psychology.* New York: Houghton, 1926.

8. CHARTERS, W., The discovery of executive talent. *Annual Convention Series,* American Management Association, 1927, 69, 10-13.

9. DANIELS, H. and OTIS, J., A method of analyzing employment interviews. *Personnel Psychol.,* 1950, 3, 425-444.

10. FEAR, R., *The Evaluation Interview: Prediction of Job Performance in Business and Industry.* New York: McGraw-Hill, 1958.

11. GHISELLI, E. and BROWN, C., *Personnel and Industrial Psychology.* New York: McGraw-Hill, 1955.

12. KENAGY, H. and YOAKUM, C., *The Selection and Training of Salesmen.* New York: McGraw-Hill, 1925.

13. KEPHART, N., *The Employment Interview in Industry.* New York: McGraw-Hill, 1952.

14. KURTZ, A., Selecting salesmen by personal history items. *Psych. Bull.,* 1939, 36, 528.

15. SCOTT, W., BINGHAM, W., and WHIPPLE, G., Scientific selection of salesmen. *Salesmanship,* 1916, 4, 106-108.

16. STEAD, W., SHARTLE, C., and associates. *Occupational Counseling Techniques.* New York: American Book, 1940.

17. SUPER, D., *Appraising Vocational Fitness by Means of Psychological Tests.* New York: Harper, 1949.

18. THOMPSON, L., *Interview Aids and Trade Questions for Employment Offices.* New York: Harper, 1936.

19. UNITED STATES EMPLOYMENT SERVICE. *Dictionary of Occupational Titles.* Washington: U. S. Government Printing Office, 1949.

20. VITELES, M., *Industrial Psychology.* New York: Norton, 1932.

21. WEAKLY, F., *Applied Personnel Procedure.* New York: McGraw-Hill, 1923.

22. WOODWORTH, D., BARRON, F., and MACKINNON, D., An analysis of life history interviewer's ratings for 100 Air Force captains. ASTIA Document No. AD 146 401. Office of Technical Services, Department of Commerce, Washington, D.C., 1956.

6. Oral Examining
in the Civil Service

WHEN an employment interview takes on the somewhat formal aspect of an oral examination, the interviewer's problems are multiplied. To supply a thread through this maze is the aim of this chapter. It pictures the unique functions of the oral examination and its place among the other instruments of personnel selection. Procedures followed in planning and conducting oral tests are then described. The spotlight is turned on the difficulties of making certain that such examinations are helpful both to the applicant and to the employing agency. Studies and experiments which have resolved some of these difficulties are summarized. Ways of training oral examiners in the performance of their exacting duties receive special emphasis; for here is an area in which distinct contributions to personnel management have recently been made.

The personnel agencies of government shoulder a heavy task of recruitment and selection. They must find and choose upward of a hundred thousand men and women a year for positions in the federal service (5), while state and local governments absorb an even larger supply. The openings range from the most routine clerical and labor classifications all the way to the highly technical, professional, and administrative. Applicants for appointment in some of these categories —postal clerk, family visitor, or junior typist, for instance—may be greatly in excess of the number of anticipated vacancies; on the other hand, a recruiting agency may have to spend several months in search of one fully qualified expert—such as a chief psychiatrist for a great municipal hospital—who can be persuaded to file an application.

Throughout the process of recruitment and selection, the personal interview should, and frequently does, serve identically the same purposes as in industrial employment. But the principle of open competition—one of the foundation stones of public policy within the civil service—introduces complications which set the competitive oral examination somewhat apart from the ordinary employment interview. Applications must be received from all eligible citizens who may wish to be considered; and the selective process must be conducted in a manner obviously fair to all. Safeguards against charges of bias, favoritism, or political influence are imperative. The procedures followed in sifting applicants and arranging lists of eligibles in order of merit must be so adequate and sound that they will command public confidence and, if necessary, stand the scrutiny of judicial review in the event of appeal.

In adapting the personal interview to meet these requirements of public policy, civil service administrators have had to think deeply about the problems involved and have carried forward experiments which shed light on the whole subject of employment interviewing. Practical suggestions extracted from their hard-won experience are pertinent not only within the civil service but in the fields of industry, education, and social work as well. (2, 3)

Purpose of the Oral Examination

The oral examination is ordinarily but one among several instruments used in ascertaining the relative merits of applicants. First, the recorded facts with respect to their schooling, occupational experience, and personal history are carefully weighed and rated. Then when necessary a written examination is given to measure their knowledge of the special field and their competence in dealing with its problems. Skills and proficiencies may be measured by standardized tests of performance; while tests of intelligence are frequently applied in order to measure their alertness, mental adaptability, and capacity to learn. Those who surmount these hurdles may be given a physical test or a medical examination, after which a character investigation explores their reputations and their records for integrity and dependability. For numerous routine jobs, and for more responsible posts, which do not call for special ability with people, the experience ratings, written examinations, and performance tests usually serve adequately to ascertain the qualifications of the applicants. But for those classes of positions which demand a high order of ability to deal personally with subordinates, associates, or public, an oral test is regarded as an indispensable step in the competitive process. The responsible representatives of an employer or a qualifying agency want an opportunity to see the candidate in action, to observe how he conducts himself during the give-and-take of a personal conference, and to question him in such a way as to draw out reliable indications of fitness which may not have been fully disclosed by other forms of test. That is the purpose of the oral examination.

The proper place and scope of the oral examination can, perhaps, best be appreciated after bringing freshly to mind four crucial questions which any employer would like to have answered before he makes a selection among the applicants for a position. Regarding each candidate he asks, "How well can he do the work, now?" Next, he wants to know about the applicant's aptitudes and educability. He asks, "How readily can he learn new duties and make progress in his occupation?" In other words, he wants first the facts as to the candidate's present abilities, and then as to his capacities or potentialities for growth. Information regarding past achievements in school and on the job, together with scores on standardized tests and written examinations, furnish answers to these two questions.

But this is not all. The employer wants to know whether the candidate *will* do the work. What is his attitude toward it? Many an able employee has chosen to devote his best ingenuity and industry to activities unconnected with his job. He may be highly competent, but lazy or indifferent. He may have demonstrated that he can turn out an enormous quantity of accurate work under pressure, and still be habitually inaccurate and dilatory. His attitudes, interests, temperament, and traits of character, then, are factors of relative fitness quite as important as are his abilities and capacities. It is necessary to find out not only what he *can* do, but also what he *does* do. His characteristic tendencies and ways of behavior are in question. What is the likelihood that he will do satisfactorily the job he is able to do? Here again, the evidence from past experience is weighty.

A fourth question remains to be raised even after the first three have been answered to the employer's satisfaction. It is this: "Will the candidate *fit into* the organization?" Every enterprise, every office, every gang of workers, every public commission is a social system. The effectiveness with which its basic purpose is carried forward depends in no small part on the ability of its chief and his associates to maintain social equilibrium within the organization, and also within larger systems of social relationships, with public, customers, or co-operating agencies (1, 6). A worker, a supervisor, an administrative aide, or a chemist who irritates his associates, annoys his superiors, or otherwise fails to win acceptance as an integral collaborating unit in his organization may seriously hamper the enterprise even though he completes the specific duties of his position with conspicuous ability. No wonder that employers make every effort to learn the answer to this fourth question: "Will the candidate fit in?"

Evidence regarding a candidate's patterns of conduct, his dominant motives, his attitudes, and his social adaptability assumes, then, an importance comparable with evidence regarding his knowledge and training. These attitudes and behavior patterns are not usually disclosed in a written examination, nor are they reflected in a merely quantitative record of experience. Therefore, civil service agencies have increasingly turned to the oral examination for answers to the third and fourth of the basic questions regarding an applicant's qualifications. Indeed, most examiners agree that for testing essential factors of personal suitability, no other technique can entirely take the place of the oral test.

In the qualitative evaluation of the candidate's experience, too, the oral examination provides an effective approach. Examiners have long recognized that "exposure" to education and time "occupied" in relevant employment are not conclusive evidences of competence any more than of personality. They want to know what traits and abilities needed on the job each candidate possesses—acquired, they care not how, from the sum total of his experience of life. Qualifications such as ability to gain cooperation or to accomplish objectives in the face of opposition may be the product of personality and experience. The oral examination can be so planned and conducted as to draw out verifiable evidence of demonstrated qualifications such as these. It is now systematically employed in some jurisdictions to supplement preliminary ratings of the candidates' records of education and experience, serving in this way the same function as the industrial employment interview during which the questioner checks over the applicant's personal history as entered on the application form and asks searching questions about his experience and training.

Evidences obtainable during an oral examination are of two sorts. First are the verifiable statements of fact, similar in nature to the testimony drawn from a witness in court. Detailed answers to questions regarding the candidate's accomplishments and training, for instance, provide this kind of evidence of his qualifications and fitness. In addition, the examiners observe his behavior during the conference. They see at first hand what kind of impression he makes on others. They note his poise or excessive nervousness; his forcefulness of expression; the modest self-assurance or the braggadocio with which he recounts his experiences; his alertness or obtuseness in grasping the point of a question and discussing it intelligently; and his command of language, particularly the fluency and flavor of his oral as contrasted with his written vocabulary. They test his ability to talk to the point instead of wandering volubly, and to impress others with his competence and good judgment regarding matters of importance within his special field. Here, too, his self-control, his poise, his emotional stability or his nervousness are seen, together with the convincingness and impressiveness of his bearing, and similar characteristics observable under the conditions of an interview. These behavioristic data, trivial though many of them may be, nevertheless weigh in the examiners' scales along with the testimony regarding verifiable facts which their questions elicit.

All these evidences cumulatively shape the examiners' conception of the candidate as a person and of his suitability for employment in the kind of work for which he is applying. The details of the observations which contribute to this conception are frequently difficult if not impossible to describe. Who but a consummate artist with words can record with precision the particular gestures, postures, or inflections which generate in the observer a conviction of the interviewee's forcefulness, for example? The conference should, nevertheless, leave the examiners with well-founded convictions as to the way in which the applicant impresses those with whom he comes in contact.[1] In so doing, it makes a definite contribution to the selective process.

[1] To quote from a letter by A. W. Kornhauser: "The elements which enter into our estimate of a given quality are indefinitely varied and numerous. There is an enormous range of functionally equivalent indicators of given traits and abilities. Significant comparison of candidates is not feasible by a simple direct comparison of the specific evidence, but should be feasible with respect to the traits inferred from the varied fragments of evidence. If we place the emphasis on trying to satisfy legal requirements for review, I fear we shall merely induce interviewers to record elaborate observations which serve as convenient excuses for their ratings—and worse, we may cause the interviewers to shy away from some of their conclusions concerning a candidate simply because they are unable to conveniently specify items of evidence which led to the final evaluation."

Conclusions from Data on Oral Examinations

The possibilities and limitations of the competitive interview are illustrated in the following brief account of a vast program of oral examinations which was carried through in 1938 by the Employment Board for the Pennsylvania Department of Public Assistance.

There were 60,000 applicants for 5,000 positions, some of them clerical. The largest number of openings, however, was as social investigator, or "visitor" so called, the duties being to establish and maintain intimate contact with needy families and to dispense public relief funds to these families judiciously, in conformity with established policies and regulations. In order to carry these responsibilities to the satisfaction of clients, taxpayers, and public authorities, visitors obviously needed certain abilities and personal traits in addition to those measured by marks in written tests. Success in supervisory and administrative positions likewise is conditioned partly by personal factors, some of which it was deemed necessary to evaluate by means of oral examinations.

Well-constructed written tests eliminated all but about 11,000 of the applicants for the administrative, supervisory, and public-contact positions. Each of these applicants was then brought before one of many boards of oral examiners for rating on traits observable during interview and deemed to be of value in the position for which he was a candidate. Each examiner recorded also an over-all rating on the candidate's "personal fitness for the position." These ratings were based, not upon extended acquaintance or upon casual observation, but on such evidences as could be brought to light during an informal conference of 20 to 45 minutes with each candidate.

The 800 examiners had been selected for their knowledge of employment practice, or of social work, or of conditions in the locality, as well as for general competence and political disinterestedness. The three or five members of each board were instructed in the nature and purposes of the examination and in the responsibilities of the position in question. They also rehearsed the procedures to be followed. Practice interviews and rating of pseudo-candidates preceded examination of actual candidates.

The graphic rating forms used with candidates for major administrative positions called for ratings on ten traits: speaking voice; appearance; command of language; poise, bearing, and tact; presentation of ideas; freedom from bias; ability to plan and organize; ability to direct and supervise; ability to interpret the organization to the community; and finally, personal fitness for the position. The forms used in rating candidates for positions as visitor listed eight traits: voice; appearance; language; alertness; ability to present ideas; poise, bearing, and tact; judgment; and personal fitness. Each trait was defined as succinctly as possible in a brief paragraph.

The rating sheets were similar in form to the one reproduced in Figs. 1 and 2. Some were hand-scored; 31,000 of them were fed to an International Test Scoring Machine—the first time this equipment had been adapted to the purpose of computing and combining graphic ratings. The machine electrically reads the rating recorded on each scale, measures its numerical value, multiplies this value by its predetermined weighting, and averages the separate trait ratings all in a moment, with inaccuracies of less than 1 per cent.

Detailed analyses of the data regarding certain of these ratings point toward several conclusions or hypotheses which should be kept in mind and tested thoroughly in subsequent studies of interviewers' ratings:

1. As to reliability: under conditions such as prevailed in these oral examinations, the ratings given to a candidate by the several members of an interviewing board do not differ greatly. Seldom is there a rating on any trait which diverges more than one-fifth of the scale length from the average of the ratings on that trait given to that candidate by the other examiners. In the samples studied, the average deviation from the consensus is about one-ninth of the scale.

2. There is, however, plenty of evidence of independence of judgment on the part of the interviewers. They do not slavishly follow the judgment of a leader or of the majority.

3. Examiners differ in susceptibility to halo. Thanks to the brief but effective precautions taken when the interviewers were being introduced to their duties, not many of them yielded to the impulse to rate a candidate high in all traits, or average, or low. There were, however, a few instances in which an interviewer rated a candidate a trifle lower than the consensus on every trait, and rated some other candidate higher than the consensus on nearly every trait, indicating halo in judgments carefully and conscientiously recorded (4).

4. Examiners differ in the fineness of the discriminations they try to make. The ratings given by one interviewer on a specified trait may be distributed fairly normally over the scale, while the ratings

INSTRUCTIONS TO INTERVIEWERS AND ORAL EXAMINERS

You are to rate the candidate on certain characteristics which have a bearing on the likelihood that he will be successful in the position for which he is an applicant but which are not measured by a rating of his experience and training, nor by his performance in a written examination, but which can be observed when you talk with him face to face.

Keeping in mind the kinds of duties the candidate will be called upon to perform, consider whether his personal characteristics, as they reveal themselves during the interview, will be an asset or a liability in filling such a position. Do not rate him on his technical knowledge or lack of knowledge of the job. Do not let your estimates of his personal qualities be colored by what he may tell you about his experience or lack of experience.

If his voice, for example, is so rasping or weak that it would give to those with whom he talks an unfavorable impression, you will rate him low in this trait, toward the left end of that scale. If it is neither noticeably pleasant nor unpleasant, you should rate him at or near the middle of the scale. If his speech is free from disturbing peculiarities of accent and his voice so clear and resonant that it would be a distinct asset in the work he will do, rate him somewhere on the right half of the scale.

Similarly, rate the candidate on each of the other traits, keeping in mind the definitions of these traits as given on the Rating Form. If a candidate has made no impression on you whatever, either favorable or unfavorable, so far as one of these traits is concerned, rate him at the midpoint of that particular scale. Record your tentative rating on each trait, by putting a check-mark (✓) on the proper scale at the point where, in your judgment, the candidate belongs.

A rating need not fall exactly at one of the subdivisions of the scale. You may place it at either extreme, or anywhere between.

Base your estimates of the applicant's characteristics solely on evidences observed during the interview.

Be sure to record your rating of the applicant on each of the traits. Do not omit any.

When rating the last trait, "Personal Fitness," If—quite apart from any inexperience or lack of technical knowledge which he may have revealed—you consider him definitely unsuited for the position, rate him far to the left. If he barely qualifies, that is, if you are prepared to endorse him as personally suited for this work but can endorse him only with some hesitance, mark him midway between the lower end and the middle of the scale. If you can endorse him with confidence, or with enthusiasm, place your check mark well to the right of the middle.

After you have interviewed several candidates and discussed the evidences of their personal suitability with other examiners, you are at liberty to revise your ratings. This is done by putting your initials above each new check-mark you make. You may use for comments the appropriate spaces to the right.

SPACE FOR COMMENT

1   VOICE AND SPEECH

2. APPEARANCE

3. ALERTNESS

4   ABILITY TO PRESENT IDEAS

5   JUDGMENT

6   EMOTIONAL STABILITY

7. SELF-CONFIDENCE

8. FRIENDLINESS

9. PERSONAL FITNESS FOR THE POSITION

    SUGGESTIONS

Fig. 1. (One-fourth actual size)

RATING FORM FOR USE OF INTERVIEWERS AND ORAL EXAMINERS — 2 — 1938

Applicant's Name or
Identification Number .... Date ....

Kind of work for which his
suitability is appraised ....

INSTRUCTIONS: Ask yourself how this applicant compares with those who are doing work of this kind. Consider whether his voice, appearance, etc., would be a liability or an asset in such a position. Rate him by making a check ("✓") at that point on each scale where, in your judgment, the applicant stands. Rate the following traits:

1. **VOICE AND SPEECH.** Is the applicant's voice irritating, or pleasant? Can you easily hear what he says? Does he mumble, or talk with an accent which offends or baffles the listener? Or is his speech clear and distinct, his voice so rich, resonant and well-modulated that it would be a valuable asset in this position?

2. **APPEARANCE.** What sort of first impression does he make? Does he look like a well-set-up, healthy, energetic person? Has he bodily or facial characteristics which might seriously hamper him? Is he well-groomed or slovenly? Erect or slouchy? Attractive or unattractive in appearance?

3. **ALERTNESS.** How readily does he grasp the meaning of a question? Is he slow to apprehend even the more obvious points, or does he understand quickly, even though the idea is new, involved or difficult?

4. **ABILITY TO PRESENT IDEAS.** Does he speak logically and convincingly? Or does he tend to be vague, confused or illogical?

5. **JUDGMENT.** Does he impress you as a person whose judgment would be dependable even under stress? Or is he hasty erratic, biased, swayed by his feelings?

6. **EMOTIONAL STABILITY.** How well poised is he emotionally? Is he touchy, sensitive to criticism, easily upset? Is he irritated or impatient when things go wrong? Or does he keep an even keel?

7. **SELF-CONFIDENCE.** Does he seem to be uncertain of himself, hesitant, lacking in assurance, easily bluffed? Or is he wholesomely self-confident and assured?

8. **FRIENDLINESS.** Is he a likeable person? Will his fellow-workers and subordinates be drawn to him, or kept at a distance? Does he command personal loyalty and devotion?

9. **PERSONAL FITNESS FOR THE POSITION.** In the light of all the evidence regarding this person's characteristics (whether mentioned above or not) how do you rate his personal suitability for work such as he is considering? Recalling that it is in his best interest to recommend him for a position if he is better suited for something else, would you urge him to undertake this work? Do you endorse his application?

Fuller instructions and space for comments on applicant's behavior will be found on the back of this sheet.

Irritating or Indistinct	Understandable but rather unpleasant	Neither conspicuously pleasant nor unpleasant	Definitely pleasant and distinct	Exceptionally clear and pleasing
Unprepossessing or Unsuitable	Creates rather unfavorable impression	Suitable Acceptable	Creates distinctly favorable impression	Impressive Commands admiration
Slow to understand or Unintelligible	Slow in grasping the obvious, Often misunderstands, Requires explanation of questions	Nearly always grasps intent of interviewer's questions	Rather quick in grasping questions and new ideas	Exceptionally keen and quick to understand
Confused and Illogical	Tends to scatter or to become involved	Usually gets his ideas across well	Shows superior ability to express himself	Unusually lucid clear and convincing
Notably lacking in balance and restraint	Shows some tendency to react impulsively and without restraint	Acts judiciously under ordinary circumstances Might be hasty in emergencies	Gives reassuring evidence of considered judgment	Inspires unusual confidence in probable soundness of judgment
Over-sensitive Easily disconcerted	Occasionally impatient or irritated	Well poised most of the time	Superior self-command	Shows exceptional poise, calmness and good humor under stress
Timid, Hesitant Easily influenced	Appears to be over-self-conscious	Ordinarily self-confident of himself	Wholesomely self-confident	Shows superb self-assurance
Keeps people at a distance	Does not easily attract friends	Approachable Likeable	Draws many friends to him	An inspirer of personal devotion and loyalty
Unsuited for this work, Not endorsed	Might do well, Endorsed with hesitation	Endorsed	Endorsed with confidence	Endorsed with enthusiasm

SIGNATURE OF RATER

This rating form prepared from suggestions furnished by W. V. Bingham.
Copyright, 1938, by the International Business Machines Corporation. All rights reserved.

FIG. 2

of another interviewer may be grouped into two or three modes, one tall mode ordinarily being near the middle of the scale and another midway between the middle and the upper limit, with little use of intermediate values, showing that sharp discrimination has not been exercised and that there should be more instruction and practice in the use of the rating form.

5. Examiners differ in their ability to estimate different kinds of traits.

6. Examiners differ in the range of the values they employ, some of them tending to distribute ratings over only a small part of the scale so that their marks automatically carry little weight if averaged with ratings of examiners who use a wide range of values.

7. A majority of the examiners tend to use a relatively restricted range of values on the scales for "voice," "appearance," and "command of language," while judgments on more important and highly complex traits such as "ability to plan and organize" and "ability to interpret an organization to the community" are spread over a much wider range, giving these judgments greater weight when ratings on all the traits are averaged.

8. There is, surprisingly, closer agreement among interviewers in their ratings on these latter, more complicated traits than on the former, more obvious ones. If closeness of agreement among raters be taken as a measure of relative objectivity, then judgments regarding a candidate's "appearance" are less objective than judgments as to his "ability to plan and organize." Probably the wider average deviations from the consensus when "appearance" is being rated are traceable in part to greater differences among the interviewers in their tastes and standards as to satisfactory appearance, and in part to the fact that they give relatively little time and thought to the rating of a trait which seems easy to evaluate and not of great importance. Whatever the explanation, there is no doubt that judgments on "voice," "appearance," and "command of language" were more subjective—in the sense that agreement among the interviewers was less close—than when traits farther down the list were appraised. The traits most reliably rated were "ability to plan and organize," "presentation of ideas," and "personal fitness for the position."

9. There was a marked tendency for examiners to rate nearly all candidates above the middle of the scale on the less significant traits —"voice," "appearance" and "command of language"— and to mark

all but the ablest of them at or below the middle of the scale on other traits. This tendency is partly due to the way the descriptive phrases are distributed along the different scales; but it is also true that interviewers tended to be particularly cautious and conservative when rating those traits which were deemed most necessary for efficient performance of the duties of the position.

10. As to the passing mark, the members of each examining board were clearly able to arrive at a common standard. On the final crucial judgment regarding personal suitability, they almost invariably were in agreement as to whether a candidate should or should not be endorsed.

11. Unfortunately there is no guarantee that the passing standards adopted by different boards examining candidates for similar positions are identical. How to ensure that such boards start from the same bench marks and maintain the same standards of excellence is no easy nut to crack.

12. Use of a graphic rating form for recording judgments presented few difficulties. To be sure, many interviewers at first expressed preference for numerical ratings, but only rarely was an examiner found who had difficulty in learning how to record his judgments by placing check marks on graphic scales.

13. As to internal weightings, it was thought advisable to find out what differences in final rank order among the candidates would result from assignment of different weights to the separate traits. Civil service authorities had suggested several alternative ways of weighting. Other schemes were proposed by social work administrators, personnel executives, and psychologists. At one extreme was a weighing method which ignored entirely the over-all judgment, on the ground that it only duplicated the specific ratings. At the other extreme were schemes which gave to this item a weight equal to the sum of all the other ratings combined. As a matter of fact, each of these proposed methods of internal weighing gave almost the same rank order as the others. The only shifts in position were instances in which candidates were nearly tied, the differences between their ratings being too small to have statistical significance. To understand how this could be possible, it must be borne in mind that each single rating on any trait represents a judgment upon the candidate's suitability. While the interviewer's attention shifts from one trait to another, candidate and job remain the same. Therefore, significant positive correlations between ratings on traits felt to be

essential to success in the position are to be expected. When such correlations are at all close, weightings assigned to the separate traits have little effect on the final rank-order positions of the candidates.

14. These oral examinations tested abilities other than—or additional to—those measured by the written examinations; for, while most of the candidates in the lowest 10 per cent of those who passed the written test also ranked low in the oral test, this close correspondence did not hold above that point.[2]

The question as to what particular traits interviewers should be called upon to rate is of secondary importance, although the traits should be obviously relevant to the responsibilities of the position. The list should not be a long one. It should, of course, include only traits observable during interview. To call for ratings on characteristics like personal courage, or common honesty in money matters is asking the impossible. Evidence regarding such traits—if they are needed on the job in question—should be sought during the character investigation, not during the usual oral examination.

Why not—it may be asked—abandon all ratings of specific traits and simply ask examiners to express a single judgment, namely, as to the personal suitability of the candidate for the position? A sufficient answer is, that this crucially important judgment is more likely to be correct if made after the rater's attention has been focused successively on several of the candidate's specific traits. Even though the ratings on these traits are subsequently ignored and only the ratings on "personal suitability for the position" taken into account, the over-all judgments are probably more discriminating and dependable when recorded by interviewers who have framed their questions and made their observations in such a way as to be able to report specific trait ratings also.

The experience of the Employment Board for the Department of Public Assistance was a revelation to hundreds of examiners, convincing them of the possibility of carrying through an enterprise of this character without injecting questions as to political affiliations of the candidates. Incidentally, while getting acquainted with the duties of the positions for which examinations were to be held and

[2] For instance, in a sample consisting of 148 candidates for the position of junior visitor, the coefficient of correlation between oral ratings and written examination marks was only $+ .15 \pm .05$; in a sample of 67 candidates for visitor it was negative, $- .08 \pm .08$; and in a sample of 80 candidates for senior visitor it was $+ .20 \pm .07$.

while questioning the applicants, many an interviewer had his eyes opened to the nature and aims of public relief and gained a vivid appreciation of ways in which he could help to speed its efficient administration in his own community.

The board succeeded in commandeering, without remuneration, the services of a large number of able persons willing to devote time as examiners to a task which they recognized as a real service to the commonwealth. They were chosen for intelligence and ability as well as for conscientiousness and freedom from suspicion of political entanglements. If the rating of candidates is to be judicious, discriminating, and fair, it is necessary to secure the services of such examiners, at once competent and distinterested.

Next in importance is the training of these interviewers. Adequate preliminary training took more time than has ordinarily been provided by administrators of oral examinations. Hours rather than minutes are required in which to make certain that purposes, processes, and techniques are thoroughly grasped. This can scarcely be assured without providing opportunity for *preliminary practice* in the conduct of such examinations. Rehearsal of interviewers during or following a period of preparatory instruction increases the facility with which the examinations are carried out and unquestionably heightens the reliability of the ratings reported. Indeed, the attention or lack of attention given to training the interviewers affects the final outcome far more than does the particular system adopted for rating traits and recording judgments.

REFERENCES

1. BARNHARD, C., *The Functions of the Executive.* Cambridge: Harvard University Press, 1939.
2. BINGHAM, W., Halo, invalid and valid. *J. appl. Psychol.,* 1939, 23, 221-228.
3. BINGHAM, W., Oral examinations in Civil Service recruitment. Pamphlet No. 13, Civil Service Assembly, Chicago, 1939.
4. ORDWAY, S., *et al.* Oral examinations. Civil Service Assembly, Chicago, 1941.
5. O'ROURKE, L., *Opportunities in Government Employment.* New York: Garden City, 1940.
6. ROETHLISBERGER, F. and Dickson, W., *Management and the Worker.* Cambridge: Harvard University Press, 1939.

Part III

Interviewing for
Facts and Opinions

7. Public Opinion Polls and Commercial Surveys

POLLING PUBLIC ATTITUDES

"Do you like President Roosevelt's idea of having Thanksgiving a week earlier this year?"

This query was put to 2,000 people during the course of interviews conducted by the Psychological Corporation and 428 said, "Yes"; but the question was also put by the same interviewers to an equivalent population in this form: "Do you like the idea of having Thanksgiving a week earlier this year?" and only 334 gave an affirmative response. So much for Rooseveltian prestige.

In another referendum, the question, "Are you willing to have an increase in prices with the hope that it will bring back prosperity?" drew 70 per cent affirmative replies, while an additional 11 per cent said "Yes" when the question was worded: "Are you willing to have a reasonable increase in prices with the hope that it will bring back prosperity?"

These differences in response are statistically significant. They are not accidental. They are not chargeable to errors of sampling. The interviewers asked other questions at the same time without any change of wording, and the proportions of "Yes" responses varied but slightly between the two halves of the total population interviewed.

Studenski (33) asked the question: "Should every worker be forced to join a union?" Then he reworded it as follows, in a way that offers four specific options: "Is it proper for a union to require all wage earners in an industrial enterprise to join the union (a) under any circumstances, (b) when the union controls a majority of the employees, (c) when it controls a minority of the employees; or is it improper under any circumstances?" The proportion entirely opposed to unionization dropped from 88.9 per cent in the first wording to 45 per cent in the second. Here the wide difference in the results of the two polls is due partly to the form of the question, partly to its wording. The specific options made it easier to say "Yes"; also the omission of the emotionally charged word "forced."

The vital need of attention to techniques of interviewing has perhaps been most clearly demonstrated in connection with such polls of public opinion, and in market surveys which undertake to measure changing trends of buying habits and consumer preferences. It is now well recognized that polls and surveys, if they are not to mislead, have to be planned with the utmost skill and care. The questionnaire must be standardized not only with reference to the form and the precise wording of the questions used, but also as to the order in which the questions are presented and the manner in which they are asked. The interviews must be numerous enough to yield statistically reliable data; and the persons to be interviewed must be expertly selected so as to constitute a truly representative cross section of the particular population whose opinions or behavior is to be sampled.

Mere size of the population sample is, to be sure, of minor consequence compared with its representativeness. The *Literary Digest's* forecast of a Landon victory in 1936 carried the weight of numbers —two and a half million replies to a postcard poll of ten million voters; but the lowest income groups had not been reached. The sample of opinion was enormous but not representative.

An inspector grading a carload of flax need not look at, smell, feel of, sift, and weigh a thousand separate handfuls. But he is not content to inspect the top layer only. Instead, he runs his slender trier clear down to the floor of the car and draws out a tiny cross section of every stratum. A few well-directed thrusts supply him with all that he needs in order to appraise the quality and condition of the flax. His sample may constitute less than one twenty-thousandth of the total; but when it has been weighed, shaken through several kinds of sieves, and reweighed, he estimates, with a high degree of reliability, the proportion of mustardseed, straw, and dirt in the entire carload.

So it is with the skilled appraiser of public opinion. His chosen cross section of the population whose attitudes are in question need not be large but it must be representative, an unbiased sample. No volume of responses, however vast, can compensate for slipshod planning or for failure to employ correct statistical controls.

Abundant proof of the need for extreme precautions in conducting surveys of public attitude has been brought forward, notably by Blankenship, Roslow, Lazarsfeld, Cantril, Gallup, Roper, and others. Significant experiments in questionnaire construction directed to this end were admirably summarized by Jenkins (20) and by Hyman *et al.* (18). The evidence convincingly supports two general conclusions. The first is that the planning of an inventory of opinion or preference is a technical matter requiring the skill and wisdom of disinterested specialists who are in a position to make repeated preliminary trials or pre-tests of the proposed schedule of questions in order to eliminate all ambiguities and the effects of suggestion; from which it follows that the preparation of a questionnaire is not a suitable assignment for a busy executive, a social worker, or a graduate student who has not had rigorous training in this field, nor, indeed, for a professional psychologist or statistician who has not specialized in questionnaire construction.

A second conclusion, of serious consequence to the public welfare, follows inescapably. It is that the opinion poll, intentionally or unintentionally manipulated in the interest of a sponsoring group, may lead to popular misconception of a dangerous sort. As Wechsler (34) points out, publication at a critical legislative moment of the results of a poorly worded, badly arranged, unrepresentative, or miscounted poll inevitably has damaging repercussions proportionate to the influence of the polling agency. On the other hand, the technically sound, disinterested survey has made for itself a place of undoubted value in the realm of public affairs, as well as in the study of buyers' preferences and of employees' attitudes toward working conditions, supervision, and policies of management.

Making Commercial Surveys and Market Studies

The term "commercial survey" includes a series of fact-finding interviews to ascertain the existing and potential market for competitive products or to establish a basis upon which to estimate the probable success of a new product or plan of marketing. The data from such interviews are used by banks, manufacturers, sales executives, and advertising agencies, in developing their promotional plans for some particular product or in deciding whether to finance or manufacture it. Speed is required to secure reliable firsthand information simultaneously from many sources in widely scattered areas; so considerable effort has been expended in developing and standardizing this form of interview.

We shall differentiate the various kinds of information required in a commercial survey and the types of interviewer needed, and then describe how surveys are planned, schedules of questions prepared, and interviewers trained. Finally, we shall see how different types of interview are carried out, including the interview for securing confidential business data from an executive who is at first unwilling to co-operate.

Several kinds of information are sought in a commercial survey. The chief points of interest are general business conditions in the field where the product is to be marketed; consumption volume and trends; present and potential consumer classes; their attitudes and buying habits with reference to the commodity and competing brands; the retail, wholesale, and jobbing situation in the distribution of the product; manufacturing conditions; advertising policies and media; and the financial standing and personnel of competitive companies.

Two general types of interviews are required: (1) interviews based upon a list of questions prepared in advance and (2) informal conversational interviews. Attitudes of consumers or potential consumers of the product, for example, and of distributors employed in getting the product to these consumers are ascertained by interviews which follow closely the questions listed in two questionnaires —one applying to the consumers and the other to the vendors. In order that a comprehensive study may be made of territorial differences in consumption and distribution, key cities in the various population classes in all sections of the country are covered in this questionnaire investigation. Manufacturing conditions, advertising and selling policies and plans, price maintenance situation, standing of the various competitive companies, and other basic data are secured through informal interviews with executives in the leading companies and with other authorities. In the commercial survey, as in other types of fact-finding inquiry, the questionnaire interview is found to be the best method of securing a consensus of opinion on a specific matter. The friendly informal interview, on the other hand, is thought to be the most efficient means of securing complete data on general conditions based upon actual experience of those engaged in the line of business under investigation. It is a different genus from the questionnaire inquiry.

Sometimes a third type of interview, known as service shopping, is included in the program of inquiry. The interviewer becomes a customer making actual purchases. He goes to various stores to compare the goods in question, noting quality and variety of stock, prices, style tendencies, quality of service, talking points used by the salesperson, and similar information. Service shopping, however, is not an essential feature of all commercial surveys, so we shall here merely call attention to publications which describe in detail the methods of training shoppers and of evaluating the data they secure (21, 25, 35).

Planning the commercial survey

To make a comprehensive survey in about three weeks of, let us say, the automobile tire industry, with manufacturers and distributors scattered throughout the United States, with a highly competitive consumption situation, and with decided territorial preferences is a sizable task, especially as it involves also a study of the current motor car situation. Every step, therefore, must be planned in advance to avoid all waste motion.

The first move, naturally, is to assemble, systematize, and analyze all available information about the product and its marketing. This is secured from government reports, from trade journals, and from statistics furnished by trade organizations, such as, in the case of automobile tires, the United States Automobile Chamber of Commerce. Data from these sources, however, are used only in a preliminary way to gain insight into the general situation. For several reasons they cannot be considered complete or final. Because of the rapid growth and constantly changing conditions of business, published statistics are frequently out of date by the time they are off the press. To secure later figures as a basis for a reliable statistical estimate, interviews with their authors or with other authorities in the field are essential. Moreover, government reports are limited to such companies as file their data; the classifications are often confused or include irrelevant items; and the recorded value of the products is generally low. Many census figures need checking. Articles in trade papers and magazines are frequently written by persons who are biased or who are familiar with the subject only as it pertains to their own more or less restricted experience. However, all of these kinds of information are assembled and digested before personal interviews are attempted.

Preparing the schedule of questions

The second step is the preparation of a questionnaire. To make a good schedule of questions, it is evident that there must be not only a clear understanding of the purpose of the survey and the exact type of data required, but also a knowledge of the sources from which such data can be secured, so that the questions may be developed from the interviewee's point of view.

With these two points clearly in mind as to the precise aim of the survey and the sources of the information, the questionnaire is prepared so that it will yield the necessary data and so that there will be no confusion as to their meaning. The questions are simple and direct, only one point being covered by each question. They follow in natural order, one leading easily to the next. They are also worded so that one checks another. Two questions may be asked to cover one important point from different angles; then, if the answer to one yields a certain piece of information, the second should verify it. If a contradiction appears, the replies are rechecked.

The length of the questionnaire also raises problems. There was a time when pollsters tried to keep the interview schedules short— a page or less—so that interviewers might readily memorize them. This is no longer true although care is taken to keep the schedule as brief as possible so that interviewees will not feel that too much time is being asked of them. Also, interviewers are instructed *not* to memorize the questions but rather to read them. This prevents the introduction of even those slight modifications which might change the meaning or tone of the questionnaire.

The Psychological Corporation, which, in co-operation with associated psychologists throughout the country, conducts experimental and commercial studies among consumers and dealers, has made analyses showing how variations in the wording of a question may produce considerable differences in the answers obtained. A question on the value of the NRA when asked one way led 41 per cent of the people interviewed to answer "Yes." But when asked in another way, 92 per cent gave a favorable reply.

The order of arrangement of questions, too, affects the responses. Thus, a disconcertingly large proportion of "Don't know" answers are given to a question regarding personal preference or attitude when it follows two or three questions of a more objective sort to which precise factual answers are readily made.

The effect of suggestion has also been studied and controlled, to ensure impartial findings. For example, in ascertaining from grocers and druggists what forms of advertising they considered most effective—billboards, newspapers, magazines, radio broadcasts, window displays, or circulars—the interviewers asked, "Can you tell from these questions which of these forms of advertising we are particularly interested in? . . . Which do you think it is?" During the preliminary tryouts of the interview form, analysis of these replies led to repeated revisions until all questions were freed from suggestion. When the nation-wide study was finally made, this key question was included so that it became possible to show statistically to the client, the National Broadcasting Company, that the questionnaire was strictly impartial.

"The critical point in all market surveys," according to Link (23), "is the obtaining of information worth tabulating. Beautifully prepared reports, dozens of charts and tables, thorough statistical treatment, thousands of interviews, are worse than useless if the information on which they are based is inaccurate or is affected by an inherent fallacy of procedure. No multiplication of answers to an unreliable questionnaire would compensate for its inherent unreliability." This is why there is so much need for psychological wisdom as well as for preliminary tryout and painstaking revision of items and their arrangement. When a schedule so devised finally passes muster, it can be entrusted to interviewers in many scattered centers of population, provided they have been schooled in following instructions precisely and in avoiding any casual remark, gesture, inflection, or emphasis that might give even the slightest of hints as to their own attitudes.[1]

Two types of interviewers

In making a commercial survey two types of interviewers are required: one to interview users as to preferences and consumption trends and the other to interview business executives and other authorities in order to secure basic facts about the industry. The first secures answers to the questionnaires; the second uses the conversational interview.

[1] Relevant to the need for these precautions are Blankenship's findings (2). Also, see Hyman *et al.* (18).

The questionnaire interviewer does not need to be an analyst, as the returns are tabulated and analyzed by the statisticians of the organization. The principal requirement is ability to ask questions in the prescribed manner and to note answers correctly. The characteristics looked for are an acceptable personality, robust health and energy, initiative in gaining interviews, good memory, and truthfulness or accuracy of report. Also important is what might best be called social presence, the ability to meet and deal quickly and effectively with many different kinds of people. With such a foundation, brief training in the technique of interviewing is usually all that is needed to develop a capable questionnaire interviewer. Periodic supervision is also important.

For the second type of interviewer, who secures statistics and other information about general conditions in the field through the medium of the more informal interview, these personal characteristics need to be supplemented by ability to express himself clearly in writing. He should have good judgment, imagination under control, and special education in business research, so that he can be readily trained to digest facts as they are given to him and to make deductions promptly. As there is seldom time for him to make a second call on his interviewee, he should be able to get a complete picture in one interview.

Because of the peculiar nature of this kind of fact finding, a high type of personal and business integrity is required. Such an interviewer must of necessity work without supervision in arranging his time and in conducting his interviews. He meets and talks with many people in the course of his work, and the organization he represents is judged by the impression he makes. If he lacks faith in his employers, in their methods, or in his own work, he creates a feeling of distrust in the mind of the interviewee. Therefore, a commercial research organization or department usually has a clearly defined policy as to its object, methods of securing information, and purposes for which it is to be used. For example, if its aim is to be recognized as a clearinghouse for commercial data, statistics, and consensus of experience, as a means of studying and bettering business conditions, this ideal is impressed upon every employee and client.

The interviewer's manner, too, influences his success. He must be resourceful enough to gain an interview, yet avoid being so self-assertive that his attitude repels. He must know how to be diplomatic if the interviewee disagrees with him, and never let a discussion become an argument. Another pitfall he must guard against is the know-it-all attitude. Interviewers sometimes assume the rôle of teacher in conducting an interview, which usually antagonizes the interviewee. He resents having an outsider tell him things he should —and feels he does—know about his own line of business.

The training of an interviewer is most important. He benefits by being coached so that his approach and conduct will create a favorable impression. To send him out to make interviews without proper preparation is a waste of time. Even though he may have had several years of interviewing experience, when he joins a new organization he requires special instruction in its methods. Furthermore, each assignment presents problems which require advice and special coaching. In these conferences, pitfalls encountered in previous interviews are reviewed in connection with subsequent interviews of similar character.

The novice frequently carries out questionnaire interviews as part of his training for the more difficult type of informal friendly interview.

Conducting questionnaire interviews

In the questionnaire investigation, the interviewer before starting out studies his schedule carefully, not to memorize the questions, but to familiarize himself with the purpose of the survey as a whole, and to be prepared to answer any questions that may be asked. The executive in charge coaches him as to the best method of procedure and goes over each question with him. He is not always required to follow a stereotyped plan in his approach, as the best results are secured when the tone of the interviewer is adapted to the personality of each interviewee. Indeed, it is impossible to lay down hard and fast rules governing every step of an interview; but much fumbling, discouragement, and waste of time are avoided if methods of approach and details of conducting the interview are rehearsed in advance. At the same time, it is essential that the interviewer ask the questions in the way that they were prepared. Even a slight change in the wording or the word order, while not appearing to be important, may change the essential content of the question and therefore affect the reply.

Interviewers are instructed not to be content with indefinite answers, such as "yes and no," "in some cases," "occasionally," and so on. When an interviewee makes such vague replies, he is asked under what conditions his action is in one direction or the other, and only the definite answer is noted. Also the interviewer is warned to guard against suggesting an answer by supplementary questions, implication, or manner. He must make every effort to secure the interviewee's real opinion or practice. Many persons hesitate to admit that they do not understand a question. Some answer without thinking. In interviewing a housewife to ascertain her preference in brands of a certain food product, she may say "I always use the X—— brand," but further questioning reveals that she does not use it because she prefers it to others, but because it is the only one carried at the shop most convenient to her home. So she must be given an opportunity to express her *preference*. The fact of use and the reason for it are covered in separate questions.

One point to be considered in advance is whether the questionnaire blank is to be shown or whether the interviewer is to ask the questions in a conversational manner and fill in the replies after the interview. This depends largely upon the kind of information sought. When it is of a technical nature, frequently the quickest and most satisfactory method is for the interviewee to fill in the answers himself. In such instances the interviewer, after leaving, writes a brief supplementary report in the space reserved for "Comments." Such comments are limited to pertinent facts which add value to the categorical answers to questions.

An interviewer seeking more general types of information may either show the questionnaire and jot down the answers at once or else fill them in later, depending upon circumstances. If he shows the questionnaire, he makes it a point to have a single copy in readiness and does not display a large number.

Many interviewers feel that it is easier to induce the interviewee to talk freely when a questionnaire is not shown and questions are answered in the course of conversation. Nevertheless, the data are more concrete and trustworthy when the answers are noted in the presence of the interviewee, who then knows exactly what information he is giving. The advantages of both methods are combined by first talking in a friendly way which gains the interviewee's interest and his general point of view toward the various questions, then producing a copy of the questionnaire, repeating each question, and noting the answers as they are made.

It sometimes happens in commercial surveys that the signature of the interviewee is required to authenticate the interview. To secure such a signature requires some diplomacy. Most people dislike to sign their names to information they have given, or else become so cautious that it is too indefinite and general to be of much value. Because of this hesitancy, space for the name of the interviewee is provided at the end of the questionnaire. The explanation that the signature is for record in the files, and that the information will be included in a statistical abstract or consensus of opinion, is usually sufficient to overcome objections.

The work of the questionnaire interviewer is facilitated by a letter of authority signed by an officer of the organization employing him, to be shown if there is any question as to purpose.

Conducting the informal interview

A printed questionnaire is too limited for use in the informal interview with major business executives and other authorities, but it is customary to outline in advance the points to be brought out. This outline is usually in the form of brief notes in a pocket memorandum book. During the interview it is then a simple matter to refer to these notes to make sure that all points are being adequately covered. The interviewer also uses this notebook to jot down figures, so that he does not have to depend entirely on his memory.

The interviewer studies all preliminary information available. He lists the persons who are considered authorities on the subject under investigation in the order in which the interviews are to be made, grouping them according to accessibility of location and importance as sources of information. Then appointments at suitable intervals are arranged by telephone, making sure that one does not overlap another or that one interview does not have to be rushed in order to be on time for the next. By making appointments in advance, time is saved in seeing interviewees promptly and in shortening preliminary explanations, and the interviewer knows that the appointment meets with his interviewee's convenience. It is usually advisable to make appointments for this type of interview not more than a day in advance. Interviews held in the forenoon or early afternoon are found to bring better results than those held toward the close of the day. Then, too, the interviewer has an opportunity to use the late afternoon hours to write up his reports and to make appointments for the following day.

In asking for an interview, a frank explanation is made as to the purpose of the survey and the use to which the information is to be put. The interviewer gives his name distinctly, and the name of the organization employing him. If this organization is not well known to the interviewee, its business is explained briefly. The interviewee is usually reassured when he learns that the interviewer has nothing to sell.

In a commercial survey the interviewer starts with a handicap rarely present in other types of interview. To be of value, the information he seeks must be concrete, up to date, and secured at first hand from men actually engaged in business in the field under investigation. The interviewer is thus placed in the position of asking an executive to give him the benefit of years of experience with no tangible profit to himself and with the knowledge that the information may be used, in some cases, for the benefit of a competitor. Further, such interviews are held during the hours when time is taken from his regular business.

These considerations affect interviewers in different ways, according to their temperaments. Some develop an apologetic, almost cringing manner, feeling that they are asking a great favor. Others approach the interviewee with a defensive attitude, or with defiant determination to force him to give up the desired information. Some women interviewers are inclined to adopt a flirtatious or wheedling attitude. But the well-trained, experienced interviewer with pride in his calling has no difficulty in impressing a businessman with his sincerity of purpose and in securing his co-operation. The average executive is familiar with the advantages of such investigations and frequently feels flattered by being accepted as an authority in his field. If, however, such business research is new to him, the interviewer introduces into the conversation facts indicating progress resulting from the broad study of business conditions, the exchange of information, and the publishing of statistics, as compared with earlier secretive methods of competition. To strengthen his position, he makes it a point to keep informed of recent developments and pithy instances of new applications of commercial research, to illustrate its value. On the whole, it has been found that, the more progressive and successful an industry or company is, the more willing it is to pass on to others the benefit of its experience. When an interviewee implies that he should have something in exchange for his contribution to the survey, the interviewer might volunteer to send him a summary of the particular findings in which he is interested.

The first few minutes of an interview are often crucial; for it is during this time that the relationship of friendly interest is established. But this opening step must not be prolonged. An interview during business hours should not be regarded as a social call. The interviewer shows his appreciation of the valuable time given him by coming directly to the point, securing without delay all the information he can, and then closing the interview promptly. The experienced interviewer knows exactly what information he is seeking and loses no time in getting to the main points at issue, so there is rarely any necessity for a long-drawn-out conversation. If the interviewee shows impatience, the interviewer usually suggests an appointment for a more opportune time, in preference to forcing through a halfhearted conference.

On the other hand, every interviewer occasionally encounters the talkative person who enjoys a friendly chat and proceeds to discuss irrelevant subjects and personal interests. One of the fine points in interviewing is to know how and when to check this irrelevant conversation and how to keep on the subject of the interview without giving offense. If friendly conversation is indulged in freely, it is likely that the interviewee will soon have other visitors and telephone calls or that his business will demand attention and he will terminate the conference. The interviewer then finds that he has not secured the information he came for, but only a few hurried, incomplete, and thoughtless comments that are practically useless.

The most successful interviewer is the one who, knowing his subject, its problems, and the methods of handling them, can temporarily file that knowledge in the back of his head and approach each interview with an open mind which apprehends readily the interviewee's point of view. Then, as the interview progresses, he discusses essential points, using what is necessary of the information he has gained from other sources to guide his questions. There is, however, a danger to be guarded against here, namely, that the interviewer actually will forget points brought out in previous interviews, and will accept each succeeding interview as a complete statement of facts; or he may let varying opinions lead him into confusion. To avoid these dangers, it is customary for the interviewer to write a detailed report immediately following each interview, with the date and the name of the interviewee. Then, when he starts to write his final report, he analyzes the statements of each authority interviewed, compares them, and draws tentative conclusions or arrives at a consensus of opinion.

Securing confidential information

In many instances a commercial survey involves the securing of information not freely divulged, such as sales figures, profits, costs, and payroll. Companies often do not care to make public such information, for the situation may involve income tax returns; competitors might use the figures to the detriment of the company; employees might demand higher wages based on what appear to be large profits; or the company may regard such statistics as nobody's business but its own. Some interviewers, when delegated to get this type of information, are tempted to use underhand methods. Ambitious to complete a difficult assignment, they adopt detective tactics or such means as newspaper reporters are sometimes supposed to employ to "get the story." They try to secure the figures from an unsuspecting employee, or by reading papers on the interviewee's desk, or by telling an untruth as to their affiliations and the purpose of the inquiry.

Such tricky methods generally fail, and if for no other reason, this should be enough to discourage the practice. The interviewer soon learns that the man who has sufficient ability to build up a successful business or to rise to an executive position is not unwary enough to be deceived into giving confidential information, and furthermore that employees are usually loyal to their employers. They see through the attempted deception and resent having their intelligence underestimated.

Another result of permitting an interviewer to use dishonest methods in securing information is that it usually acts as a boomerang. If he is encouraged to use such tactics, he loses his sense of loyalty to his own organization. He develops habits of deceit so that his work is influenced by his shifty and inaccurate methods of thinking, and the information he gathers is not dependable. Interviewers who are permitted to "get the story" by whatever means they think best are likely to use the same type of imagination in deceiving their employers as to how they spend their time when not supervised, and injecting their own opinions into the report of the interview, and in being otherwise unreliable in their dealings with their organization.

The conviction has become general, with the growth of business research through personal interviews, that it is unethical to ask a man to give information and specific data pertaining to his business without first informing him frankly of the true purpose for which they are to be used. If then the actual figures are not forthcoming, the interviewer asks for estimates, based upon an analysis of percentages and averages. Estimates arrived at by statistical experts show the general trend and may be reliable enough to serve all ordinary purposes. Such estimates are freely given. Then they are sometimes backed up by the actual figures of the company, the very data which had in the first instance been witheld.

The interviewer who makes a straightforward statement of his purposes and follows it with a reasonable request usually secures wholehearted co-operation and comes back with the information required.

One new development in market research, which many workers are inclined to regard as something of a fad, is motivation research. It has received considerable attention in the popular press as well as in professional and trade publications.

Widely associated with its developer, Ernest Dichter, motivation research relies on the so-called depth interview. Dichter and others who utilize motivation research rely heavily on the theories and constructs of psychoanalysis. The assumption is that consumer behavior is understandable only in terms of deep, usually unconscious feelings and motives. Rather than relying on the brief replies to relatively superficial questions by a large sample of respondents, motivation research utilizes intensive interviews with a comparatively small sample. The goal of these interviews is to probe the dynamics of the subjects so that those motivational characteristics related to purchasing behavior may be brought to light.

The results of these interviews are then used in planning advertising and product development campaigns. For instance, if one is trying to sell a cake of soap, there are several approaches. Price might be emphasized. Motivation research might suggest, however, that subtle references to the product's ability to reduce guilt-produced feelings of dirtiness would be more effective. The notion that the convertible automobile is a symbol of virile masculinity is another example.

It is true that unconscious motivations influence our behavior more than most realize. On that basis, motivation research may be on the right track. More evaluative research needs to be done before a final judgment of the effectiveness of this approach can be entered. Moreover, any such indirect approach through the unconscious involves ethical issues which have been the subject of wide spread discussion.

Conclusion

We have seen that business has come to place increasing reliance on market analyses, surveys of consumer preference, psychological brand barometers sensitive to changing trends in buying habits, and studies of business conditions affecting the sale of a particular product; and that personal interviews are indispensable in securing quickly the facts essential to such commercial surveys.

These interviews are of two kinds: (1) a short, well-systematized inquiry which follows closely the outline of a specific questionnaire, for securing information from consumers and from dealers; (2) a more informal interview, to secure from major executives or statistical experts important data regarding their own concerns, and information bearing on general business trends.

Both kinds of interview have to be carefully planned. Indeed, the thoroughness with which preparation is made in advance may well give pause to interviewers in other fields. Based on analytical studies of data obtained from many published sources, the inquiry is mapped out. Decision is made as to the size and distribution of the various samples of the population to be interviewed. The specific questions to be answered are chosen, and so phrased as to be unambiguous and free from implications that might suggest one answer rather than another, but so designed that answers to some of them will serve to check the correctness of others. These questions are then arranged in a natural sequence. The interviewers are selected with reference to their particular duties, instructed in the subject matter of the inquiry, and coached in the procedures to be followed in approaching interviewees, in securing the desired information, and in reporting the results. Meanwhile, seasoned investigators of superior ability make thorough preparation for informal interviews with business experts and executives of various, perhaps competing, firms. They map their campaigns, choose their interviewees with discrimination, and schedule appointments in advance. Their success in securing valuable and frequently confidential data depends not at all on their cleverness in concealing the purpose of the study, but on their straightforward manner of telling the precise object of the visit. In commercial surveys no less than in studies of industrial relations, strict honesty in interviewing has proved to be the best policy.

In the following chapter, we shall deal with opinion and attitude measurement in the industrial situation. Considerable time and effort has been spent in finding out about attitudes and opinions, which have been widely recognized as being critical to employee performance and morale. In these surveys of attitudes, the interview has been the essential technique used.

REFERENCES

1. AMERICAN MARKETING SOCIETY COMMITTEE ON MARKETING RESEARCH TECHNIQUES. *Technique of Marketing Research*. New York: McGraw-Hill, 1937.
2. BLANKENSHIP, A., The effect of the interviewer upon the response in a public opinion poll. *J. consult. Psychol.*, 1940, 4, 134-136.
3. BLANKENSHIP, A., The choice of words in poll questions. *Sociol. soc. Res.*, 1940, 4, 110-113.
4. BLANKENSHIP, A., The influence of the question form upon the response in a public opinion poll. *Psychol. Rec.*, 1940, 3, 345-424.
5. BLANKENSHIP, A., A source of interviewer bias. *Int. J. Opin. Attit. Res.*, 1949, 3, 75-98.
6. BRADLEY, J., *Survey bias as a function of respondent-interviewer interaction*. Unpublished Ph.D. dissertation, Pennsylvania State University, 1952.
7. BRITT, S., The strategy of consumer motivation. *J. Marketing.*, 1950, 666-674.
8. CAMPBELL, A., The uses of interview surveys in federal administration. *J. soc. Issues*, 1946, 2, 14-22.
9. CANTRIL, H., Experiments in the wording of questions. *Publ. Opin. Quart.*, 1940, 4, 330-332.
10. CANTRIL, H. *Gauging Public Opinion*. Princeton: Princeton University Press, 1944.
11. FERBER, R. and WALES, H., Detection and correction of interview bias. *Publ. Opin. Quart.*, 1952, 16, 107-127.
12. FESTINGER, L. and KATZ, D. (Ed.), *Research Methods in the Behavioral Sciences*. New York: Dryden Press, 1953.
13. GALLUP, G. and RAE, F., *The Pulse of Democracy*. New York: Simon and Schuster, 1940.

14. GUEST, L., A study of interviewer competence. *Int. J. Opin. Attitude Res.*, 1947, 1, 17-30.

15. HARRIS, N. and CONNELLY, G., A symposium on interviewing problems. *Int. J. Opin. Attitude Res.*, 1948, 2, 69-84.

16. HYMAN, H., Problems in the collection of opinion-research data. *Amer. J. Sociol.*, 1950, 55, 367-370.

17. HYMAN, H., Trends in public opinion polling since 1948 and their probable effects on 1952 election predictions. In Proceedings, 1952 Conference on Testing Problems, Educational Testing Service. Princeton: Educational Testing Service, 1953.

18. HYMAN, H., et al. *Interviewing in Social Research.* Chicago: University of Chicago Press, 1953.

19. JAHODA, M., et al. *Research Methods in Social Relations.* New York: Dryden 1951.

20. JENKINS, J., Characteristics of the question as determinants of dependability. *J. consult. Psychol.*, 1941, 5, 164-169.

21. KNEELAND, N., The interview in training salespeople: Techniques for instruction based on errors, ratings, and service shopping reports. *Personnel J.*, 1929, 8, 47-52.

22. LIKERT, R., The sample interview survey: a fundamental research tool in social sciences. In Dennis, W. (Ed.) *Current Trends in Psychology.* Pittsburgh: University of Pittsburgh Press, 1947.

23. LINK, H., A new method for testing advertising and a psychological sales barometer. *J. appl. Psychol.*, 1934, 18, 1-26.

24. METZNER, H. and MANN, F., A limited comparison of two methods of data collection: the fixed alternative questionnaire and the open-ended interview. *Amer. sociol. Rev.*, 1952, 17, 486-491.

25. MOCKETT, J., Service shopping in stores. *J. Personnel Res.*, 1924, 3, 338-346.

26. ROSLOW, S. and BLANKENSHIP, A., Phrasing the question in consumer research. *J. appl. Psychol.*, 1939, 23, 612-622.

27. SHEATSLEY, P., An analysis of interviewer characteristics and their relationship to performance. *Int. J. Opin. Attitude Res.*, 1950, 4, 473-498.

28. SHEATSLEY, P., An analysis of interviewer characteristics and their relationship to performance: part II. *Int. J. Opin. Attitude Res.*, 1951, 5, 79-94.

29. SMITH, H. and HYMAN, H., The biasing effect of interviewer expectations on survey results. *Publ. Opin. Quart.*, 1950, 14, 491-506.

30. SMITH, M., BRUNER, J., and WHITE, R., A group research project on the dynamics and measurement of opinion. *Int. J. Opin. Attitude Res.*, 1947, 1, 78-82.

31. STEMBER, H. and HYMAN, H., How interviewer effects operate through question form. *Int. J. Opin. Attitude Res.,* 1949, 3, 493, 511.

32. STOUFFER, S., *et al. The American Soldier. Volume 4. Measurement and Prediction.* Princeton: Princeton University Press, 1950.

33. STUDENSKI, P., How polls can mislead. *Harper's Magazine,* 1938, 180, December, 97-104.

34. WECHSLER, J., Polling America. *Nation,* 1940, January 20, 64-67.

35. WHITE, P., *Market Analysis.* New York: McGraw-Hill, 1925.

8. Interviewing Workers about Employer-Employee Relationships

THE attitudes and emotionally toned ideas of workers and their supervisors are potent in shaping employer-employee relations. Such factors largely determine, for instance, the extent to which the provisions of the National Labor Relations Act facilitate co-operation or precipitate conflict. Attitudes and beliefs cannot be taken for granted. They should be skillfully and accurately ascertained. Leaders of labor and of management alike need to uncover and to assay the facts as to workers' feelings of insecurity, annoyance, frustration, fear, suspicion, and antagonism as well as their preferences, ambitions, loyalties, and satisfactions in the job. Only in the light of such understanding can industrial statesmanship forestall unnecessary conflict and build an enduring structure of sound co-operative relations between employer and employee.

In this book's first edition, the authors reported in detail an experiment in interviewing 511 textile workers on strike in New Bedford. The personal interview proved to be a feasible means for revealing attitudes in this kind of industrial situation. As there employed, it was found to be practicable and fairly reliable. Given a frank, open-minded approach, with precautions against errors resulting from mutual misunderstanding of terms, the reliability of the interview for revealing attitudes is higher than has commonly been supposed; higher, indeed, than its reliability in ascertaining facts of a more objective sort, such as dates, or number of fellow workers in a plant.

The interview designed to reveal attitudes of workers toward the conditions under which they work and the relations they sustained to fellow workers, to supervisors, and to management, often meets with the greatest success when the interviewer obtrudes himself least—when, in other words, he maintains the rôle of listener. When he learns to be skillful in that rôle, his interviews become most rewarding.

Problems investigated by employment relations interviews

The types of problems most often investigated by means of the employment relations interview will now be described, with illustrations of the different ways in which they are approached and of the means taken to increase the skill of interviewers in being good listeners.

An affluent employer wanted to find out how much his employees appreciated all the fine things his company was doing for them and which of these they prized most. He was interested to know not only how contented they were with their good wages, reasonable hours, steady employment, healthful working conditions, and opportunities for promotion; he was even more anxious to learn whether they fully appreciated the sick benefits, pensions, group insurance, opportunity for stock purchase, and vacations with pay, not to mention hospital service and rest rooms, company restaurants, evening classes, and all the athletic facilities, picnics, and parties which he delighted to provide. After an extensive inquiry had been made at his request by an outside agency, he was amazed to learn that the very features of his employment relations program of which he was proudest and on which he gladly spent the most money were either resented or held in slight esteem by the majority of his employees. Matters which to him had seemed trivial or unworthy of attention, such as provision for some participation by the employees themselves in determining what these employment relations policies and expenditures should be, loomed large in the minds of the workers. He was brought up short.

This incident is not unique in the history of business, or of government. Rulers and legislators, as well as employers and labor leaders, have from time to time throughout the centuries awakened with a start on discovering that the feelings of their people were the opposite of what they had supposed. The need for correct understanding of real preferences and attitudes requires no elaboration here. It is obviously indispensable to sound management and satisfactory employee relations. We shall, then, ask what function the interview has as a means to such understanding, and how it may be most effectively used to that end.

The employment relations interview has several uses in addition to its obvious one of enlightening management as to what is on the worker's mind, indicating environmental conditions to be corrected, improvements to be introduced, or hindrances to smooth operation which can be removed. It can be made a valuable instrument for building morale, and also for developing more competent supervision; for, rightly employed, the very process of interviewing benefits both interviewer and interviewee. It enables the employee or the supervisor whose views are solicited to get off his chest any irritation he may have been nursing—a wholesome catharsis which tends to bring at once a new release of energy, good will, and zest for work. The manager or his representative who does the interviewing likewise benefits. He learns. He gets fresh insight into the springs of action and the varied manifestations of human nature. And he accumulates a wealth of specific incidents and vivid expressions of attitude invaluable as concrete illustrations for use in training other leaders as well as himself. Industry is learning how to capitalize at its full value the employment relations interview as a mine of instructional material for discussion in supervisory conferences. From interviews which yield such educative materials, and which at the same time have immediate values for therapy as well as for fact finding, both management and worker may profit.

Let us see how personal interviews are used to accomplish this threefold purpose of supplying management with information regarding conditions and attitudes, releasing the will to work among employees and supervisors interviewed, and building up a supply of valuable case material to be brought to the attention of supervisors and executives in the course of their training for higher responsibility.

Techniques in the employee management relations interview

Wide differences are noted in type, character, and length of interviews. They vary all the way from the casual conversation, that just happens, to the systematized questionnaire. They may be formal or informal; specific or general; stereotyped or free. The best interview often begins as an informal conversation on some matter of immediate interest such as the effect of the damp weather on fluctuations in output, progress of the children in school, or yesterday's baseball victory. Then its course is determined for a time by the interviewee, not by the interviewer who, only by being interested but otherwise passive, can get an indication of attitudes and feeling states and permit the emergence of whatever is uppermost in the employee's thoughts. During this free conversational stage, the successful interviewer resists his natural impulse to suggest topics or ask questions which will lead the course of the discussion toward particular points; but he is alert to notice clues to dominant interests, preferences, sources of irritation, or obsessions. Does the conversation turn a second time to the topic of the time-study man? Or is there a note of discouragement in a remark about the difficulty of getting ahead? While evincing a genuine interest in the interviewee and so encouraging him to a measure of self-revelation, it tests the mettle of an interviewer to have to keep his hand off the tiller and let the conversation drift; but only so are deep currents detected.

Following upon this free and unguided stage of the interview, the interviewer takes the helm. He first asks questions to draw out details regarding significant points that have been touched upon; and then other questions, to secure reactions with reference to topics on which he is making a systematic inquiry. This catechizing, if it is done at all, follows but does not precede the informal, undirected conversation. It has been repeatedly demonstrated by controlled experiments in the psychology of testimony—as we shall see in the chapter on the Interview for Legal Evidence—that the free narrative report which is afterwards supplemented by specific questions, carefully worded so as to avoid implication or suggestion, yields the most accurate picture of the facts; so, in getting the picture of a worker's attitude, his free conversational statements should proceed specific questioning. The final stage of such an interview is again a free and informal one. The interviewer is still alert, for not infrequently it is during this apparently inconsequential after-conversation that the most revealing comments of all are dropped.

Immediately following such an interview it should be written up fully, preserving so far as possible the actual words and expressions used.

An employment relations interview of the type described takes time, patience, and skill. It is rewarding but expensive. It is not used when the purpose is a less general one and information is sought only as to preferences regarding a specific policy, such as adoption of the three-day week in preference to a 50 per cent layoff during a slack period, or as to feelings regarding the relative importance of several of the firm's policies of personnel management. In such inquiries, a clear statement of purpose and a brief discussion of the points at issue lead directly to the categorical questions. Even here, however, opportunity should be given the interviewee to amplify and qualify his answers. As we found in an investigation of employees' attitudes toward an employment guarantee plan in a Holyoke paper mill, these comments and qualifications throw valuable light on categorical answers. This same investigation showed how close is the similarity of returns obtained by interview and those secured by secret ballot on the question at issue. But the interviews revealed shades of opinion and partial exceptions to an otherwise favorable attitude which the ballot necessarily smothered. When, as in this instance, the distribution of preferences regarding a particular policy is to be ascertained, recourse to the relatively expensive and time-consuming method of the interview rather than to the ballot cannot be recommended, but its use with a representative sampling of those whose attitude is in question, as a supplement to the ballot, is strongly urged.

The same position may be taken regarding the relative value of the personal interview in comparison with the printed questionnaire. Mass data of a most illuminating sort regarding employee attitudes have been gathered expeditiously by means of questionnaires, clearly constructed and specific. But such inquiries need to be preceded and followed by interviews with a sufficient number of employees to make certain that the questions are correctly understood and that they are taken seriously. These interviews at the same time serve to interpret and illuminate the questionnaire data. Indeed, it must not be forgotten that often the employment relations interview has its chief usefulness as a supplementary aid to other methods of inquiry. It can suggest hypotheses, supply leads, reveal avenues of approach to be followed; and it has its uses also in checking the findings of other types of investigation, statistical or experimental. The fact that it usually raises more questions than it answers is not wholly to the discredit of the interview.

Interviews for revealing employee attitudes and learning about employment conditions have much in common with several types of interview to which reference was made in preceding chapters. The employment manager's interview with the leaving employee at time of separation is distinctly of this sort. The personnel executive who is successful in getting at real reasons for leaving rather than those first alleged will also succeeed in uncovering real grievances or sources of unrest in plant or office. In his follow-up interviews with employees recently hired, and in his talks with employees seeking transfer or promotion, he also has good opportunities to sound out employee opinion and gather suggestions of value to the management.

The interviewer may, for example, hear of a drill press not kept in repair or of a belt placed so that it is an unnecessary hazard to passing workers. Sometimes it is the piece rate, or the pace of the machine, that leads to dissatisfaction. More often the trouble is alleged to be with a supervisor who cannot or does not teach, or with a foreman who is felt to be abusive or not "on the square." The interviewer uses such information with discretion, first making certain that it is correct and then making it available to those who are in a position to do something about it, provided this can be done in such a way that there is no chance of reprisal or annoyance to the particular employees from whom the information came.

The interview for job analysis as a basis for the establishment of standard practice and personnel specifications has for many years served to yield also as a valuable by-product information regarding employee opinions, attitudes, satisfactions, anxieties, and resentments. This interview aims to secure a full list of a man's duties and responsibilities. The crucial question is "Just what do you do?" When the analysis is complete, it shows the specific knowledge, skills, and personal qualifications needed in order to do these things and to fill this position satisfactorily. The interviewing may be carried out by a specialist from the personnel department. Often it is done in part at least by the employee's immediate superior, with the guidance of the analyst. No such intimate study can be made without revealing the worker's attitude toward his work. Conditions calling for adjustment are often brought into the open during the course of a job analysis.

A similar source of significant information about attitudes is the interview conducted in connection with the making of a personnel audit—a systematic inventory of a firm's human assets and liabilities. One purpose of such an audit is to enable the management to budget its personnel requirements and plan for future needs. Since the inventory begins at the top and includes officials and staff executives as well as office force, salesmen, engineers, operating executives, supervisors, and employees, skilled and unskilled, it provides an unparalleled opportunity for securing a complete cross section of representative attitudes throughout the organization.

A firm sometimes undertakes, in addition to the personnel audits, to make a complete survey of its employer-employee relations. Whether such an inquiry is carried out by the management's own personnel staff or by an outside agency specializing in such service, the interview is obviously one of the essential methods employed. It is never the main reliance. Often it is used chiefly as a means of defining problems and as a lead to sources of more objective data. Wage sheets, labor turnover figures classified by departments and causes of leaving, records of absence, illness, accidents, discharges, complaints, suggestions received and acted upon, minutes of supervisors' conferences and employee organizations, joint agreements, arbitrations, and statistics as to employee stock ownership, thrift, and participation in insurance and benefit plans, tell more about the pulse of employee relations than any amount of personal interviewing can reveal. But these cold records and statistics never contain the whole story. The fact remains that only through direct personal contact with employees and officials can an appraisal be made of the true status of employee relations in some of its aspects. On the one hand are sure to be unreported grievances, apprehensions, dissatisfactions; and on the other, loyalties and good will not fully measured by any of the personnel statistics. These liabilities and assets can to some degree be brought to light in the employment relations interview. Moreover, if these interviews are planned and systematized to that end, they can, as Houser has shown, be made to yield a reliable index of morale.

We have deferred specific reference to the use of the interview in investigations of joint relations—the relations of employees as a group to employer, or to employers as a group. The questions at issue are often controversial: wage standards, hours, working conditions; recognition of the employees' right to organize and to conduct negotiations with employers through union officials; open shop *vs.* closed shop; craft unions *vs.* industrial unions; unadjusted grievances, unfair practices, and the like. Such investigations are often carried forward of necessity in the heat of conflict, in an atmosphere of antagonism or industrial war. In no other aspect of employee relations has the interview as a method of inquiry been used more widely or scrutinized more closely as to its validity and techniques. And rightly so. For the questions to be answered are vital and many of the facts on which sound conclusions can be based are obtainable in no other way. When, however, the conflict of interests is intense and controversy is hottest, the method of the personal interview is put to its severest test, the test of ability to arrive at truth in spite of bias, prejudice, and fundamental differences of attitude on the part of those interviewed. And not only is the bias of self-interest of the interviewee, whether worker or employer, to be reckoned with. The investigator as well comes to his task with predilections born of his social philosophy, his own economic and social status, his past experience and present affiliations. Hence, the peculiar need in this field of labor controversy for precautions by means of which to safeguard the integrity of the personal interview and to ensure reliable, disinterested fact finding.

In preparation, then, for such an inquiry, the employment relations investigator will first quite objectively ascertain his own bias, and take care that it is not allowed to color his questions, his attitude in interviewing, or his report. He will define the issue clearly and determine in advance what facts obtainable by interview are significant and relevant to a solution. He will map his campaign in general and in detail, outlining the specific topics of inquiry, and formulating in advance the precise wording of key questions. He will choose his interviewees with care, making certain that he gets access to a sufficient number of representatives of each of the conflicting points of view. He will establish his status with both groups and win their confidence while maintaining an evident disinterestedness and impartiality.

In carrying forward the inquiry, the interviewer must be able to win and deserve the confidence of those he questions, for only so can he count on frankness and sincerity from them.

When making notes of interviews, he scrupulously keeps the record of facts observed and of statements made to him separate from any inferences or interpretations of his own.

Important interviews he reduces to writing and later has the essential substance of them confirmed by the interviewees.

As the investigation progresses, he summarizes it from time to time, and before it is completed, submits his tentative findings to each of the contending parties for correction and comment; but he reserves for himself the responsibility of final summary, interpretation, and conclusion.

Such is the course the interviewer takes in charting his way through troubled waters of industrial conflict. He is a skillful mariner who escapes shipwreck in the whirlpool of suspicion or on the jagged rocks of his own preconception. But when he does succeed in steering between Scylla and Charybdis, he makes port with a rich cargo.

No interviewer has written more illuminatingly of these and other hazards of industrial investigation than Mary van Kleeck, director of industrial studies of the Russell Sage Foundation. To her publications the serious student of interviewing in the employment relations field is particularly recommended (13).

Having noted the range of uses which the employment relations interview serves and the many forms it assumes, attention turns to certain questions of specific procedure. How is it possible to gain that degree of confidence without which the interview must surely fail? How can the interviewer learn to listen—patiently, interestedly, alertly? Who makes the best interviewer—an inside man or a stranger, an executive or a fellow worker? How should the results of interviews be digested, summarized, used? What pitfalls peculiar to this kind of interviewing can be identified and guarded against?

Gaining confidence of the interviewee

There is no single simple formula for winning confidence, but there are several points, more or less obvious perhaps, which may here be touched upon because unfortunately they are sometimes overlooked.

The one best way to gain a man's confidence is to deserve it. The successful interviewer steels himself against the natural impulse to talk over with his acquaintances choice bits of personal information that come to him in the course of his interviewing. He is no bearer of tales. The intention of personal integrity in this intimate relationship is not enough. It has to be a habit. Many an interviewer has damaged his usefulness in an industrial situation through a chance remark that eventually reached the ears of his interviewee or of a supervisor who proceeded to use the information to the annoyance or disadvantage of the one most concerned. The temptation to tell is sometimes strong. Many a manager is anxious to find out just who it is who thinks the foreman has double-crossed him or who is arguing for a closed shop. Indeed, the old practice of maintaining spies, stool pigeons, or secret-service men for the precise purpose of locating and discharging disgruntled employees and troublemakers became shamefully prevalent again in some industries during the 1930's, as the LaFollette Senatorial Investigation revealed. That such practices continue is suggested by the recent McClelland committee hearings.

Particularly reprehensible is the policy of shortsighted overseers who pride themselves on having a few personally loyal men among the employees who covertly spy on their fellow workers and report any laxness or disaffection. There may be situations, as in the railway business, in which undercover men are needed to check up on employees entrusted with the collection of money. The fact that conductors know they may be caught in any attempted peculations may be a wholesome deterrent. But as a source of information regarding employee attitudes in general, the undercover man is notoriously unreliable; and the manager who is known to depend upon information obtained through stealth forthwith forfeits any expectation of confidence and respect. As with manager or labor leader, so with interviewer: it pays to be forthright. Sincere straightforwardness on his part engenders a similar attitude in those with whom he talks, just as surely as sly cleverness breeds suspicion. The rôle of detective is wholly foreign to real mutual understanding.

For these reasons the employment relations interviewer does not delay in letting the interviewee know what his purpose is, if there is any room for doubt. He wants no misunderstanding on that score. At the same time, he aims to do this in a way that relates his purpose to the interviewee's interests. This is relatively simple provided his inquiry is not partisan but rather a genuinely disinterested effort to reach the truth as a basis for mutual understanding.

The interviewer's personal interest in the employee with whom he talks must be real and not assumed. Nothing is more irritating to a worker than to glimpse in the interviewer an artificial, insincere show of interest in him and in what he is saying. No one can successfully pretend to an interest he does not feel.

The interviewer will naturally wish to learn in advance enough about the interviewee and his work so that he can talk the worker's language and can start from a natural point of contact. When this advance information is not readily secured, it is often well to begin with a few direct questions about the worker's present occupation. "What are you doing now? . . . How is the work going? . . . What job did you have before that? . . . Do you like this work better?" and the conversation is launched.

While some interviewers are naturally more skillful than others in stating the purpose of the interview and more competent in tapping a copious flow of comment and suggestions, all who are selected for this work benefit from at least a minimum of specialized training. This training covers the approach, including, when necessary, a guarantee of anonymity, and practice in recording interviews so as to preserve the essential features while deleting items which would serve to identify to others the source of the information. Special pains must be taken to instruct the interviewer to keep hands off and let the interviewee talk freely once he is under way. Equally important is some preliminary training in noticing apparently insignificant references and comments which in spite of their casual nature contain indications of anxieties, obsessions, or fears. This may be done with the use of illustrative material already gathered. The interviewer needs to be cautioned, however, against the danger of letting his attention run exclusively along grooves suggested by these particular illustrations or by lists of items which may have been gone over in the course of the training. He usually needs to be reminded that no two people are alike, that what weighs heavily with one is trivial to another, and that his duty is to get the real picture of the situation as it appears to the person to whom he listens.

The interviewer usually needs to be especially cautioned not to argue or instruct. It is no function of his to moralize or to try then and there to correct an attitude which he may feel to be wrong. His duty is to listen and to understand.

The art of listening can be practiced during the interview; but after all, the interview is only a beginning. In writing up accounts of interviews and later studying these reports, the attitude of listeners still needs to be cultivated, for most people have a strong proclivity to impose their own interpretations on what is said, rather than to take the other person's point of view, and read into the narrative what he intended.

The ability to take the rôle of listener is one of the outstanding characteristics of successful leadership as well as of successful research.

Systematic surveys of employee attitude cannot always be carried out by experienced masters of the art of interviewing connected with organizations specializing in this type of investigation. Indeed, a great deal may be said for inquiries conducted by the management itself. In these instances the question arises whether the most value is to be secured from interviewing done directly by executives or managers, by foremen and supervisors close to the daily problems of shop or office, or by personnel specialists in the industrial relations department. Some firms have chosen interviewers with a background of training in psychiatric social work. Others have placed the responsibility on a nurse attached to the plant hospital who seizes the opportunity to talk with employees who come for treatment, medical or optical examination, or first aid. As between the interviewer who comes from the outside and the one who knows the plant from within and also has the advantage of being already well and favorably known to the workers, no good evidence has been adduced that there are marked advantages either way. Indeed, success depends much more on the ability and training of the individual interviewer than on his status and connection or on his intimate familiarity with the particular industrial setting.

Examples from industry

The Western Electric Company in its Hawthorne Works took a bold step in past years in selecting the interviewers from among the ranks of the workers themselves. For these workers, the learning of the interviewing process then becomes a stage in their development as future supervisors. This plan makes it easy for the employee to talk frankly in conversation with someone of his own status. The status, to be sure, is not precisely the same, because the interviewer, although himself a worker, has been designated as a representative of the management in this particular relationship. But the thousands of employees who have now been interviewed in this way apparently find the relationship quite satisfactory. Many of them are glad of the opportunity to tell what they think and to offer suggestions, for improvement of conditions. The results of the program of employee interviewing as carried out in the Hawthorne plant far surpassed expectations in improvement of morale, increase in earning power, and better understanding between employees and management.

This particular experiment of the Western Electric Company in the systematic use of the employment relations interview has been one of the notable developments of industrial management practice. It was first described by G. A. Pennock, M. L. Putnam, and Elton Mayo in the *Personnel Journal* for February, 1930, and in Mayo's *Human Problems of an Industrial Civilization* (8). A later and more complete statement is found in *Management and the Worker* by

Roethlisberger and Dickson (11). It had its origin, curiously, in an effort to determine by controlled experiments the effect of increased illumination on output. One question led to another. In order to be able to observe and measure the effect of different influences affecting individual variations in production, a small group of women relay assemblers were isolated from the other employees doing this work, and special equipment installed which automatically recorded their performance minute by minute.

Every effort was made to keep as nearly constant as possible all external conditions and incentives. Then after a basic period of five weeks, one factor after another was varied and its effect noted. The first change was in the wage incentive, a special method of group payment being adopted. Eight weeks later, rest periods of five minutes each were introduced, at ten o'clock and at two. After five weeks the length of these rest periods was doubled. Then six rests of five minutes each were tried for a month. In this way observations were made of changes in workers' performance which followed other modifications of working conditions, including, at various times, provision for a midforenoon lunch, a shorter working day, and a five-day week. Some physiological measurements were made at various times, including vascular skin reaction, systolic and diastolic blood pressure, blood count, and other indicators of fatigue and metabolic balance. These served to assure the investigators that no excessive fatigue or other harmful physiological effects were resulting from the work. Indeed, general health improved.

All this time the supervisor noted remarks made in conversations, and the girls were interviewed quite informally as to their attitude toward their work and the prevailing conditions. Matters of health, diet, sleep, recreation, and irritations or anxieties caused by home conditions were recognized from time to time as accounting in part for fluctuations in the records of individual performance.

This interviewing was done partly by a nurse trained to observe and listen as well as to question. Officials and supervisor also naturally showed a keen interest in these employees and in their expressions of attitude. But no pressure to speed up was at any time exerted. The instructions were always for the assemblers to maintain their natural pace.

The results were astonishing. They were measured not only in terms of output, which on the whole increased prodigiously, but also in terms of promptness and regularity of attendance, and of employees' satisfactions and morale as observed and as ascertained in personal interview. Obviously factors far more potent than any of the external conditions, such as rest periods, wage incentives, or length of working day, were operating. Eventually it became unmistakably clear that the most powerful of these favorable influences was the type of supervision exercised—friendly, informal, free from pressure or harsh order giving—coupled with the keen personal interest in each employee shown by interviewers and managers.

This principle of management, that the most potent of all incentives to good work is genuinely interested personal supervision of the kind that listens rather than shouts orders, was no new discovery. Wise managers and overseers have always known and practiced it in some degree. They have kept the door open to any employee with a complaint. They have gladly listened and undertaken to straighten out the difficulty. They have tried to know their workers personally, to have and to show a genuine interest in each of them as a fellow human being rather than as a cog in the great machine. But never before has the truth of this basic principle of sound employee relations been more clearly and strikingly demonstrated.

The management, then, was confronted by a practical problem. How could the benefits of this investigation be spread to all the 30,000 employees in the plant? Could they be assured an opportunity to unburden themselves if they wished, to express themselves quite freely about conditions and personal relations? And the foremen, supervisors, gang bosses—2,000 of them—how could they all be trained to listen, to understand, to stop yelling and domineering, and to take a real personal interest in each of their people?

Two main steps were taken to accomplish these ends. The first was to provide a new avenue of personal contact between workers and management. Some sixty workers were chosen and trained as interviewers. They were then sent into other departments than their own to interview workers there. Each employee interviewed was told that the management wanted to learn what he thought about conditions, what he liked and disliked about his work and circumstances, and anything else he cared to say. He was promised anonymity, and given entire freedom in choice of topics to be talked about. Sometimes no complaints, dissatisfactions or suggestions were forthcoming. Often the conversation went far afield. Always the interviewer tried to avoid guiding the interview toward particular subjects, but kept himself on the alert for any indications however obscure, of worries or dissatisfactions as well as of favorable attitudes. Although sometimes there was reticence or suspicion, these opportunities to talk openly and frankly with a fellow employee who represented the management were welcomed by most of the workers. Many were ready and eager to unburden themselves of minor irritations or long-harbored resentments. Many had specific suggestions for bettering working conditions. Indeed, these interviews not only supplied a safety valve for blowing off steam; they furnished the management with valuable indications of shop conditions, material and personal, which could at once be improved.

Of course, the guarantee of anonymity was scrupulously respected. Otherwise the whole experiment would have led only to disaster. The interviewer wrote up the significant parts of each interview, preserving so far as possible the worker's own phraseology, but carefully omitting or disguising details which might lead to identification. These reports were further scrutinized and modified to this end by members of the industrial research staff.

When a sufficient number of interviews had been completed in several different departments, the reports were analyzed, complaints and suggestions were classified and counted, and brought to the attention of the authorities who could in many instances remedy the situations in question. Thus an exceptional number of comments about the temperature in one room led to the discovery that in installing the new heating system there had been an error in computing the radiating surface required to provide a temperature suitable for the kind of sedentary work then being done in that room. In such ways both management and workers found the interviewing valuable.

The second essential step in extending widely the benefits of the industrial investigations was taken in connection with the program of supervisory training. The aim was to teach all the supervisors how to deal with their workers in the essentially friendly, personal ways which the investigation had demonstrated to be so vital to employee morale. This was not done by lecturing them. The research staff first selected and edited a variety of typical interviews. These were mimeographed. Then the supervisors were brought together biweekly in groups of sixteen, under the leadership of one of their number or of a member of the training staff, to read one of these interviews and to discuss it among themselves.

These supervisory conferences led to results no less amazing than those of the original experimental investigation. Some of the more capable supervisors, to be sure, already had little need of the illumination which these intimately revealing human documents supplied. Others, temperamentally of a different type, failed to be interested or to profit from the discussions. But by and large a new impetus was given to intelligent supervision, a readier recognition of difference between workers, and an understanding of the personal values they cherish. The conferences continue to carry over into the daily practice of the supervisors the essential point of view, the concrete knowledge of human nature at work, and the habit of listening.

Here and there, other firms have taken an attitude similar to that of the management at Hawthorne, and have more or less systematically undertaken to enrich their supervisory training with fresh concrete materials secured through employee interviews. In one Pennsylvania factory 243 employees were interviewed by five instructors from the Extension Department of Pennsylvania State College. In describing the findings, Richards (10) attributes a preponderance of unfavorable over favorable comments from the workers to a natural tendency under such circumstances to mention unsatisfactory conditions and to take satisfactory conditions for granted. Marked differences among the interviewers were noted in their ability to avoid leading questions and suggestions of topics.

Sometimes supervision involves the interview for reprimand. This is more effective if it is in the form of constructive criticism or instruction. Interviews by supervisors with employees which center around general impressions are likely to accomplish very little. Flanagan and Burns (1) reported the use of an Employee Performance Record, on which the foreman records incidents indicating significant achievement or failure on the job. When using this record the foreman makes no over-all judgments. He merely cites the incidents he has observed and recorded with the time and circumstances of each, and discusses both the causes and the consequences of these types of performances. If the foreman is experienced and has acquired skill in presenting such facts, the employee is quick to agree that these are the facts and to proceed to a discussion of their importance, their basis, and their implications for his future plans and conduct. Foremen have found by experience that prompt daily recording of incidents results in many more incidents being recorded and more effective supervision.

One of the most interesting recent discussions of supervision is in the book by Maier, Solem, and Maier (7). This contains a number of cases drawn from industry and sets forth in detail the technique of role playing as another method found useful in employee relations.

These studies indicate a new trend in the understanding of attitudes of employees. The techniques used are similar to those of the clinic. Industry is on the brink of widespread realization that mental mechanisms studied in the clinic operate also in the individual's everyday experiences, no matter what his occupation, circumstances, and habits.

Appreciation of this point of view is illustrated in Hersey's (5) unique investigation of workers' efforts and emotions as related to their working conditions, health, recreations, and family life. This inquiry had to do with a study of satisfactions and other affective changes in a group of seventeen workers in a railroad shop. The aim was to discover evidence of recurring relationships between personal or environmental factors affecting the individual worker, on the one hand, and, on the other, his behavior, whether objective or emotional, while at work. The method entailed an informal but intimate interview or conversation, continuing from day to day for the better part of a year. "In the relationship which the investigator has sought to develop between the workmen and himself," says Hersey, writing of this study, "there is an approach to psychoanalytic methods and techniques; but there is an important difference in that these relationships are built up within the actual surroundings in which the experiences studied take place. The investigator has *lived with* his subjects in the shop, and so far as possible become an accepted and familiar visitor in their homes." There was the definite attempt, however, to get each worker to "explode his thoughts." During the year, with two intervals of eight and four weeks inserted as breathing spells, the investigator spent every working day and many evenings and Sundays with the workers. He both observed the men and received oral reports from them each day in regard to their physical condition, sensations of fatigue, efficiency in production, use of leisure time, and many other details related directly or indirectly to their success and satisfaction in their work. Upon reaching the shop each day the investigator procured from each man an account of all of his important activities since the preceding day. The working day itself was divided into quarters of two forenoon and two afternoon periods. Data were obtained from all the workers for each quarter of the day. The workers' statements for each period of the day were compared with objective measures of production, and occasionally with chemical analyses of their blood, and with blood pressure tests, prone and standing, taken at the beginning and at the end of the work day. One significant finding which depended largely on data secured through interview related to emotional changes of these normal workers. Indications were found that all these men went through regular periodic emotional cycles—ups and downs of mood somewhat analogous to manic and depressed states—the periods being from three to nine weeks long. The length of the cycle varied with different individuals, but was more or less constant for each worker.

In this study of conditions, internal and external, influencing a worker's feelings and attitudes, the interview as a means of ascertaining these subjective states was indispensable. The light it shed on shop conditions and personal relations between employees and their supervisors, as well as on the fluctuations of emotional attitude above described, has since given fresh vividness and practicality to the foremen's training conferences in this shop. Hersey subsequently made similar studies of attitudes, feelings, and fluctuations of output of workers in four shops of the German State Railways.

The employment relations interview is not only a tool for research, nor is its use restricted to investigators and interviewers specially trained. It is an instrument for continuous service, available to all. The understanding of human relations is an integral function of management. Almost every working day in the year, every supervisor, foreman, and executive has, or ought to have, interviews with his subordinates—conversations to give him intimate knowledge of how they feel as well as what they are doing. Like the function of training one's subordinates, it must be performed in the main not by any specially constituted staff, but by each executive personally. But again, like training, this function is usually better done if the executive has the help of staff specialists. Both by way of the personnel department and through the doorway to every office, the employee should find access to a ready listener. Not to his immediate superior alone but to anyone he chooses as confidant should he be privileged to talk; and the supervisor should not be irritated if the worker sometimes goes over his head to someone higher up. To old-line bosses, brought up in the military school of authoritative control, this is preposterous doctrine, subversive of all discipline and sound organization. Complaints, they say, should be made to the foreman, and come up through regular channels; and so they will, ordinarily, if the foreman has learned to listen. In any event, the employee's need for unburdening himself is vastly less frequent and insistent in those plants where the opportunities to talk it out are not restricted. Where this enlightened policy prevails, the management has less unrest to deal with among employees because it has more complete and accurate information about their attitudes, because it can better anticipate and forestall difficult situations, and because the employees, easily relieved of pent-up feelings, actually have a far better spirit and fewer causes of dissatisfaction.

In conclusion, the main principles applicable to the employee relations interview may be briefly recapitulated:

The process of unburdening is in itself a wholesome experience. Impulsions can be talked out instead of acted out.

The interviewer should listen, not argue.

He should show his interest, and this means that he must really be interested.

When the subject is a controversial one, he should discover his own bias, and abandon it for a strictly impartial point of view.

In recording his interviews he should keep his data clearly separate from any interpretations of his own.

The interview yields information which may be useful in remedying conditions, removing anxieties, and bringing about better personal relationships.

It enables management to sound out employees' attitudes, anticipating troubles and resentments before they become acute.

Findings secured through interview may be tabulated by departments or divisions, and also by topics mentioned in the course of the interview. In this way the management secures indications of the relative importance of different matters brought to light, and of where remedies should be applied.

The interview is most effective when the person interviewed has confidence that what he says will not be used to his disadvantage.

To win confidence, the interviewer should deserve it.

A guarantee that an interview will be kept in confidence, once given or implied, must under no circumstances be violated.

Concrete instances gathered by personal interview and disguised to ensure anonymity, furnish valuable material for illustrative use in supervisory training.

The person who does the interviewing learns much about human nature and about industrial conditions which cannot be adequately reduced to writing. The experience of interviewing thus constitutes a valuable feature of the training of supervisors and prospective supervisors.

Hence, when employees are selected to do the interviewing they are receiving exceptional training for future responsibility.

Personal interviewing is not only the task of the personnel specialist but of everyone with supervisory and executive responsibility. Rightly done, it helps to allay industrial unrest, for it forestalls irritations, disarms hostility, makes friends, and releases the will to work.

In the employment relations interview, perhaps more than in any other, the success of the interviewer depends on how well he is able to listen. His judgments must be based on what he has learned directly from the interviewee. His own opinions must be laid aside, leaving his mind as unprejudiced as a photographic plate. This difficult task, if well learned, will make him more competent in many fields of interviewing.

REFERENCES

1. FLANAGAN, J. and BURNS, R., The employee performance record: a new appraisal and development tool. *Harvard Business Rev.*, 1955, 33, 95-102.
2. GARDINER, G., *How to Handle Grievances.* Elliott Service Co., New York, 1937.
3. GILSON, M., *What's Past is Prologue.* New York: Harper, 1940.
4. HADER, J. and LINDEMAN, E., *Dynamic Social Research.* New York: Harcourt, 1933.
5. HERSEY, B. *Workers' Emotions in Shop and Home.* Philadelphia: University of Pennsylvania Press, 1932.
6. LANSBURGH, R. and SPRIEGEL, W., *Industrial Management.* (Third Edition) New York: Wiley, 1940.
7. MAIER, N., SOLEM, A., and MAIER, A., *Supervisory and Executive Development.* New York: Wiley, 1957.
8. MAYO, E., *The Human Problems of an Industrial Civilization.* New York: Macmillan, 1933.

9. MERIAM, R,. Employee interviewing and employee representation. *Management Rev.*, 1931, 20, 308.
10. RICHARDS, J., Interviewing industrial employees: a source of foreman training material. *Personnel J.*, 1930, 9, 281-289.
11. ROETHLISBERGER, F. and DICKSON, W., *Management and the Worker.* Cambridge: Harvard University Press, 1939.
12. TEAD, O., *The Art of Leadership.* New York: McGraw-Hill, 1935.
13. VAN KLEECK, M., Procedure followed in studying the industrial representation plan of the Colorado Fuel and Iron Company. *J. Personnel Res.*, 1925, 4, 133, 154.
14. WEBB, B., *My Apprenticeship.* New York: Longmans, 1926.

9. The Interview in Journalism

THERE is one marked difference between the foregoing types of interview and a reporter's interview, the purpose of which is to get the news or materials for a feature article. This difference is in the locus of interest; for the journalistic interview is conducted primarily in the interest not of the person interviewed nor of the interviewer, but of the general reader. The emphasis is on *interesting facts,* that is, facts of concern to an audience quite remote from the immediate situation. The person interviewed may or may not want to help out or to place his information before the reading public. The reporter may or may not be personally intrigued by the material he gathers. But he must not lose sight of his audience. He learns to ask himself intuitively and constantly: "Is this a matter of any moment to our readers? Will it whet their curiosity, challenge their attention by its novelty or strangeness, appeal to them as important, or supply them with needed facts?" How can he train himself to know instantly what is important and interesting? How can he develop a news sense? This center of reference furnishes the key to the peculiar nature of the journalistic interview, and defines its major problem as follows: How can the reporter best get what he needs from a possibly reluctant interviewee who is under no compulsion or obligation to talk?

Many problems of interviewing in journalism do not differ essentially from those in other callings in which it is essential to gather facts and opinions and to verify their correctness. Some of these points, developed at length in other chapters, need only be touched upon here. In the interview for legal evidence, for example, one of the objectives is the eliciting of actual and crucial facts irrespective of the interviewee's wish in the matter. So a reporter profits by the contributions to interviewing made in the legal field, and by study of findings with reference to reliability of testimony. The employment relations interview has in common with the interview in journalism the problem of building up an attitude of confidence and of readiness to talk. The mechanisms observed in clinical interviews and in psychiatric practice are valuable to the reporter, making him aware of latent attitudes and the nature of resistances which he may encounter. No less than in the vocational interview, the importance of a well-planned schedule is recognized, or at least a clear formulation in advance of the direction which the interview may take; and, as in the chapter on the interview in commercial surveys, the value of preparation for the journalistic interview through review of relevant facts is obvious. Toward effective reportorial work each of these fields makes a specific contribution.

Even in the requirement that the interviewer must often secure his materials from a reluctant or passive interviewee, the journalistic interview is not unique or wholly different from many other interviews. But since this requirement is distinctly characteristic of the reporter's work, it will be developed here in a way which may be suggestive to other interviewers as well.

Getting the interviewee to talk

To secure an interviewee's co-operation, to get him to talk, to lead him to talk about what the reader wants to know—these are problems of motivation not wholly different from those of salesmanship. Indeed, the development of thought in relation to interviewing in the field of journalism has in many respects been analogous to the growth of a psychology of advertising and selling. When writers first discussed the subject, empirical conclusions were stated in the form of many specific warnings and admonitions, illustrated by anecdotes. After these so-called principles had been multiplied, and it was evident that none would apply to all interviews, a reaction set in and it was commonly stated that there could be no general principles: the method to be used depended almost exclusively upon the individual case. With a better understanding of the psychology of human interests and motives, however, it came to be realized that the fundamental principles of motivation underlie the successful interview as well as the sale. Just as the salesman must start with the buyer's point of view, so must the journalist start with the interests of the person he interviews. As one interviewer remarked:

You will never succeed until you learn to put yourself in the place of the man you are dealing with. . . . I have frequently had occasion to observe that to win the favor of a certain type of man, it is necessary, in so far as possible, to make even one's language correspond to his.

Later, another wrote:

The reporter and the salesman have much the same problems. Both must be able to reach their man, to gain and hold his attention, to direct his mind along the way they want it to travel, and finally to show that it will pay him to talk. . . . There is always a way of exploding the reservoirs of silence and making eager, flowing sentences grow where only lifted eyebrows and cautious monosyllables grew before.

How to find and tap a man's real interest, and so sweep away his inhibitions—that becomes the practical question. In his book, *Getting the News,* Maulsby (9) has brought together specific suggestions for different occasions. Some of these need only a change of phrase to apply with equal pertinence to interviewing situations in fields other than journalism.

The reporter's problem is not so much to know how to talk as to know how to listen. The reporter must be able to get facts and opinions from persons who may be total strangers to him. The stranger must be induced to tell everything he knows. . . . People like to talk about themselves. All that is necessary is that the conditions surrounding the conversation be right. The interviewer must understand the interviewee's language, the interviewer must be sympathetic and interested, and the interviewer must impress the interviewee as being discreet. There is no sure way for a reporter to *appear* intelligent, interested, and discreet unless he *is.* . . . To be an intelligent listener on any and all subjects requires a broad general knowledge and a vast fund of experience. . . . But admit ignorance where it exists or the interviewee will perceive it and cease to confide important details. For a reporter to be interested, sympathetic, and enthusiastic depends upon his attitude. If a reporter wants to be interested, he can be and show it in a natural way.

When a reporter engages a man in conversation, it is with the idea of ascertaining definite facts, of acquiring information that will give the background necessary for understanding the situation at issue. Usually the reporter knows, before the conversation begins, what sort of material he may expect from it. He gives the person with whom he talks a chance to furnish not only their own ideas and opinions, but also correct facts which may help him better to understand the situation.

The interviewer, of course, must know enough about differences in human nature to judge what attitude on his part will bring forth the liveliest reaction from the particular interviewee. Sometimes the reporter has to be more optimistic than the man he is interviewing; sometimes it pays to be decidedly pessimistic about one of his subject's pet projects; sometimes, if a reaction to a particular phase of a topic is wanted, it is desirable to ask leading questions that almost put words into the interviewee's mouth.

Good interviewers, if they value spontaneity above precision of report, do not ordinarily show pencil or paper during their conversations; for sight of pen or pencil makes some people feel as if a grim teacher had unexpectedly demanded that they recite a lesson for which there had been no preparation, with the result that they forget whatever they know. The chief reason for not using the pencil is to avoid interrupting the speaker's train of thought.

Some reporters make out in advance a tentative list of questions. The best story, however, is likely to come from things that turn up unexpectedly in the conversation; but to get it, the reporter must be continually on the alert, since the most important facts often put in an appearance obscurely and incidentally. If written questions have been prepared, they should not be produced until the end of the interview, and then with a wrank statement that it is done to make sure that nothing has been forgotten.

Different approaches for different types of persons

There are for the reporter three different sorts of approach for three different classes of persons: for those of the reporter's own intellectual or social level, for those above, and for those below him. The interviewer, however, should always be himself. He should act as if he knew what he was doing and had the best reason in the world for doing it. There is no need to cringe or to truckle. In talking to persons of his own social level, the interviewer should act naturally and treat the one interviewed as he would a friend. When in doubt as to the interviewee's status, he should act as if approximate equals, with the interviewee in perhaps the slightly higher position. Treat what he says with respect; otherwise he will pass on some false or misleading information. Dealing with social or intellectual inferiors is difficult, not because the reporter feels any superiority but because the other man thinks the reporter does. If the reporter permits the interviewee to feel that he is inferior, he will not gain his objective, as the interviewee will put obstacles in his way. Nothing induces reticence and inhibitions more certainly than a sense of inferiority.

Bogardus, a social investigator, notes that different types of persons are interested and motivated to talk by different devices. The naïve person says whatever he is stimulated to say in a simple, normal way. The self-centered interviewee opens floodgates when his ego is appealed to. The confessional mechanism may be put in motion when rather special rapport has been set up. With some, the scientific habit mechanism, the interest in truth for the sake of science, can be brought into action. Those with a sophisticated habit mechanism, such as is often found in lawyers and in police who are habitually on the defensive, must be drawn away from their daily environment before they will talk freely in a fair exchange of ideas. "To urge the interviewee to be frank," Bogardus says, "or to over-urge him, is inhibiting. It is better for the interviewer to create the atmosphere of frankness rather than to urge frankness."[1]

Interviewing those who are aware of their own superior knowledge is a problem. Experts have no time to waste. Time is money to them. Authorities on any subject want to get down to facts during business hours. The interviewer should, therefore, know exactly what he wants to ask, and keep away from nonessentials. On the other hand, the expert is often eager to enlighten the world on matters in his chosen field. Also, he sometimes welcomes proper publicity. The reporter, therefore, should convince him that he, as an interviewer, is a channel through which a message can reach the public. The more eminent the man the easier it is to get a message from him.

If the interviewer is uninformed on the matter about which he is interviewing, he should not hesitate to admit ignorance. The person who knows is usually glad to enlighten him. But the reporter should prepare himself just as thoroughly as possible beforehand on the subject to be discussed. He should familiarize himself with the vocabulary. If, after the interview is over, he finds he has missed some important facts, the only thing to do is to go back and get them.

Maulsby agrees that celebrities as a rule are not hard to approach. The difficulty is to get them to say anything of real value. The reporter's first object in interviewing a prominent person is to induce him to begin talking naturally and without restraint—whether about

---

[1] Bogardus, E. S., "Social Research Interview," *Journal of Applied Sociology,* 1925, 10:69-82.

his health or the state of his business—with the idea that once he gets warmed up, he is bound to say something that the public will be glad to read.

One method is for the reporter to say nothing after he has introduced himself. If the celebrity is accustomed to being interviewed, he may say, "I suppose you have come to get my views on . . ." If he is unaccustomed to talking for publication, the reporter's silence makes him feel that he has to put his best foot forward or else shame himself forever. Sometimes a reporter can say: "I'm here to interview you. You have had more experience in being interviewed than I have had in interviewing anyone as important as you are. Go ahead and say something."

Differences between well-prepared, intelligent, attentive interviewers and the less professionally competent, are pictured by an anonymous author in the *Scientific American* (1). Writing from the point of view of the person being interviewed, he says:

The man who is frequently interviewed will say that there are good and bad interviewers, and that whether an interview is to be a painless or painful process depends upon the reporter. He who has not formulated in his own mind the subject on which he seeks light and who accordingly goes into the presence with but a hazy idea of what it is that he wants to know is doomed to failure before he starts. His victim will perhaps pursue him from point to point eager to locate and supply his need, but he will succeed only by chance, because the other has not taken the trouble to identify it himself. An equally discourteous type is the interviewer who is constitutionally incapable of paying attention to what one tells him. There is no limit to the number of times which such a man may hear a thing without heeding it.

On the other hand, it takes two to make a successful interview. The interviewer may be as patient and as skillful and as courteous as he pleases, but he is helpless when confronted by the man who is constitutionally incapable of being interviewed.

Difficult interviewees

The difficult interviewee may be one of four types: (1) The man who will not let the interviewer get started but begins to talk himself, never on the subject of interest to the interviewer. (2) The man who lets the interviewer start the attack, but no more. He breaks into the middle of sentences, and completes sentences with a different meaning of his own. (3) The man who hears the interviewer out, but is diverted into a byway. (4) The man who answers with a great many qualifications. All of them tax to the utmost the ingenuity of the reporter. He must size up his man promptly, and be prepared to shift his attitude accordingly. Experience brings the necessary flexibility more quickly if the young reporter makes mental note of his procedures in unsuccessful as well as successful interviews, and critically thinks them through in detail afterwards.

This observation holds not only of procedures for inducing the person interviewed to discourse on topics of interest to readers, but applies equally to techniques of verification, without which it is often impossible to secure information known to be correct as well as readable. No attempt is made in this chapter to describe these processes of verification, indispensable to good reporting. They differ little from those already presented, especially in the chapters dealing with the interview in employment investigations and in commercial surveys. In the legal interview, which will be studied next, questions of verification and dependability of report are prominent. They have received much more rigorous analysis than has as yet been accorded to questions of how to motivate an interviewee to talk.

Not all interviews in journalism, of course, have the search for specific facts as their purpose. The feature interview, for instance, is concerned with particular facts only as they pertain to the interviewee. This is the sort of interview printed about anyone who is catapulted into prominence overnight. The aim is to get the person interviewed to say anything at all, and to make the story more of a character sketch than an answer to definite questions.

In general, the journalistic interview, in common with the interview for legal evidence, seeks, as we have seen, to gain information from an informant who is often reluctant to give it. The reporter's peculiar task is, then, to induce him to talk even though he is under no compulsion to do so. The interviewer must grip his interest and help him to see that it is to his own benefit to divulge the facts—facts not only correct but important, and above all interesting and significant to that absent audience, the reading public.

REFERENCES

1. ANON., The art of being interviewed. *Scientific Amer.*, 1918, 119-184.
2. BARBER, N., *Newspaper Reporting*. Pitman, 1936.
3. BELL, E., Interviewing—its principals and functions. *Proceedings,*

American Society of Newspaper Editors, Washington, D.C., 1927, 169-175.

4. BRENNECKE, E. and CLARK, D., *Magazine Article Writing.* New York: Macmillan, 1930.

5. CHARNLEY, M. and CONVERSE, B., *Magazine Writing and Editing.* The Cordon Co., 1938.

6. CRAWFORD, R., *The Magazine Article.* New York: McGraw-Hill, 1931.

7. HALL, W., *Reporting News.* New York: Heath, 1936.

8. HARRINGTON, H. and WATSON, E., *Modern Feature Writing.* New York: Harper, 1935.

9. MAULSBY, W., *Getting the News.* New York: Harcourt, 1925.

10. PATTERSON, H., *Writing and Selling Special Feature Articles.* New York: Prentice-Hall, 1939.

11. PORTER, P. and LUXON, N., *Reporter and the News.* New York: Appleton-Century, 1935.

12. REED, P., *Writing Journalistic Features.* New York: McGraw-Hill, 1931.

13. WARREN, C., *Modern News Reporting.* New York: Harper, 1934.

10. The Interview in Legal Practice and Law Enforcement

UNLIKE the counseling interview or the interview in the clinic, the interview for legal evidence is not always conducted primarily in the interest of the person interviewed. A witness may or may not be involved and intensely interested in the issues of the controversy before the court, so the interviewer may have the problem of eliciting facts from him in spite of reticence or reluctance on his part. Often the interest of society, expressed through the action of the court, far outweighs any individual considerations. The object of the interview for legal evidence is to ascertain crucial facts. This must be done irrespective of the interviewee's wish in the matter.

Up to the present time, the most important studies of the interview in law are those relating to the dependence which can be placed on the testimony of witnesses. The use of the interview in legal practice, however, is not confined to the examination of witnesses. The interview between the lawyer and his client is of first importance. A lawyer's success depends in a measure on his skill in getting a comprehensive and accurate understanding of his client's case, at the same time establishing confidence. Thus, much that has been stated in connection with other types of interview applies also to those used in the practice of law and need not be repeated here. The research contributions peculiar to this field are the findings from psychological studies of the reliability of testimony. And they are significant for all interviewers who have to sift the true from the false. A description of one simple experiment will indicate the nature of these investigations and of what they have disclosed.

An experimental study of a traditional assumption

An assumption commonly made in regard to the reliability of testimony is that when a number of persons report upon the same matter, those details upon which there is agreement may in general be considered as substantiated. Experiments have shown, however, that there is a tendency for the same errors to appear in testimony of different individuals, and that, quite apart from any collusion, agreement of testimony is no proof of dependability. There are constant errors of observation and report. Variation in a habitual sequence of events or in a familiar setting is particularly likely to pass unnoticed, as in an experiment reported by Otto (9):

For eight weeks, seventy-five young men and women, largely upperclassmen, had been studying logic, when, without warning, a carefully rehearsed disturbance took place in the classroom. Student Jones struck student Brown with his fist, whereupon the latter hit his assailant with a book. These students were seated next the outside aisle of a large classroom [of amphitheater type] and halfway from the front. At the first sign of disorder, student Smith, occupying a seat in the front row and five seats from the outside aisle, threw two silver dollars into the air, and scrambled to recover them as they fell to the floor. The instructor, who was collecting papers from the class when the altercation began, ordered the three students from the room. Taking advantage of this tense moment while the three students were preparing to go and were leaving, the instructor went to the platform in the front of the room, and with his back to the class, looked at his watch, wrote "9:45" on the blackboard, erased the figures, repeated these actions, then faced the class just as the last man to go was at the door. Before there could be any interchange of opinions, he asked the class to write as fair and complete a statement as possible of what had happened. And that the testimony might be of practical use, certain definite questions were agreed upon as the basis of the reports. (The students at the University of Wisconsin are on a self-government basis. They knew that the testimony they gave might be used as evidence in the student court, and that they might be called upon to stand by it. Many of them afterwards stated that they expected their testimony to be so used.)

. . . In answer to the important question, "Where was the instructor when the disturbance began?" the testimony is as follows: According to 22, he was near the front of the room; according to 20, in just about the middle; while 21 say that he was in the rear. The variation becomes still more striking if we try to locate the instructor more exactly. Of those who insist that he was in the front of the room, one is sure that he was opposite the first row of seats west of the center aisle; another that it was the second row; another that it was the third row, and on the other side of the aisle. Furthermore, each of five different students report, and according to later interviews, would have felt forced to testify under oath, that when the disturbance began the instructor was just in the act of taking his particular paper and was thus opposite to the seat in which he sat. These seats are located on both sides of the center aisle, and from the front to the rear of the room.

Testimony like this shows that the hop-skip-and-jump nature of attention may not be regarded as a light matter in the weighing of evidence, and for this important reason: The breaks in observation do not remain in memory as so many blanks. On the contrary, the snatches [of the sequence of events] that are noticed slide together, and the resulting whole is accepted by the witness himself as a faithful record of what actually took place in his presence. Only the student in seat 26 was quite correct in her statement that "the instructor was just passing the seat that I occupy when I heard a noise of fighting on my left"; but she felt no more certain of the truth of her statement than did the young men in seats, 92, 74, 58, 40, who were wrong. It takes time to collect papers from seventy-five students in a large room, but for these four men all that had occurred from the time they had handed their papers to the instructor to the time when the disturbance began not only dropped out of existence but left no trace of its ever having been. . . .

It will be recalled that while the men who were ordered from the room were leaving, the instructor stood with his back to the class, writing on the blackboard, until the last of the three "culprits" was nearing the door. Only five of the seventy-five observed this with even approximate completeness; their attention was fixed elsewhere. Still in answer to the question, "Where was the instructor and what was he doing when the students left the room?" only six say they do not know. The other 64 give very definite testimony as to his whereabouts and actions. Three state that the instructor went to the door and held it open for the students to pass out; one that he stood in the center aisle muttering, "I'll break this up, or know the reason why"; three have him seated dejectedly at his desk, his face buried in his hands; while the remaining fifty-seven essentially agree that he was seated at his desk, "toying with the papers that he had collected" (or with class cards, watch chain, piece of chalk, etc.), "as if not knowing what to do," and that "his face wore an expression of embarrassment and uneasiness."

Now granting that the instructor's face testified to embarrassment, it was at the time invisible to most of the students. Their reports here as in their description of his position and actions are a composite of past experience and what they saw when their attention returned to the instructor. What the witness thinks he saw is actually largely a fiction, having its roots in part in his own emotional nature, and in part in idiosyncrasies and habits of this or other instructors, now vicariously doing duty for the unobserved.

The two mental characteristics so far considered play into the hands of a proclivity to make a story of the observed. The snatches retained of an occurrence are not kept in isolation like so many loose beads of knowledge, but are strung on a thread; are combined into what is meant to be a harmonious narrative. It will be recalled that the two men who began the disturbance occupied seats next to the outside aisle of a large room, and halfway back. As soon as the disorder was underway, student Smith, who was seated five rows to the front and five seats from the outside aisle, dropped some money and scrambled to pick it up. Now the interesting fact is that in the testimony these two events are brought together in the relation of cause and effect, and thus become incidents in a story which harmonized them. Two of the accounts will illustrate: "One of the students," reads a report, "either Jones or Brown, dropped some money. A scramble immediately took place between them, while the money rolled toward the front of the room where it was grabbed by Smith who made considerable noise doing it." It was quite natural for this witness to introduce a bit of stage business which gives still more unity to his conception of the disturbance. . . .

In the other account the two occurrences are united under the influence of a common student experience. The seats in the university classrooms are equipped with adjustable desk-arms. Sometimes the mechanism fails to work when the student tries to adjust the arm, and occasionally in such cases the arm is broken off and a little steel ratchet ball falls to the floor. Although at this time no seat-arm was broken off, reports of students sitting in different parts of the room agree in substance with the following: "Brown said something to Jones and then in a minute a scrap was on. In the tussle a seat-arm broke off, and Brown tried to poke Jones with it, but it fell to the floor. I heard the little iron ball from the ball-bearing roll to the front of the room. Smith made a grab for it and so he too got into trouble." It is striking that among those who found this particular connection between what Jones and Brown did and what Smith did, is the immediate neighbor of the latter, whom one would expect to be a reliable witness of Smith's part in the affair. But instead of seeing Smith drop money he saw "a little steel ball come rolling out between Smith's feet, and Smith grabbed it and put it into his pocket." He was never convinced that this was fiction, and when last heard from insisted that if called into court he would be compelled to stick to his original story in spite of what others claimed to have seen. . . .

When the members of this class in due time learned of the various discrepancies in their testimony, some of the most puzzled individuals were those who claimed to have heard the little steel ball roll along the floor. It now appeared indisputable that no steel ball had fallen to the floor, and yet the experience of its having fallen would not fade for all that. As one of them expressed it later: "It is positively uncanny. I could swear I heard that little ball bound from step to step as it rolled to the front."

A single experiment such as this cannot yield generalizations to be accepted without further scientific study and verification. But taken together with other studies it indicates how the psychology of testimony contributes to fact finding in many fields. Based on similar experiments, Schultz[1] has presented an analysis of some of the psychological processes in observation and report of episodes. (1) In observation, whatever is noted depends partly upon the observer's mental state at the time, and partly on the objective complex in which things occur. If an observer expects or fears that one man will attack another, movements of the arms may be seen as blows. (2) Attention is caught by novelty and by the logical significance of the impression. A fight in a classroom is a novel occurrence, and a bright rolling object is seen logically as a ball from a broken tablet arm. (3) The number of items reported is larger than the observer was attentively noting; there is a "spread" of observation outside the main objects of attention. Although watching the fight, observers saw bright objects rolling. (4) Optimal conditions for observation are present when novelty supplies a motive; but if there are familiar details, they assist comprehension. (5) When a strange event suddenly irrupts into a familiar and commonplace setting, a certain amount of time is necessary before attention can be readjusted to the new situation. For this period of readjustment, reports are inaccurate. (6) Reports show the presence of perseveration tendencies, enough to make probable that "perseveration plays an important rôle in the errors of witnesses." When a witness is cross-examined, he tends to preserve, consciously or unconsciously, the errors in his first report. Since this tendency decreases with time, it follows that reports given directly after an event need not be the best. (7) Reports are affected by the process of logical elaboration, such as emphasis on essentials and dropping of unessentials, illustrating a principle of economy of consciousness. (8) Descriptions of persons tend to fall into more or less precon-

[1] Schultz, G.: "Zur Aussagepsychologie," *Zeitschrift für Psychologie,* 1913, 7:547-574.

ceived types.[2] (9) Some persons embellish their reports to secure better literary form and may thus distort them unintentionally. (10) Emotion produces decided distortion, especially of verbal items such as quotations, often resulting in exaggeration. (11) Better reports are secured when the reporter believes himself seriously responsible for his statements.

Knowledge of the mental tendencies involved in observation and report helps in understanding the errors to which testimony is subject. Inaccuracies are much more frequent than is commonly recognized. Indeed, careful studies have shown that only 2 per cent of free narrative reports are without error. By a free narrative is meant a report in which the narrator is not subject to questions or suggestions of any kind. Only ½ of 1 per cent of depositions are error-less, and these accurate narratives and depositions are, in the main, limited in scope. Thus, they are errorless only because they are given by persons who confine their statements to a few facts of which they are certain.

Assuming free narrative reports obtained without any suggestive questions to increase the error of testimony, what per cent of the material so secured is accurate? It has been found that about 75 per cent of testimony is accurate on the average, although individual reports vary considerably.

Attestation, or the religious oath, does not guarantee accuracy, but it reduces error about one-half, chiefly by making the witness feel his responsibility. Even then, an average of at least 10 per cent of such testimony is inaccurate.

NATURE AND SOURCE OF ERRORS

The practical value of experimental studies lies in the light they throw on the nature and sources of error. Most errors can be classified under the following headings:

TESTABILITY. Some testimony cannot be accepted as dependable because it is not testable, or capable of proof by evidence. In other words, the facts with which such so-called testimony deals are not susceptible to testimony. A witness obviously could not give testimony on what an automobile driver intended to do at the time of an accident.

---

[2] This is illustrated in the results of Rice's study of Stereotypes, described in Chapter One.

He could give an accurate report only on what the driver actually did. This kind of error may occur in connection with the error of confusing inference with fact. What is stated is not a testable fact, but an inference.

MEMORABILITY. Memorability refers to that quality of a fact which provokes promptness and accuracy of recall. Hollingworth studied this subject in connection with advertising and found that the ease of remembering facts was in the following order: mere presence of things; number of people, when number is small; space relations; conditions of objects; order of events; color; size and quantity; sounds; duration of time.

ERRORS OF APPREHENSION. Errors of apprehension are due to inadequate sensory data or to misinterpretation of these data.

1. *Defects of sense organs.* A defect of vision or hearing may limit the experience of an individual in a given instance, and his testimony would be correspondingly limited or erroneous. Color blindness has sometimes led to a confusion of railway signals. Obviously a person with color defect might unwittingly give distorted or at least incomplete testimony when interviewed in regard to an accident.

2. *Perceptive incapacity and illusions.* Even though the sense organs function adequately, there may be inadequate or erroneous interpretation of the data supplied through the senses. The value of testimony is necessarily limited by such misapprehensions. Susceptibility to illusion seems to be increased when the observer is in a crowd. Under such circumstances of heightened suggestibility, agreement of witnesses is no guarantee against errors of apprehension.

3. *Paramnesia.* A not uncommon phenomenon called paramnesia is the consciousness of familiarity which sometimes accompanies a new experience. It is due to the presence, in the new, of unanalyzed elements that are part of a familiar experience. It is especially noticeable when one sees a city or street for the first time, but looks on it with recognition. Paramnesia is essentially a special form of illusion and may lead to erroneous statement.

LIMITATIONS AND ERRORS OF RECALL. The most common limitations of testimony are due to difficulties of recall. Not only does the witness forget rapidly, especially at first, after experiencing the fact to be reported, but he is subject to various errors:

1. *Omissions.* Omissions of some facts or parts of an experience are found in practically all reports. Omissions are more frequent in

free narratives than in reports elicited by systematic questioning.

2. *Additions.* Additions, elaborations, and exaggerations are also found in nearly every report, but not so extensively as omissions. When a witness is reporting an experience, questions help him to remember, but they also suggest additions and elaborations which did not accompany the original experience. Therefore, for accuracy, the free narrative report is preferable. Even in free report, error of fantasy or retouching of the recollection creeps in. This is aggravated by too great credulity, suggestibility, or lack of purpose to scrutinize each idea as it comes to mind.

3. *Substitutions.* Substitutions might be considered a combination of omissions and additions in which irrelevant but often subtly similar items displace true elements of the incident reported.

4. *Romance.* Romance or fantasy is an exaggerated form of elaboration often found in testimony given by an individual who has lived much to himself, who has been thwarted in the realization of some strong wish, or who for other reasons has constructed for himself a world of imagination more or less remote from reality.

5. *Untrue confessions.* Another extreme form of fabricated testimony is the untrue confession. This is often the result of insistent suggestion and similar influences brought to bear in cross-examination or in the *third degree.* Untrue confessions are more likely to be made by highly suggestible or hysterical persons.

6. *Transpositions.* Transpositions sometimes occur, in which all the facts are given but not in proper relation. Questioning, particularly cross-examination, often increases the susceptibility to interchange events in order of time.

CONSTANT ERRORS. Constant errors of various kinds are common. There is, for instance, as we shall see below under paragraph 9, a general tendency to underestimate long distances or periods of time but to overestimate short distances or periods of time. Other forms include the halo effect, and the tendency to minimize or omit reference to unpleasant facts.

FACTORS AFFECTING ACCURACY OF REPORT. Many studies have been made of the factors affecting accuracy and dependability of report. Some of the more significant conclusions are summarized here, chiefly from Whipple's surveys published in the *Psychological Bulletin* during the decade 1909 to 1918.

1. *Sex of reporter.* Some experimenters have found that reports

from men tend to be more accurate than those from women, but they also tend to be less extended or complete. Other experimenters, however, have found practically no difference either in quality or in range of reports.

2. *Age of reporter.* Reports from children are very inferior; but, as stated above, because they are less sophisticated, they sometimes reveal leads that might otherwise be concealed. Gross (5) states that the testimony of a healthy half-grown boy is likely to be free from prejudice and erroneous interpretation.

3. *Intelligence of reporter.* Studies of the relation between intelligence of the reporter and reliability of report are not conclusive; but the evidence indicates that reliability is partly dependent on intelligence. Errors are probably not so much in observation as in recall and in critical organization and formulation of what is observed.

4. *Time interval after event.* Lengthening of the time interval between experience and report decreases range and accuracy of testimony, but these losses are not so great as those shown in the well-known curves of forgetting based on laboratory experiments with nonsense syllables. Indeed, with some reporters the accuracy of testimony seems to be somewhat improved after several days have elapsed. This might well be, if the reporter was at first still in a state of emotional excitement caused by the experience.

Assurance does not decrease with time, and may even increase. Thus, warranted assurance and warranted tendency to oath decline with the lapse of time.

5. *Contents or features of report.* In general, persons and their acts, objects, things, and spatial relations are reported with an accuracy often as high as 85 to 90 per cent; whereas secondary features, especially quantities and colors, are reported with greater inaccuracy. Reports on colors have an error of from 40 to 50 per cent. In reporting items about a person, a witness's account is unconsciously altered to accord with his general knowledge of the person.

6. *Form of report.* All authorities agree that use of the interrogatory form of report—one obtained by questioning—increases the range and decreases the accuracy of the report. Thus, in comparison with the narrative, the range of the interrogatory may be 50 per cent greater, while the inaccuracy may be as much as 550 per cent greater.

Many experiments have been made to determine the effect of questioning on testimony. One by Cady and Gault (4) is typical. An episode was prepared for observation by students in a classroom. Two hundred and seventy-two students saw a man enter, speak about a test, and show a chart. Then half of the students were asked to write in detail what they had seen, and the other half were given 42 questions on the incident. For both groups the reports on the oral part of the episode were on the whole better than the reports on the general happenings or on the printed material. More errors occurred in the reports of students who were asked to answer questions than in the reports of those who were free to choose their own details. Facts mentioned in the narrative reports were likely to be mentioned correctly either in general or in detail, while reports made in answer to a list of questions were affected both by the range of the list and by the directness of the questions. The range of items covered in the narrative reports was much greater than the range of the question-answer reports. The students making the narrative reports omitted more details than they remembered to relate, one group omitting as much as 74 per cent of the details.

According to these investigators, the material most often correctly reported is (1) that which has been best presented and (2) that which falls into a general scheme of organization and can be reported upon with generalizations. The matter reported upon with the greatest number of errors is that which deals with facts which we habitually treat in a standardized manner. These statements are in accord with our own deductions from a study of the interview for fact finding in employment relations, described on page 154. As to form of question, the most dangerous leading questions are those which suggest the wrong answers and do not imply the correct answers. The most satisfactory methods of obtaining dependable reports are, in order of merit:

1. Combination of free narrative and question-answer, with the free narrative report given first.
2. Surprise episodes in which there has been no warning that a report is to be called for.
3. Report following an episode for which warning of a required report was given.
4. Question-answer report followed by a free narrative.

7. *Type of question.* The introduction of leading or suggestive questions noticeably decreases the accuracy of report among children, and unless the conditions of report are quite favorable, even among adults. Muscio's valuable study of the effect of form of question is described earlier.

8. *Hearsay vs. eyewitness evidence.* When the account of a given experience is transmitted from one person to another by serial repetition, the effect is to produce exaggerations and a "lessened delicacy of expression such that what are at first mere possibilities or inferences become unqualified actualities. The effect is to reduce range and accuracy, similar to that of a longtime interval."

9. *Estimates of duration and magnitude.* Evidence indicates that brief periods, up to two minutes, are much overestimated, and that this tendency diminishes until at five minutes it is inappreciable, while from ten minutes on there appears a slowly increasing tendency to underestimation. As regards spatial magnitude, Stern (10) concludes that within a certain range of dimensions—one to four meters, like the size of a window—estimates are fairly accurate, while smaller sizes, as the dimensions of a book are overestimated and larger dimensions, up to fifty meters, are underestimated.

It has been alleged that there is a general tendency to overestimate sizes of objects not seen for years. This aggrandizement of the memory image, as Mark Baldwin called it, is strikingly noticeable when a mature person returns to scenes of his youth and is astonished at the smallness of houses and hills. This phenomenon is not wholly explained by reference to changed standards of comparison due to bodily growth of the observer in the meantime; for it occurs even when the young person was fully grown at the time when he originally knew the remembered scene. Neither is it due to a general tendency for memory images to increase in size. Niagara does not seem to shrink between visits. The man who returns to rugged Vermont, after years on the rolling prairies of Iowa, finds the hilltops higher, the cliffs more abrupt, the roads more winding than he had remembered them. The more inclusive generalization is that memories tend to vary in the direction of a mode or central tendency for the class of experiences to which the remembered object belongs.

10. *Effect of repeating a report.* When a person is called upon to make a report several times, the effect of this repetition is complex. It tends, in part, to establish in mind the items reported, whether they be true or false; and it tends also to induce some departure in the later reports, because these are based upon memory of verbal statements of the earlier reports as well as upon the original experience itself; that is, the later reports undergo distortion on account of the flexibility of verbal expression. Repeated reports show a perseverative tendency.

11. *Effect of practice.* Mere practice in reporting, even without special training or conscious effort to improve, facilitates and betters a report in every way. On the other hand, repetition of the same incident or repetition of the report results in little improvement if not actual distortion.

EVALUATION OF TESTIMONY FOR FACT FINDING AND JUDGMENT. Jurists and others have written at length on fact finding from legal evidence, but only a few experimental studies have been made. Marston (7) has compared the findings of fact from testimony by single judges, male juries, and female juries. A report of his experimental study is pertinent here.

Marston's investigation was undertaken to determine whether the alleged percentages of testimonial error, as found in laboratory experiments, do really, in trial, lead to erroneous verdicts. Preliminary studies were made for roughly determining, first, the possible psycholegal causes of testimonial error; and second, what possible psychological relations may exist between the findings of judge and jury and the original testimony upon which such findings were based.

The first study compared methods of eliciting testimony by free narration, direct examination, and cross-examination. The incident used was a natural one with no unusual features, but one that could have legal significance. A boy entered the room and delivered an envelope containing a message. Under his arm he carried three books of different colors, and also held a second envelope in his hand. While the message was being read by the lecturer, the boy, facing the audience, drew and opened a long pocketknife and scraped his thumb with it. The predetermined plot was to try the boy for stabbing an acquaintance, the books to be found at the scene of the crime.

It was noteworthy that among the eighteen witnesses not a single one noticed the knife at all.

Free narrative was uniformly less complete but more accurate than either direct or cross-examination. Direct examination gave results both more complete and more accurate than cross-examination. Cross-examination caused greater caution than direct examination, but without any gain in completeness or accuracy. In individual results, caution showed a correlation with both completeness and accuracy. "It seems a rough but certain indicator of the probable value of any witness's testimony."

The second experiment was designed to compare the testimony on expected and unexpected incidents. The same incident was performed before a second group of twelve lawyers who realized that it was an experiment and that they would be asked to report on it. The entire group of witnesses, as compared with the first group, showed gain in completeness, but a small loss in accuracy, and considerable loss in caution.

In the third experiment testimony of all witnesses in both experiments was given to an eminent jurist, Dean J. H. Wigmore, to a male jury, and to a female jury. In summary, the findings of the experiment were as follows:

1. A single trained judge was more successful than a jury in finding the facts from given testimony. He excelled in completeness, and also, though not to so great an extent, in accuracy.

2. The female jury excelled the male, both in completeness and in accuracy of report.

3. Professional training and experience increased success in finding facts.

In the fourth experiment, the purpose was to compare written testimony with oral testimony as a basis for findings of facts by juries. Each of the twelve witnesses in the second experiment, one at a time came face to face with female and male juries and gave their testimony orally. The findings of these juries were compared with those based on the written testimony. The findings based on testimony written immediately after the occurrence were superior, in both completeness and accuracy, to those based on oral testimony three months after the event. Self-confidence or self-assertiveness of a witness on the stand, even though the witness was obviously unreliable, was found to have a larger influence on jurors of both sexes than did the logical or psychological probability of other testimony.

Finally, the findings of fact by the judge and by the juries were compared with the testimony on which the findings were based. The results may be summarized in six statements:

1. All finders of fact, averaged together, slightly excelled the average witness in completeness of report, and, to a less degree, in accuracy of report.

2. Accuracy of findings of fact does not seem to depend upon the accuracy of that testimony on which the findings were based.

3. Completeness of findings of fact does not seem to parallel, even roughly, the completeness of the original testimony.

4. Findings of fact, by juries, based upon oral testimony, are consistently less complete than is the testimony of the average witness. Such jury findings do not differ significantly in accuracy from the testimony of the average witness.

5. The total averages of six juries of both sexes showed these juries to be slightly more complete, and slightly less accurate in their results, on the average, than were the thirty witnesses on whose testimony the juries' findings were based.

6. The total average scores of three judges (two of whom had no legal training) significantly excelled the average scores of the thirty witnesses, both in completeness and in accuracy.

JUDGING THE CHARACTER OF WITNESSES. Evaluation of testimony tends to involve appraisal of the witness. It raises in particular the question of his sincerity and truthfulness. To aid in making such judgments, Osborn (8) has described seven signs, observable in the witness's behavior, which indicate untruthfulness: (1) hangdog appearance; (2) tendency to repeat questions; (3) talking in almost inaudible tones and acting as though he wishes the experience were over with; (4) unnatural emphasis; (5) defensive smile or nervous laugh; (6) unnecessarily minute accuracy; (7) repeated statement of desire to be truthful and frank, and uncalled-for swearing of truth.

Accurate appraisal of character is a difficult and elusive goal. It cannot be reached by reliance on inferences from the shape of the head or the contour of the physiognomy. But close observation of actual behavior, including posture, voice, eyes, and facial expression during the interview, yields clues which must not be ignored.

SUMMARY

In actual court practice many principles and rules have been established to safeguard the taking of testimony and to increase the reliability of inferences from it. Some of these rules have been verified by experiment as well as by practice. A summary of such principles follows:

1. Some testimony cannot be accepted as reliable because it is not testable or capable of proof. This is a safeguard against the error of confusing inference with fact.

2. The witness is subject to errors of apprehension owing to inadequate sensory impressions or to misinterpretation of such impres-

sions. What is noted depends partly on the observer's mental state at the time, and partly on the complex external situation in which the events occur. Attention is caught by novelty as well as by the logical significance of the impression received. The facts most often correctly reported are (1) those which have been most vividly presented, (2) those which concern most directly the reporter, and (3) those which fall readily into some scheme of organization and can be presented in the form of generalizations. The facts reported with the greatest number of errors are those which the reporter habitually treats in a standardized manner.

3. The accuracy of a report depends partly on the nature of the items covered. In general, persons and their acts, objects, things, and spatial relations are reported with an accuracy which may be as high as 85 or 90 per cent, whereas secondary features, especially quantities and colors, are more inaccurately reported.

4. Accuracy of report is subject to limitations and errors of recall. Omissions are found to be more frequent in free narrative than in a report elicited by systematic questioning. Additions, elaborations, and exaggerations, however, are increased by use of questions. Therefore, for accuracy, the free narrative report is preferable; and for completeness, it should be followed by questions.

5. The correct recall of one feature of an object or event does not guarantee the correct recall of other features of the same object or event, even though these features seem logically bound together.

6. When a number of persons report upon the same matter, those details upon which there is agreement may, in general, be considered as correct. Experiments show, however, that there is a strong tendency for the same errors to appear in testimony of different individuals. Variation in a habitual sequence of events or in a habitual setting is particularly likely to pass unnoticed and the consequent error to appear uniformly in the testimony of different individuals.

7. The witness's denial of having seen, heard, or been aware of some object or part of an episode which he reasonably should have been aware of may be a truthful statement, and yet it should not be considered a denial of the existence of such an object or event.

8. Professional training and experience in finding facts through oral examination markedly increases success.

9. A single trained judge is more successful than an inexperienced jury in sifting the facts from given testimony, as regards both the

completeness and the accuracy of findings.

10. Some divergence in the testimony of two witnesses is one indication that there has not been collusion or coaching.

These investigations in the field of legal practice as to reliability of statements and conclusions drawn in the process of examining witnesses, form an extremely valuable contribution to our study of the interview. A thorough familiarity with the varied factors controlling reliability of report is a vital part of the lawyer's equipment. But of what use to others are the principles derived from a study of the interview for legal evidence?

First, such a study tends to make any interviewer cautious about always accepting as reliable even the most obviously sincere statements of fact made to him by an interviewee.

Second, it ought to put him on his guard particularly with reference to the various kinds of more common errors of report described in this chapter.

Third, and specifically, it should encourage the practice of securing from the interviewee a complete free narrative report or description of the whole situation before an attempt is made to question him in detail.[3]

REFERENCES

1. BRITT, H., The rules of evidence—an empirical study in psychology and the law. *Cornell Law Quarterly.*, 1940, 25, 556-580.
2. BURTT, H., *Legal Psychology*. New York: Prentice-Hall, 1931.
3. BURTT, H. and GASKILL, H., Suggestibility and the form of the question. *J. appl. Psychol.*, 1932, 16, 315-373.
4. CADY, H. and GAULT, R., On the psychology of testimony. *Amer. J. Psychol.*, 1924, 36, 110-112.

[3] The authors cannot do greater service to the student of the fact-finding interview than to urge him to browse widely in Dean Wigmore's monumental treatise on *Evidence,* and to make the acquaintance of Albert S. Osborn's fascinating book on *The Problem of Proof.* In the latter volume, written by an expert who has sat through many notable trials, the interviewer will value particularly Chapters XII, XIII, XV, and XVI: Cross-Examination from the Standpoint of the Lawyer; Memory and the Proof of Facts; Advocacy; and Persuasion and Practical Psychology in Courts of Law. Interviewees as well as interviewers will relish Chapter XI on Cross-Examination from the Standpoint of the Witness.

5. DUDYCHA, G., et al., Psychology for Law Enforcement Officers. Springfield, Ill.; Charles C Thomas, 1955.

6. GROSS, H., Criminal Psychology. Translated from the fourth German edition by Horace M. Kallen. New York: Little, Brown, 1911.

7. MARSTON, W., Studies in testimony. J. crim. law criminol., 1924, 15, 5-31.

8. OSBORN, A., The Problem of Proof. Bender, 1922.

9. OTTO, M., Testimony and human nature. J. crim. law criminol., 1918, 9, 98-104.

10. STERN, W., Lectures on the psychology of testimony and on the study of individuality. Amer. J. Psychol., 1910, 21, 270-282.

11. WELLMAN, F., Art of Cross-Examination. (Fourth Edition) New York: Macmillan, 1936.

12. WHIPPLE, G., Psychology of testimony and report. Psych. Bull., 1914, 11, 245-250.

13. WHIPPLE, G., Psychology of testimony. Psych. Bull., 1915, 12, 221-224.

14. WHIPPLE, G., Psychology of testimony. Psych. Bull., 1917, 14, 234-236.

15. WHIPPLE, G., The obtaining of information: psychology of observation and report. Psych. Bull., 1918, 15, 217-248.

16. WIGMORE, J., A Treatise on the Anglo-American System of Evidence in Trial at Common Law. New York: Little, Brown, 1923.

17. WIGMORE, J., A Student's Textbook of the Law of Evidence. Foundation Press, 1935.

Part IV

The Counseling Interview

11. The Case Study

THE INTERVIEW, we have said, is but one device for obtaining information. It is by no means the only one, and, in many cases, it is not the best technique. Moreover, interview data and processes themselves are best understood against a background of other kinds of information. For these reasons, interviewers, especially those whose work is helping others, ordinarily attempt to develop a systematic case study of the interviewee.

The case study involves much more than merely asking the interviewee to complete a standard history form. Often, the interviewer or someone else on the staff whose special job it is makes field visits to family members, employers, and others who might have something to add to the picture being developed about the client. Frequently, these contacts yield information above and beyond that initially sought. For example, one of the writers was once involved in counseling with a student who was having academic difficulties. He called on the professor in the one course which was giving the client the most trouble. Ostensibly, the visit was for the purpose of discussing specific methods for helping the student to overcome certain areas of deficiency. In the interview, however, the professor told the writer that he had wondered about the student, had become increasingly concerned about his mental health. The student, it seems, constantly stared out of the window in class, seemed unable to recite in class, and on examinations "blew up" on more than one occasion and left before the examination hour was over. With these leads, the counselor began further exploration into the area of the student's adjustment and uncovered what had previously been missed: a fairly severe anxiety problem. Once that was cleared up through extended counseling, the classroom behavior changed, and the student's grades improved.

Fundamentally, when one is working in the counseling, clinical, or social casework setting, the initial problem is to understand accurately and completely the problem which the client presents. We have mentioned before that the presented problem—the one which the client *says* troubles him—is very often not the real or basic problem. In many cases, the client simply does not know what the real problem is. Alcoholism is an example of this. It constitutes a real problem, but it is often only a symptom of something underneath which impels the person to seek escape through overuse of alcohol. In preparing to help such a person, it is essential that as much as possible be known about his total pattern of behavior, past and present. None of this should be taken to indicate that the interview is any less useful than we have maintained; rather, it is to say that the interview must take its place with other techniques for studying and helping the individual.

The systematic case study itself is based in large part upon interviews. These may be with the client, with family members and friends, with employers past and present, with representatives of other agencies, or with any who possess information of value. The case study is also based on questionnaire data, physical examination reports, medical histories, and a variety of psychological tests. Case studies made in different settings will vary because of their purposes, and the information collected and emphasized will differ correspondingly. The case study made for a vocational problem in a university will differ substantially from one made for use in prescribing therapy in a neuropsychiatric hospital.

Case study to provide a prediction

These differences are reflections of an important underlying idea: that case studies are made for a purpose and that purpose (or those purposes) will determine its character. To go a step further back, the fundamental purpose of the case study is to provide a *prediction*. When a counselor develops a case study for a vocational problem case, he is trying to find out about the client's abilities and interests, broadly, his potential. He does this because he and the client will, in the process of counseling, work through such questions as, what are promising occupations for me? what are my chances of success in job A versus job B? The answers to these questions are largely matters of prediction, and case study materials have long been felt to improve the predictions made. When the treatment team in a hospital develops a case study, it is usually trying first to understand the etiology and extent of the illness, then to decide (predict) which kind of treatment will be most efficacious for that patient.

The actual process of prediction varies from complex and sophisticated statistical procedures to rather subjective, unsystematic methods. Both approaches have their defenders, and we will have more to say about these points of view in a moment. Whichever approach is taken to the technique of prediction, there is also a problem concerning the kinds of information to include in the prediction. Until the advent of the giant electronic computers, the number of variables which could be treated statistically at any one time was severely limited. Even today, most operating clinicians, counselors, and social workers have to make do with perdiction systems based on a small number of variables. It is therefore essential that the most productive and most fruitful variables be studied. Selecting these is no easy task.

Finally, the information which is entered into a case study must be scrutinized in terms of certain fairly stringent criteria. The data must be reliable, and above all they must be valid. Validity and reliability are commonly, almost universally, evaluated with respect to psychological tests; unfortunately, the same analysis is not often made of other information which becomes a part of the case study.

Before we discuss the kinds of information which are commonly sought and made a part of the case study, we should like to spend a little time in considering these three major problems: (1) selecting the information to be included as valid for the case study; (2) evaluating it as to its accuracy or reliability, and (3) utilizing it in making the predictions which are the end goal of the case study. Obviously, these three issues involve many overlapping features, but we shall deal with them as though they were separable.

In dealing with the first question, the selection of the information to be included, we must return to information theory for a simple framework of explanation. Fundamentally, we are interested in increasing the amount of information at our disposal so that we can make a prediction which is as accurate as possible. This is not a matter of simply collecting as much information as we can lay our hands on conveniently. Rather, it is a matter of collecting that information which will substantially add to our ability to predict. An example will illustrate this.

Suppose that we are trying to decide, as did the military services during the war, which men to commission. Suppose further that we have one available commission and two applicants. We know that good officers must be reasonably intelligent. Therefore, we are interested in assessing the intellectual level of all candidates. If we know that one of our candidates had graduated with honors from a first rate university and that the other had dropped out of high school after his second year, we already have, by knowing this, some relevant information on which to base a decision, a decision which is actually a prediction. Admittedly, it is not perfectly reliable information. There may well be circumstances in which we shall wish to obtain more reliable information. The point here is that we ordinarily start with *some* information.

If this is so, then we must evaluate any further information sought in terms not only of its accuracy but also in terms of its ability to add significantly to what we already know. For example, most scholastic aptitude tests correlate about .50 with freshman grades in college. High school grade average correlates to about the same degree with the same criterion. Ignoring the correlation between these two measures for the moment, it would be logical to ask whether a scholastic aptitude test adds to the prediction which we can already make with knowledge of high school grade average. Actually, a combination of the two measures gives a better prediction than either alone. Commonly, a multiple of the two will yield a correlation of about .60. This represents, by the addition of either piece of information, a gain of about 11 per cent in predictive accuracy. We must decide, at this point, whether we need this gain badly enough to pay for it in terms of testing time.

This problem faces the developer of the case study at every step of the way whether he recognizes it explicitly or not. Usually, people recognize it quite informally and unsystematically when they decide, frequently with a fatalistic shrug, that a certain piece of information, while nice to have, would not be worth the effort to obtain it.

Evaluation of information items

One line of research which has received and continues to receive a great deal of attention is relevant here. That has to do with the development of standardized biographical information blanks. In this work, entries in a questionnaire (or a case study) are treated exactly like test items. Each individual item is evaluated against some criterion, such as success as a salesman or as an officer candidate, response to counseling or therapy, or broken parole. Those items which correlate significantly with the criterion are then weighted in terms of the magnitude and direction of the correlation. Commonly, unit weights (plus and minus one) are used, but sometimes more ambitious weighting systems are employed. Thus, scoring keys are developed so that, when a new biographical inventory is seen, it can literally be scored like a test and a prediction made from the sum of the item weights.

This research has the advantage of determining which items are useful in the sense of predicting a known criterion. It sifts out from all of the information available those pieces which do in fact relate to the questions asked. It is an interesting commentary on clinical practice that non-scored (that is, non-contributing) items are so often retained simply because some staff member feels that they tell him something. This is related to a problem we shall discuss shortly.

Evaluating items of information for reliability and validity is a process too often ignored in case study research. When a new test is put on the market, buyers look immediately for information about its validity and reliability. When someone wishes to add an item to the case study, it is as often as not accepted or rejected on the basis of whether or not it "seems" appropriate. Reliability and validity are as important for other case study items as they are for test scores. So are norms.

A common definition of reliability, seen in many textbooks, is that it refers to the consistency with which a test (or item) measures whatever it measures. This is a limited conception which has been corrected in the most recent books. Today, reliability is seen as Thorndike (17) has defined it: as a measure of the presence or absence of error in a measure. The greater the error, the lower the reliability.

The reason why consistency is too limiting a conception of reliability may be illustrated by case history data. One of the commoner methods for measuring reliability is by test-retest. Here, we demand that the individual respond in the same way on the second administration of an instrument. Suppose, however, we are studying the individual's adjustment to the job while he is undergoing psychotherapy. His adjustment is quite likely to change from month to month, perhaps from day to day. Demanding consistency would result in a loss of sensitivity. Or, suppose that we are evaluating the client's mood. Moods change, sometimes very rapidly and markedly. Utilizing an instrument which did not show such changes when they occurred would be fruitless.

On the other hand, there are many things to which we expect consistent answers. If a client is asked how much he earned on his last job, we would not want this figure to change if we asked him about it later. In general, we want consistency with respect to personal history information, but we probably do not want consistency with respect to the individual's evalution of or reactions to such information.

There are some who feel that too much attention is paid to reliability. The reason for concern with reliability—and we doubt that there can be too much concern—lies in a relationship between validity and reliability. We will discuss validity below. For the moment, it can be defined as the ability of an instrument to measure what it is supposed to measure. Validity is the crucial matter. Without it, measurement is impossible. Reliability and validity are related concepts and must be considered together. The validity of a test or item is limited by its reliability. In other words, reliability sets the upper limit for validity. Actually, this upper limit is rarely if ever reached because the criterion also contains error, but the general principle still holds.

The techniques for measuring reliability are many and varied. We will not go into them here. The reader who is interested in studying them in detail is referred to such standard texts as Thorndike (17), Cronbach (6), and Anastasi (1). Gulliksen's excellent book (11) is only for the individual who possesses considerable background in statistics.

Reliability measures the presence or absence of error. However, a measure may be free of error and still not tell us what we want to know. It is this ability to tell us something in which we are interested which is at the heart of validity. Validity is the key, the goal of measurement. We devise tests and select items in order to discover something about an individual's status on some characteristic or trait. If the test or item does not do this, it is worthless. If we wished to build a test to measure intelligence, we would not be interested in one which really measured motivation. Validity, then, refers to the extent to which a test or an item really measures what it is supposed to measure.

The processes employed in building biographical information blanks (see above) are essentially validation procedures. In determining validity, it is necessary that we relate the responses on the item or test to some independent measure of the trait in question or to the trait itself. For example, we may be interested in tendencies toward delinquent behavior. Once it has occurred, it is relatively easy to detect, but the problem may be to predict this behavior. Finding the relationship between responses to items and delinquent behavior may allow the investigator to develop a scale which will predict such behavior in advance. This is what Gough did in developing his delinquency scale for the California Personality Inventory. Once the scale or item has been shown to be related to actual criterion behavior, we need no longer wait for the behavior itself but can use the scale.

The key to the problem of validity is the need to be concerned about the criterion problem just as much as we are in test development. For example, if the case study is to be used as the basis for assignment to treatment, response to various kinds of treatment may be the best criterion. If the case study is to be used in vocational counseling, adjustment to work may be of concern. The criterion will be determined by the goal of the process under consideration.

Normative information essential

Finally, normative information is essential if case history information is to be understood and interpreted. Suppose that an individual lists his annual income as $1500. How is this to be interpreted? For the United States as a whole, it is low, but for some groups, some sub-cultures, it might be high. Or, another man, in describing his job history, might list eight or ten jobs a year. This might indicate that he is an occupational drifter, but it might point to an individual in migratory farm work. A college student might say he had two dates per month. Unless information were available about how many dates his peers averaged, it would be difficult to interpret this fact.

Many experienced social workers, psychologists, and psychiatrists maintain that they have a set of norms more or less "in their heads." That is, they can draw on their accumulated experience, gained from seeing a large number of cases. This assertion has several flaws, however. In the first place, it is extremely unlikely that any single person will deal with a truly representative sample of people. His norms will therefore be biased. Some people who, like Freud, have built personality theories on the basis of clinical practice with abnormals, are open to the charge that their theories, based on the smouldering memories of neurotic adults, correspond but little to the facts of life as far as normal personality development is concerned.

The second major difficulty with the informal, experience-based normative systems is to be found in the human memory and in selective recall and perception. Psychologists have documented very thoroughly the fact that perception is highly selective. We see—in the sense that we attend to—what we want to. What is unpleasant, threatening, or in conflict with prejudices is overlooked. Memory is also selective. People with unfavorable attitudes toward Negroes, for instance, tend to recall instances of Negroes doing things which point to their inferiority. Not to extend the argument needlessly, it seems safe to say that there is no substitute, not even experience, for objective, carefully developed, and representative normative data which can provide the interviewer with a basis for interpreting the information he gets.

Statistical probability vs. clinical intuition

This leads to the final problem with which we will deal before turning to the actual content of the case study. This has to do with the techniques employed for manipulating the information once obtained. There has been a lively controversy going on in psychology on the matter of clinical and actuarial prediction. It was probably touched off by the publication of Meehl's (14) challenging and provocative book on the subject. Fundamentally, the argument is between one group which feels that, insofar as possible, formal, statistical techniques should be used in manipulating data and the other group which, while admitting that these techniques are useful under certain circumstances, insists that the experienced clinician is a better predictive instrument than any statistical formula. Meehl's argument, buttressed by a search of the available literature, is that whenever a clinician and a prediction formula are compared with respect to their ability to predict a criterion, the formula either wins or ties. Opponents of this argue that the clinicians are handicapped in such comparisons by being unable to use the data of their choice and by being forced to predict limited and, in a sense, meaningless criteria. Although the argument continues, it seems to rest at about this point: where the criterion to be predicted is sufficiently objective and where data are available which lend themselves to statistical manipulation, formulae are as accurate or more accurate than clinicians. In the many cases where these conditions do not hold, clinicians' judgments are, if not demonstrably adequate, probably better than anything else available.

This argument has real implications for the interviewer developing and using a case study. Predictable criteria are hard to develop, require a great deal of work and imaginative planning. Reliable predictors are equally hard to develop. On the other hand, there is an unfortunate tendency prevalent in many agencies to make a virtue of necessity and to put the unsystematic interviewer's judgment on a pedestal. We must recognize that objective prediction is an ideal, a goal to be sought after, one not likely to be attained in the near future. It is, however, essential if case work of all kinds is to improve that psychologists, social workers, psychiatrists, employment interviewers, and others employing the case study keep this goal, this ideal before them. There is art in interviewing, there is some science, and there should be more.

Practically speaking, this means that people will have to follow the procedures discussed above: select items for the case study in terms of their relevance to certain specified criteria; evaluate these items for their reliability and validity; combine them, in making predictions, by using the best, most sophisticated methods available including statistical equations.

Kinds of information in a case study

In turning now to the kinds of information typically included in the case study, we must confess that they do not by any means represent items which meet the standards we have just described. To a great extent, they are items which are included in case studies because many people have felt, rightly or wrongly, that they should be included. How many of them would stand up under the kinds of analyses proposed is a moot point. It is likely that some or most would, depending on the decision to be made or the criterion to be predicted. Information about the following areas, then, is commonly included in most case studies.

1. *Intellectual capacity*. This is the psychologist's oldest, most reliable stock in trade. Estimates of intellectual capacity may be based on such secondary evidence as school achievement, but ordi-

narily, they come from psychological tests devised for the purpose.

These tests are of several kinds. First, some are individually administered, and some are group tests. Some are performance, and some are largely verbal, paper and pencil tests. Some yield a single index while others provide the worker with a variety of sub-scores. Each test has certain advantages and disadvantages. Critical reviews of most available tests are included in the series edited by Buros (3) (4) (5). Information about the administration, scoring, standardization, reliability, and validity is contained in test manuals. Additional (and often more useful) information is to be found in journal articles where studies of the tests are reported.

The selection of the correct test, administering it, scoring it, and interpreting the results is a job for the person trained in these activities. Specialists in test administration, called psychometrists, are employed by many counseling centers, clinics, and personnel offices. Clinical and counseling psychologists, some guidance workers and social case workers, many personnel workers in government and industry, a few teachers, and a few physicians are trained in testing techniques. Most test publishers will refuse to sell tests of intellectual capacity to anyone who cannot prove that he has had adequate training to handle them.

Measures of intellectual capacity are included in the case study because our society places such a premium on this trait for so many activities. Many occupations require very high levels of intellect. The decision to go or not to go to college is made in substantial part on the basis of intelligence. Potential for rehabilitation, accessibility to therapy, many things are functions of this ability. At the low end of the scale, such decisions as whether or not to commit an individual to an institution for the feeble minded are made very largely on the basis of such tests. In some states, a psychologist's report is required for such commitments. In most, it is sought and used whether required by law or not.

2. *Aptitudes*. Measures of special aptitudes are entered in case studies where decisions about education or occupational choice are to be made. Aptitudes are for the most part estimated by means of tests. These tests, like the intelligence tests, are of many kinds, such as individual and group, performance or verbal, paper and pencil, omnibus or differential. Like intelligence tests, their administration and interpretation requires considerable training and experience.

Information about these tests is available from the same sources as for intelligence tests.

There is some question as to whether aptitudes and intelligence are in fact different things. We cannot discuss this controversy here except to indicate the general positions of the people on opposite sides of the argument. One group insists that there is such a thing as general intelligence, that it can and should be measured separately from aptitudes. The other group maintains that there is no such thing as general intelligence, that what we are talking about is a conglomerate, a cluster of separate, almost unique, aptitudes. For these people, in other words, intelligence is simply a waste-basket name for the sum total of an individual's aptitudes. The theoretical problems imbedded in this argument are prodigious, and we cannot give a ready easy resolution here. In practice, both kinds of tests are used and appear to be helpful.

We mentioned omnibus and differential aptitude tests above. When aptitudes were first measured, attempts were made to build tests for such things as mechanical aptitude, sales aptitude, medical aptitude, etc. In other words, an attempt was made to assess an individual's promise for a total, complex activity. More recently, the pendulum has swung in the direction of breaking these complex activities up into their components. Thus, medical aptitude might be seen as made up of verbal reasoning, quantitative reasoning, spatial relations ability, etc. Tests were built to measure these components. The first kind of test, attempting to assess promise for the total activity with one score, is an omnibus test; the second kind, providing measures of the several component parts, is a differential test. Each has its advantages and disadvantages, its opponents and supporters. The decision about which kind to use must be made by someone familiar with the strengths and weaknesses of both.

Aptitude measures are included in many case studies because aptitudes have been shown to predict either success in training or on the job. In many cases, decisions about admission or rejection are made solely or largely on the basis of such tests. The counselor, working with a student who is trying to decide between engineering and medicine, needs to be able to predict the student's capacity to learn in both fields. If it is significantly higher in one than the other, the direction may, all other things being equal, be indicated. Bingham's book (2) on this subject is still standard reading for those interested in the field.

3. *Achievement*. Although achievement might refer to many kinds of activities, it is ordinarily taken to refer to school achievement. Occupational achievement or success is customarily included in another section of the case study. Achievement is usually measured by one of two means: school grades and standardized tests.

An increasing number of school systems now maintain cumulative records of student progress including grades. The transcript of grades is kept by almost every college and university. Unfortunately, this information is, particularly for older people, often hard to get. In such cases, the interviewer must rely on client reports. These reports are probably not very accurate. A great deal of information may be gleaned from a transcript of grades. Average grade in high school is still as good a *single* predictor of college success as anything available. More than grade average, however, the interviewer may be interested in patterns of success and failure. Did the client do well in mathematics and science, poorly in English and languages? Did he do his best work in shop? Did his grades suddenly improve or suddenly deteriorate? These questions can often lead to interesting hypotheses about the client.

Standardized tests of achievement are being increasingly used to evaluate achievement. One reason for this is the non-comparability of school grades. A grade of A in one school may reveal a level of knowledge equivalent to a grade of C in another school. One school may, in its English course, emphasize grammar and mechanics while another may emphasize composition. Standardized achievement tests, by comparing subjects on the same materials and putting them on the same base line, overcome many of these difficulties.

Achievement tests may be written, verbal, or performance; they may be omnibus or diagnostic. Information about these tests is available from the same sources as for aptitude and intelligence tests: reviews, manuals, and articles as well as texts. Oral trade tests, which we discussed in an earlier chapter, are one widely used example of achievement tests.

4. *Interests*. Individuals may have abilities but not employ them, not make the best use of them. There is, in other words, something besides sheer ability which goes to make up promise of success. That something is felt to be motivation. Unfortunately, motivation, while

much discussed and studied, is still but little understood. Actually, motivation can be subsumed under the general heading of personality. For certain practical reasons, we separate tests of personality and motivation from tests of interests.

Interests have been studied and measured for about forty years. Moore, in his doctoral dissertation, opened the way for Strong's work which has dominated this field. The serious student of interest measurement will find Strong's books (15) (16) and the one by Darley and Hagenah (7) required reading. By interests is usually meant a tendency to like or dislike some activity such as a job, job duty, hobby, recreational activity, etc. To say that one is interested in something means that he likes it, finds it intriguing, wants to do it. He is, in other words, positively motivated toward the object or activity.

While instruments have been built to measure interests in recreational and social activities, their commonest concern has been with occupations. Interests are commonly assessed by such techniques as tests, inventories, self report, and activity records. Self reports have been shown to be rather unreliable. It is strange but true that many people do not know what they really like. Tests have been built on the assumption that people will learn more about things in which they are interested. This assumption has not been widely substantiated. Activity records suffer as measures of interests because opportunity plays such a large part in them. Given a chance, many people find themselves fascinated by activities they had never tried before. The greatest success has come with inventoried interests. Here, individuals indicate their reactions to a wide variety of activities. Their responses are scored according to the relationship their responses have to a criterion. This criterion, in the most widely used instrument (the Strong Vocational Interest Blank), is the responses of successfully employed men and women in certain occupations.

5. *Personality*. As we indicated above, personality is such an all-encompassing term that it almost loses its distinctive meaning. Interests, in the sense of liking or disliking certain things, is certainly a part of it. So, really, are intelligence, achievement, and aptitudes. Traditionally, however, the term is restricted to the *affective* aspects of the person, such as, how he feels about himself and others, his moods, the way he reacts to stress, and his level of anxiety.

Estimates of these and other aspects of personality may be and usually are obtained in a variety of ways. Perhaps the commonest still is the interview. The way the individual reacts, what he says, how he says it are all observed by the interviewer who forms an opinion of the individual. Another commonly used method is observation. This is most often used with children in play and school settings, but it can be and is used with adults also. In hospitals, for instance, nurses and attendants ordinarily keep records of how patients seem to feel, how they behave, and how they get along with other patients. Teachers often do the same with pupils. A third source of information about personality comes from reports by others. Family members, friends, teachers, employers, and others may be asked their opinions. The interview is usually the method for obtaining this information. It must be remembered that this is information twice removed; once as seen by the observer, once as recorded and interpreted by the interviewer. The other commonly used technique, one which has gained increasing acceptance, is psychological tests of personality.

These are of several types. Some are verbal, some are written, some are performance. Some are objective (where the individual's answers are limited), and some are projective (where the responses are quite free). A wide variety of stimulus material is used, ranging from statements such as "I often feel unhappy," through pictures and ink blots, to toys and odd shaped colored pieces of wood. Some are individually administered, and some may be given to large groups. Once again, the selection of the measuring instrument is a matter of careful and expert judgment.

6. *Family background.* Included in this area will be information dealing with parents, siblings, sometimes more distant relatives. Kinds of information sought vary. Education, age, occupation, marital status are quite common kinds of information sought about relatives. Frequently, socio-economic status, hobbies, religious affiliation and activity, and community activities will also be entered in the case study.

These kinds of data are ordinarily obtained either by direct interviewing or by questionnaire. Either technique may be applied to the client in question or to people who know him.

7. *Socio-economic background and status.* Insofar as this is different from family background, it will also be studied. With adults, they will usually have achieved their own socio-economic level and have some adult background or history to describe. Information may

be collected by interview or questionnaire methods. Certain aspects of it may be assessed by tests or inventories.

It is frequently important to distinguish between actual socio-economic status and perceived status. There are frequently substantial differences in both directions. Gough (9) (10) has developed scales which measure both objective status and subjective status. The Occupational Level (OL) key of the Strong Vocational Interest Blank for Men is another measure of socio-economic status, in this case desired status. Another fairly objective approach is the use of such devices as the American Home Scale.

8. *Educational history.* This may be included under achievement, but ordinarily a separate section will be devoted to it. Included will be such information as schools attended, ages of graduation, curricula followed, grades attained, number of changes, disciplinary records, social and athletic participation, teachers' notes of behavior and adjustment, failures, special promotions, and subjects liked and disliked.

In some instances, school records will furnish most of this information. In others, school officials and teachers must be interviewed or asked to complete questionnaires. Frequently, parents can provide some of the information. Sometimes, the individual in question can furnish many of these data.

9. *Marital history and status.* This section might include information on number and duration of marriages, number of children, present marital status, adjustment to spouse and family living, and the like. In some cases, such as social casework with broken or breaking families, such information will be collected in considerable detail. In others, a simple, general statement may suffice.

There are some standardized inventories and questionnaires available, but most of this information must be obtained by interview, observation, or questionnaire methods. The people queried will vary with the situation but may include the client, the spouse, the children, parents, neighbors, other relatives, and friends. Court records may sometimes furnish valuable information.

10. *Physical development and status.* In many instances, physical characteristics and conditions will color the decision about methods for assisting the individual or making decisions about him. An individual with a history of tuberculosis may have to take this into account in deciding upon an occupation. A paraplegic faces many

difficulties in economic, social, and marital adjustment. The detail in which this information is collected will vary considerably with the setting. In medical rehabilitation cases, it will be quite detailed; in most counseling with students, it need not be of great concern.

The authoritative source for such information is the medical examination and history. The physician is necessarily the one most heavily relied on for such data. If other techniques are used and if a question arises, the physician must be consulted. However, interview and questionnaire techniques are often used and, in many cases, provide sufficiently good information for the purposes at hand. One interesting problem in this connection is the often wide discrepancy between the objective, authoritative statement and the perceptions of the client or others concerned.

11. *Occupational history and status.* The importance of this information for many kinds of cases is compellingly obvious. One needs to know about the individual's job history, including part-time jobs, from the very first to the present. Such information as employer, location, job duties, salary, length of employment, and reasons for leaving is usually obtained.

In some instances, the individual can be relied on to give a fairly accurate account; in others, he cannot. He may, for instance, desire to conceal some section of his job history, especially if it was unfavorable to him. He may simply not remember in sufficient detail the information sought. In such cases, other sources of information must be resorted to. The records of previous employers may be checked; credit bureaus often have fairly good information; sometimes, family members or friends can verify or correct statements made. Occasionally, where classified information is involved, formal search procedures are used.

12. *Social history and status.* It is often seemingly important to know how the individual developed socially, just as it is sometimes important to know about his physical development. The case worker might wish to know whether the individual was a social isolate or had many friends, whether he was shy and retiring or active and aggressive in social relations, whether he participated in the kind of activities most people do at about the same age as most others.

Some school records will give some of this information. Family members and friends, acquaintances, fellow employees, and others can provide more. The individual himself is probably the best source for much of it, but it must be recognized that there are many and powerful reasons for the individual to distort the picture. Some of these reasons are conscious, and some are unconscious. A case with which one of the writers once worked illustrates this. The client was a young woman student. By her own report, she was one of the most popular and best liked girls on campus. The Dean of Women, however, had another study, one which was well documented. It turned out that the girl herself simply did not realize that she was unpopular, that her aggressive social behavior, far from gaining her friends, was making enemies.

13. *Miscellaneous.* The above categories are the ones most commonly included. There are many other kinds of information which may be of interest to the case worker. Military history is one example. Community, fraternal, church, and civic activities may be of interest. Attitudes and opinions, ordinarily not included in the section on personality, may be relevant. The list could be extended considerably.

There is one other matter which needs to be discussed briefly in connection with the case study. That has to do with the presentation of the facts. A case study becomes a permanent record, is consulted not only by the case worker but by his colleagues, by his successor if the case is reopened, by representatives of other agencies, by courts, by employers, by many other individuals who have a right to have access to the study. It is therefore important that the information collected be presented in a manner which will make it most useful.

It is no easy task to write a case history so that the essential elements are included in logical form, so that the highlights are really underscored, so that ambiguities are reduced to a minimum, so that it is readable and understandable by all who may have reason to consult it. A simple, factual summary is rarely enough. Integrated interpretations are usually necessary. These should not, however, be sheer wild guesses but should reflect the information contained in the study. Interpretive statements should, therefore, include some reference to the data on which they are based. If this is an impression gained during an interview, well and good. These are not perfectly reliable and valid, and they should be identified as impressions, but they are often the best we have at our disposal.

Most case studies are prepared for a purpose. That purpose, as we indicated earlier, may be something like deciding on the kind of treatment, on the kind and level of training to be undertaken, or on the disposition of a disrupted family situation. This being so, the information collected is ordinarily polarized around the questions involved. The same data will be interpreted in somewhat different ways depending upon the purpose of the study. It is important to keep that purpose in mind. Too many case studies become rambling, disjointed essays without special relevance to any particular problem or its solution.

The actual writing of the case study and summary presents many special and difficult problems which are often ignored. It would probably be unreasonable to insist that every psychologist, social worker, guidance counselor, and psychiatrist become a master of prose style. There are special talents and interests required for this. It does not seem unreasonable to ask, however, that these people learn how to write clear, concise, readable prose, that they become able to convey unambiguously and clearly the thoughts they have on the subject. Frequently, ability to manipulate polysyllabic jargon is mistaken for good writing. Good writing is usually simple. Technical words may be useful if they actually convey a precise shade of meaning which is needed. Simply as window dressing they are worse than useless, because they make unintelligible to many potential readers what ought to be clear and understandable. The actual and potential reading audience must be considered in writing the report. If one is certain, for example, that only his professional colleagues will read it, the common terminology of the profession—provided always that it is correctly employed—may provide the writer with a kind of shorthand. If members of other disciplines or if relative laymen are to be involved, then the language should make due allowances.

Hammond (13) has written a valuable book on writing case reports. It contains many suggestions which should be useful both to beginners and to others who perhaps have lost sight of the important fundamentals.

In this chapter, we have dealt briefly with some of the issues which seem basic to the case study. These were: the selection of items in the case study, the evaluation of items, and the use of items. We then described the major elements which are included in many case studies. Finally, we commented upon the matter of presenting the completed report.

We shall next deal with the interview in situations where individuals with various kinds of problems are helped to solve them. The case study is an essential part of such assistance, enabling the counselor, the social worker, the psychiatrist to understand better the kind of person with whom he is dealing. Hopefully, this improved understanding results in better treatment.

REFERENCES

1. ANASTASI, A., *Psychological Testing.* New York: Macmillan, 1954.
2. BINGHAM, W., *Aptitudes and Aptitude Testing.* New York: Harper, 1937.
3. BUROS, O., (Ed.), *The Nineteen Forty Mental Measurements Yearbook.* Arlington, Va.: Gryphon Press, 1945.
4. BUROS, O., (Ed.), *The Third Mental Measurements Yearbook.* New Brunswick: Rutgers University Press, 1949.
5. BUROS, O., (Ed.), *The Fourth Mental Measurements Yearbook.* Highland Park, N.J.: Gryphon Press, 1953.
6. CRONBACH, L., *Essentials of Psychological Testing.* New York: Harper, 1949.
7. DARLEY, J. and HAGENAH, T., *Vocational Interest Measurement.* Minneapolis: University of Minnesota Press, 1955.
8. FENLASON, A., *Essentials in Interviewing.* New York: Harper, 1952.
9. GOUGH, H., A new dimension of status: I. development of a personality scale. *Amer. sociol. Rev.,* 1948, 13, 401-409.
10. GOUGH, H., A short social status inventory. *J. educ. Psychol.,* 1949, 40, 52-56.
11. GULLIKSEN, H., *Theory of Mental Tests.* New York: Wiley, 1950.
12. GUSTAD, J., The evaluation interview in vocational counseling. *Pers. Guid. J.,* 1957, 242-250.
13. HAMMOND, K. and ALLEN, J., *Writing Clinical Reports.* New York: Prentice-Hall, 1953.
14. MEEHL, P., *Clinical Versus Statistical Prediction.* Minneapolis: University of Minnesota Press, 1954.
15. STRONG, E., *The Vocational Interests of Men and Women.* Stanford: Stanford University Press, 1943.
16. STRONG, E., *Vocational Interests Eighteen Years After College.* Minneapolis: University of Minnesota Press, 1955.
17. THORNDIKE, R., *Personnel Selection.* New York: Wiley, 1949.

12. The Interview in
Vocational Counseling

LITTLE has, thus far, been said about interviews intended to affect attitudes and behavior. It is true, of course, that the employment interview does have some effects on attitudes; so does the public opinion interview. But their major goals are not centered on changing the individual interviewed. The counseling interview and the clinical interview, while they deal with facts, have as their focus the goal of bringing about some changes in the interviewee. This change of focus also substantially changes the interview.

Occupational changes produce need for vocational counseling

To understand the counseling interview and the problems with which it deals, we must look to several social and economic developments. These have been going on for centuries, but the industrial revolution, beginning in the middle of the eighteenth century, accelerated them, complicated them. Since vocational counseling deals principally with the individual and his job, we must look first to changes in the occupational picture over the past two centuries.

Workers in the eighteenth century were likely to be found in a comparatively small number of occupations. Agriculture was by all odds the dominant industry, and the largest proportion of workers were to be found in it. In the cities, there was some manufacturing, but it tended to be *craft* rather than *production* manufacturing. That is, a skilled craftsman, a master, along with his journeymen and apprentices, would make objects for sale. Customarily, these were made to order. Shoe making is a good example. The shoemaker, along with his helpers, would take the customer's order, prepare the leather, cut it, sew the shoes, and do whatever else was required to prepare the final product, the pair of shoes. One man, especially a master craftsman, was perfectly capable of carrying through the whole process from beginning to end. Because shoes were made to order, there was rarely if ever any tendency to make shoes of various sizes in advance and to stock them. The same was true of other crafts where work was typically done to order by a craftsman and his assistants.

There were, in addition to farm workers and craftsmen, other kinds of jobs, but they were limited in number. There were a few professions such as the law, medicine, teaching, and the ministry. There were a few clerical workers. However, compared to the present day, the number of different ways to earn a living was limited.

Most training was accomplished through apprenticeship programs. Boys were commonly put to work as apprentices with a master craftsman. After a few years they might, if they showed promise and if they got along with the master, hope to become journeymen. Still later, some might qualify as master craftsmen. Those who did not make the grade tried other jobs until, largely by trial and error, they found something they could do.

The social structure was also different. Family position meant much. The sons of laborers could almost never rise far. By and large, they were restricted to the social class of their fathers. Sons of craftsmen commonly followed their fathers' trades; farmers' sons became farmers. Among the wealthy, eldest sons inherited the property and title; second sons frequently went into military service; third sons became ministers or entered other professions.

When the industrial revolution began to have its effects, marked changes occurred. First of all, instead of making products to order, plants were set up to manufacture for stock. That is, shoes were made in a variety of sizes and styles and were then stocked so that when a customer wanted shoes, a pair might be found in stock.

With the emphasis on manufacturing to stock, there came other changes. Efficient, speedy production began to be of concern. This meant that ways were sought and found to turn out products rapidly and cheaply. This in turn led to mass production which was accomplished by breaking up the jobs into many smaller and simpler operations. No longer did a master shoemaker make the whole shoe. Rather, semiskilled workers performed a variety of restricted functions. Some cut leather; others sewed; others polished, etc. Master craftsmen were retained for a time as supervisors, but they were increasingly outnumbered by the semiskilled workers on the production lines.

With production to stock goods there came still other changes. Whole new classes of workers were needed in the merchandising and selling areas. Manufacturers sold their products to wholesalers who in turn sold them to retailers. Selling became a major occupation. The more complicated records required led to the increase in numbers of specialists in bookkeeping.

Finally, as more and more efficient ways were sought to accomplish manufacturing, new machines were developed. Men were needed to build and maintain them. Secondary manufacturing became a major industry, as did maintenance.

There were many other similar changes, including the development of new products. It is difficult to imagine how many kinds of new jobs have been created by the invention of the automobile or by the development of the electronics and aircraft industries. The point to keep in mind, however, is that the number and variety of jobs increased at an astonishing rate. *Today, there are over 27,000 different jobs in the United States.*

Consider what this means to the young person entering the labor market. He is faced with a bewildering array of possibilities. While it is true that nobody knows about all jobs, the young man or woman entering the labor market still faces many possible decisions. It is obviously impossible to resort to simple trial and error without running the risk of wasting one's whole lifetime. Family background is no longer the guide—or the limitation—that it once was. Sons of laborers can and do aspire to become business leaders and professional men.

By the turn of the present century, there were so many people having difficulties in getting located in the world of work that the attention of a number of persons was directed to the problem. While many took the cold-blooded position that if the young man or woman could not make good it was his problem, others believed that timely help would not only prevent personal failure and disappointment but would also make available to industry the kinds of workers it needed.

The person best known for his pioneering efforts in this respect was Frank Parsons. This remarkable man, at various times an attorney (hence, the word *client* for the interviewee in vocational counseling), engineer, and social worker, worked in Boston in a social service capacity. There, he observed the many individuals who were floundering around in the world of work, never finding a job which suited their capacities and interests. He undertook to provide help for them. In his classical book, *Choosing a Vocation* (8), he outlined three steps which should be followed in helping the individual to locate a job suited to his interests and abilities. These steps were:

1. analyze the individual; find out about his abilities, interests, experience, etc.;
2. analyze the job in terms of its requirements;
3. match the information about the individual with the information about job requirements.

Experience and research over the past half century have modified Parsons' approach considerably, but the beginner would do well to read his book carefully, for much of what he said still has relevance.

The assumption underlying Parsons' book as well as most vocational counseling until very recent years was that an individual might be assisted in finding a suitable occupation if all the relevant facts about him and the world of work were systematically collected, analyzed, and compared. In Parsons' day, methods for analyzing jobs —job analysis procedures—were beginning to be fairly well developed. Unfortunately, methods for analyzing the individual were in their infancy. It was therefore necessary to rely largely on client self-report regarding such things as abilities, interests, and personality traits. Although there were grave dangers in such reliance, there was then no alternative to using what clients reported about themselves. Today, other methods are available, and most counselors use them.

From the beginning, the interview has played a central role in counseling. There was a time when it was felt to be a more or less necessary evil, something to be tolerated until better, more objective procedures might be developed. It is now seen, properly, as the core, the essential element in counseling, for it is in the interview that client attitudes and behavior are ultimately affected.

Purpose of Counseling

The interview was first used principally as a data-collection technique. It still has some of this function, because there are many important aspects of client behavior that are not yet accessible to psychological measurement. Perhaps the most important change in counseling may be seen in the purposes set for it. From Parsons' original conception, counseling has moved to a point where it is seen not solely as a means for assisting the client to make a specific choice but also, as Bordin (1) has put it, ". . . understanding of the obstacles to further personality growth and development that are typified by this person's rather specific and, for the time being, limited difficulty." (p. 9) In other words, it is assumed that most individuals, in the process of maturation, learn enough about themselves and the world of work so that they can make reasonably appropriate decisions about their occupations. A substantial number, however, either do not acquire this capacity or, through conflicts of various sorts, are unable to make effective use of it. Counseling is therefore seen as a process whereby the individual learns a set of skills that will enable him not only to solve the problem of the moment but, more importantly, similar problems as they may occur later. This is a large order.

Before we proceed with the discussion of the counseling interview, it seems necessary to try to make certain distinctions. Some readers have perhaps already wondered about the difference between counseling and psychotherapy. Both are concerned with essentially the same objective—helping people to learn more productive and effective ways of living, and both are often performed by the same individuals. Counseling psychologists frequently go well beyond a vocational problem and deal with conflicts, conscious and unconscious. Clinical psychologists and psychiatrists, in dealing with neurotic conditions, frequently deal with adjustment to the world of work. There has been an argument going on for some years as to what, if any, are the differences between counseling and psychotherapy. One of the present writers (5) has attempted to make this delineation with only moderate success.

At the present time, it seems impossible to draw any hard and final lines between the two processes. There are some broad guide lines, but there is much overlapping in any attribute on which we compare them. Generally speaking, counseling deals with the normal problems of normal people. It is typically concerned with such real problems as choosing a job or getting along in school. Ordinarily, it is not necessary to deal directly with the unconscious, although unconscious material certainly affects the counseling interaction in a great many ways. Generally speaking, counseling is of shorter duration than psychotherapy, typically lasting for from three to a half dozen interviews. Usually, counseling stresses reality factors, such as abilities, achievements, aptitudes, and job requirements more than the content of the unconscious. There seem to be differences in the interest of counselors and therapists. While counselors often do therapy and therapists often do counseling, each group tends to prefer to deal with certain kinds of problems. Whether this means that they are, in a variety of ways, different kinds of people remains to be demonstrated. There is some reason to think that this is so. Finally, psychotherapy tends to be seen by many as a medical problem; counseling is rarely if ever seen as such. Much therapy is done by non-medically trained individuals, but dealing with neurotic and psychotic conditions presents problems substantially different from those involved in dealing with occupational choices or study skills.

Another distinction that needs to be made is between counseling and guidance. To some, the terms are synonymous. There is a growing tendency to separate them. Hahn and MacLean (6) have given what is perhaps the best distinction. They say that counseling is a much more personal, individual process whereas guidance is more of an administrative procedure, much more of an intellectual, teaching process. Examples may be seen in the Veterans Administration. Within the Department of Medicine and Surgery, there is a counseling program that provides services to all hospitalized veterans. It is the kind of program described above, dealing broadly with a variety of patient problems. There is also a program in Vocational Rehabilitation and Education which has much more of the guidance flavor about it. Here, one of the major concerns is with administering benefits such as educational entitlement. Procedures are more carefully spelled out, and the range of problems dealt with is more restricted. The distinction between counseling and guidance is not intended to be at all invidious. Counseling and guidance are both essential processes in helping people.

Evaluation of counseling

To return to the counseling process itself and the interview which is its core, little is known about precisely how and why it works. There is a considerable body of literature available which suggests that counseling is fairly effective in a substantial number of cases. Even here, however, there is argument; certainly there is an urgent need for more research designed to tell us which techniques do work and in what proportion of what kinds of cases. Dressel (4) has well summed up the problem of evaluation as follows:

It has been said that giving advice is like kissing; it costs nothing and it is a pleasant thing to do. While I do not believe that counseling is synonymous with giving advice, the analogy, nevertheless, has some relevance. Counseling has further similarities to kissing in that (1) everyone feels qualified to practice kissing and most everyone does at some time; (2) the objectives of kissing are usually not clearly stated but are not entirely intangible; (3) kissing itself is apt to be so satisfying that there is little tendency to evaluate it otherwise. (p. 70)

Theories of Counseling

While nobody is really sure about what happens in the counseling interview, there are several theoretical statements which have plausibility. Not surprisingly, these positions are to a greater or lesser extent in conflict. This is probably a good thing; hopefully, out of such conflicts will come a sharper, more adequate notion about what counseling accomplishes and how it does it.

There are two positions that are commonly accepted as being at opposite ends of the scale; they really are not, but opposing them in this way may serve a useful purpose. At the one end is what Williamson (18) has called the Minnesota point of view. At the other is the Chicago school, originated by Carl Rogers. We shall try to describe these positions briefly as a prelude to dealing with recent formulations, which seem to us to be more productive.

Minnesota approach

The Minnesota point of view is in some ways the more traditional. To understand it, it is necessary to look to the man principally responsible for it, Professor Donald G. Paterson. Paterson was a psychologist for the U. S. Army during the First World War. He had a great deal to do with the development of the selection testing program. Afterward, he joined the Scott Company, founded by the late Dr. Walter D. Scott, a firm of consulting psychologists interested in industrial problems. Going to Minnesota as a professor in 1921, Paterson transplanted his interests in occupational adjustment to that environment. His interest in test construction continued, and Minnesota became, largely through his efforts and influence, one of the major centers for test research and development. During the depression, he was instrumental in establishing the Minnesota Employment Stabilization Research Institute. The section with which he was principally concerned concentrated on the analysis of the individual, trying to find out what trait differences and pattern differences predisposed some men to become early casualties of the depression while others maintained themselves in the highly competitive labor market. A counseling program was set up that dealt with large numbers of men and women presenting a wide variety of vocational problems. It was this experience with the Employment Stabilization Research Institute, along with experience garnered in the student counseling program, that crystallized and matured the approach to counseling known as the Minnesota point of view. This is not to say that this point of view is of only historical interest. It has kept developing and changing, is very much a force at the present time, but it still reflects its origins, its ultimate concern with the problems of essentially normal people.

While this approach began with and continues to have a deep and abiding concern for occupational adjustment, it has been extended to other areas. Whatever the problem, real or presented, there has always been a heavy emphasis on objective description as the basis for counseling. The use of tests of various kinds has been a cornerstone of this approach. So has the use of the systematic case study (3).

For a long time, the interview, always a fundamental tool, was used largely in two ways: first, to obtain information about the client and, second, to inform him of the results and interpretations of the information gathered. Comparatively little attention was paid to the feelings and reactions of the client. It was even possible for leading proponents of this method to suggest that, if the client resisted or rejected the counselor's interpretations, *persuasion* should be used to convince him of their correctness. This neglect of client feelings and of the subtle but important counselor-client interactions in counseling has been corrected in more recent formulations (17) (6).

The Rogerian Approach

Usually placed at the opposite pole has been the approach developed by Carl Rogers and his students. As with the Minnesota point of view, some understanding of the background of the founder helps to illuminate the system. Rogers spent the early years of his professional career in a child guidance clinic. Here, while the range of problems was great, most of them tended to involve emotional reactions. In addition, children are far less able to talk about their feelings, less able to deal with them intellectually. Finally, children and adolescents, by virtue of not having had an opportunity to solidify their problems over many years, are more likely to be able to work them through.

In his work, Rogers was influenced by the psychoanalytic writings of such major workers as Freud and Rank. Rank in particular, and especially as interpreted by Taft, had a great effect on Rogers' developing ideas. By the time he wrote his book *The Clinical Treatment of the Problem Child* (11) his notions about counseling and therapy were fairly well crystallized. Rogers' classical description of his position, *Counseling and Psychotherapy* (12), should be read by every serious student of counseling and the interview.

Where the Minnesota point of view, resting systematically on the largely statistical theory of relatively unique traits and relying heavily therefore on objective measurements of these traits, viewed counseling as a fairly intellectual kind of educative process, Rogers, basing his ideas on the main themes of psychoanalysis, saw it as a largely emotional interchange. Rogers felt that counseling should be so structured that the innate growth potentials of the individual, blocked and distorted by unfortunate environmental circumstances, could be released so that the client would be enabled to work out his own problem. This in turn led him to decree that the counselor must never impose his own ideas and evaluations or interpretations but rather should help the client to achieve these insights by himself. Rogers' point of view, for these reasons, is best known as the non-directive (Rogers has more recently indicated a preference for the term "client centered").

In this system, then, the interview is a device for fostering an emotional interchange, with the counselor assisting the client to recognize and deal with his own feelings. In doing this, the counselor attempts to stay out of the picture as an individual, to get the client to look into the mirror of the self which he, the counselor, holds up to the client. This conception is well described in the recent book by Rogers and Dymond (14).

For some years, there was considerable direct and open controversy between the proponents of the two schools. The Minnesota group was criticized for being too intellectualized, for failing to recognize the role of client emotions in all kinds of problems, for assigning to the counselor too much authority and responsibility. The Chicago group was as vehemently attacked for resting on an unproved assumption about innate growth tendencies which only awaited release, for failing to recognize the importance of the realities of client abilities and interests and job requirements in dealing with vocational problems, and for failing to assume responsibility when this seemed necessary. Rebuttal and counter-rebuttal filled the literature for several years. Out of this has come a synthesis. The Minnesota point of view has absorbed and made use of the literature and ideas on client emotional reactions in the interview. It still insists that objective measurement is essential and that reality factors must be considered, but counselors of this persuasion are more apt than formerly to make haste slowly in dealing with such matters, taking their cues from client expressions of feeling.

The newer thinking about counseling has been well described by several authors. Hahn and MacLean (6) probably best represent the continuing although modified Minnesota tradition. Pepinsky and Pepinsky (9) represent a serious attempt to extend it farther in the direction of such fundamental issues as are involved in learning theory. Bordin (1), originally trained by Rogers but no longer especially representative of that position, has dealt quite effectively with the so-called dynamic approach, one which is heavily influenced by psychoanalytic theory. The previously mentioned work by Rogers and Dymond (14) contains the most recent treatment of the non-directive position. Many points remain on which there is major disagreement. Since, however, there is still no conclusive, experimental evidence that tells us which approach is the best for which circumstances or for which clients and counselors, such disagreement is probably both inevitable and healthy.

Phases of Counseling Process

Despite the differences, there is considerable agreement about the counseling interview itself. It is now seen by most counselors as embracing all three purposes described earlier in this book: obtaining information, giving information, and changing attitudes. Emphases vary, with some counselors emphasizing one or another phase at various times and with different clients. Perhaps the point on which there is the widest agreement is that the counselor, if he is to be effective, must adapt his methods to the needs of the client with whom he is dealing.

What happens in the course of the typical vocational counseling case? Though the details are too complex to describe here, there are certain gross features which can be pictured. Ordinarily, the client comes to the counselor voluntarily, seeking help with what seems to him to be a problem. The vocational problem may not be the only one or even the most important one. This is the counselor's job to discover. Often, a vocational problem is "safe," one which is socially acceptable, which the client can admit without having at the same time to admit that he has other problems. Some counseling centers have a standard procedure which calls for an initial screening interview in which an experienced staff member tries to form an estimate about such matters.

Once counseling begins, the client and the counselor spend considerable time talking, getting acquainted, and establishing a sound working relationship. This may take one hour or several depending on the client and on the problem. A wise counselor will not rush this, will not let the client push him too rapidly into "taking the tests." Simply assigning a battery of tests and interpreting the results is not counseling. We must again recall Bordin's comment that we need to find out, fundamentally, why this client has been unable to make a decision in the first place or has made one or several wrong ones.

During such interviews, all three of the functions of the interview may come into play. The counselor seeks, directly or indirectly, information about the client. This does not mean that he asks a series of questions. Preferably, he gets the client to talking freely, because such talking reveals more than a series of direct questions is likely to do. The counselor listens not only to what is said but also to the subtle implications of what is said; and he listens for what might be said but is not. He observes. Too many counselors forget to do this, but the language of body movement is rich in meaning (10). Does the client seem tense and fidgety? Is his voice too loud? Does he drape himself over his chair; put his feet on the counselor's desk? There are many things people do which, if they do not clearly and concisely indicate feelings, at least suggest to the counselor lines of thought and exploration.

The counselor also conveys information. He tells the client about the process of counseling, the rules of the game, about the agency and, perhaps most important, about himself. Some of these things he says directly, but mostly he communicates by what he does, his tone of voice, inflections, and gestures. If the counselor's manner is timorous and hesitant, he may convey to the client a sense of uneasiness, a lack of confidence. If the counselor is brusque and overbearing, the client may feel that he will have trouble in communicating. If the counselor is too cold, polite, and formal, the client may feel that his problem is not really of any great concern. Nobody has systematically studied the language of behavior in this sense, so what we can say is not based on the kind of evidence we would like to have. Every experienced counselor has had clients tell him about some of their idiosyncracies, but there may be other problems so disturbing that clients terminate counseling rather than deal with them.

The counselor, from the beginning, changes attitudes also. At the outset, he may have to deal explicitly and implicitly with attitudes toward counseling. Some clients think of it as "taking the tests," expecting that these will pinpoint the one occupation out of thousands in which they can be successful. Others are afraid of tests, afraid of revealing things about themselves which they have hidden. Many come with the feeling that the counselor, once he is told the symptoms, will, like a physician, prescribe a magic remedy while the client need assume no active part or responsibility. There are many other attitudes toward counseling which must be dealt with if counseling is to be successful. In most cases, a frontal attack on them is neither necessary nor desirable, but dealing with them indirectly requires considerable skill and experience.

Early interviews are ordinarily spent also in developing at least the essential elements of the case study. This was discussed in detail in the preceding chapter. For the moment, it is sufficient to say that the counselor must learn a great deal about the client, about his past history, his education, his family situation, his hobbies, his vocational experience, and his health. Some of this information can and should be obtained by means of the data blank. Much of it, and particularly that part which deals with the client's feelings and reactions about the elements in his life history, must be obtained through the interview.

At some point in most vocational counseling cases, after one or many interviews, the client and the counselor see a need for obtaining information on such things as abilities, interests, aptitudes, and personality. In short, testing seems indicated. There has been considerable controversy about how to introduce testing into counseling and how to assign tests once the topic has been introduced. The pros and cons of this argument have been summarized and the results of a study on these problems have been presented by Gustad and Tuma (see Chapter Two).

Tests should be introduced, assigned, and interpreted in light of the counselor's understanding of and feeling for the motives of the client. Counseling can be ruined at this stage by wrong handling. The counselor may have spent several hours in trying to get the client to accept responsibility for making his own decisions. If he then takes back this responsibility, puts the client through several hours of mystifying and stressful testing, and acts like the Delphic oracle in interpreting the results, all may be lost.

However tests are used, it must be remembered that tests are no different in principle from other kinds of information. Most tests are in fact highly structured and standardized *interviews* in which the client is asked a series of questions or is asked to solve a series of problems. They often have greater reliability than the usual interview, and their correlations with various criteria are commonly known. They are also frequently timesaving devices such that the counselor can, by an hour's testing, obtain information which would require many hours of interviewing. Counselors often complicate their work needlessly by thinking of tests as something special and different from the normal processes of the counseling interview.

Interpreting the results of the tests is another point fraught with danger. Most clients are incapable of understanding the scores derived from a test; they need the help of the counselor to interpret all the information. At the same time, if this information is to be of use to a client struggling to see himself realistically and completely, to make his own decisions, he must be helped to incorporate it into his self-concept. Forcing him to accept a certain interpretation is likely to produce either dependence or resistance, neither of which is desirable. Simply telling the client what the test scores mean is not enough. The results must be related to his whole conception of himself, and time must be taken to allow him to work through any problems the test scores create. For example, if the client has been in the premedical curriculum and if his scholastic ability test score is, say, at the tenth percentile, it is not wise simply to tell him this and that he has no chance of making the grade in medicine. If counseling is to be successful, he must come to be able to deal with this himself, but it should be presented carefully, in full appreciation of his feelings.

Increasingly, counselors are scattering tests throughout counseling, answering a few questions at a time, rather than assigning a presumably comprehensive battery all at once. Some counselors, for instance, obtain a measure of interest first. This limits the range of further testing needed, for there is probably little point in worrying about the mechanical aptitudes of a client interested in creative writing. Next, having determined the general direction, the level may be determined by general ability measures. If the client's interests are in the biological sciences, for instance, he might be considered for medicine, biological laboratory work, or a variety of related jobs. If his ability is low, medicine is probably ruled out, leaving the counselor and client to find something else in the area which is consonant with his abilities. This approach to the assignment of tests is somewhat like the successive hurdles method employed in personnel selection.

Completion of test interpretation by no means completes counseling. Assuming that it does is one of the commonest and most serious mistakes made in counseling. There is still much to do, and most of it has to be done by means of the interview. Rarely is it possible to narrow down the vocational possibilities to a single one. Ordinarily, there are several possibilities. If the counselor turns the client loose at this point, he may enter the job market almost as confused as if he had never had counseling.

There is the matter of the client's understanding what is involved in the various jobs. This is occupational information. Counseling centers must maintain files of such information so that clients can find out in more detail than the counselor can tell them what is involved in various jobs. Merely to send the client to read is not, however, enough. After he has read, he needs the opportunity to discuss his reactions to what he has read and to raise further questions. Often, reading does not provide sufficient information. Then, the counselor may wish to arrange for the client to visit a plant or office where he can see and talk with workers employed in the jobs under consideration. In counseling college students, it is often advisable to make an appointment with the head of the department concerned. These individuals know the jobs fairly well, and they can give the client a perspective which the counselor cannot.

Sometimes, it is necessary or desirable to arrange for job try-outs. The counselor may arrange to have the client work for a time in a job, keeping in touch with him so that he may talk over the client's feelings about the work. The counselor, unlike the psychotherapist, often does his most effective work outside the interview office.

Finally, after interviewing, testing, job exploration, and follow-up, counseling may reach its completion. Terminating the counseling relationship is sometimes difficult, sometimes quite easy. Despite every effort to the contrary, the counselor may find that the client is hesitant to give up the friendly, permissive relationship with the counselor. He may have some feelings of dependency. Some clients, with these feelings, keep finding new problems. It is the counselor's job to forestall the development of such feelings in the first place. If they do develop, the best method for dealing with them is usually to treat them as symptoms of personal difficulties and work with them in a therapeutic fashion. This does not mean that intensive therapy is required, but such feelings should be recognized frankly and dealt with for what they are.

In most cases, however, the client himself senses that the problem is within his control, that he is capable of handling his problems by himself without further assistance from the counselor. He will usually say so, thank the counselor for his time, and end the relationship.

Preparation by supervised experience in counseling

The individual preparing to become a counselor must, in addition to formal, didactic training, have considerable closely supervised experience in counseling (see Chapter Four). For the person merely interested in understanding better the general processes and procedures of counseling, there are two sources of study materials which will be useful. There are case summaries available in several of the standard texts on counseling. There are also available transcriptions of recorded interviews. These latter are especially valuable in that they enable the student to follow closely the intricate patterns of interaction between the counselor and the client. Rogers (12), Snyder (15), Callis, Polmantier, and Roeber (2), Kahn and Cannell (7) and Bordin (1) are especially good sources for such materials.

We have said a number of times that there is no formula to guide the interviewer in the conduct of the interview. The interview is a subtle and complex process resting, in the final analysis, on the characteristics of the participants as they interact. At the same time, there are some general statements and suggestions which we feel are broadly applicable and widely accepted and which may be of interest especially to the beginner in the field. On the following pages, we have listed these suggestions. Probably none will hold in all situations and with all interviewees, but they do seem to hold in a high proportion of cases.

While originally developed by Stogdill (16) for the interview with students, the points listed below have utility for other counseling cases as well.

THERAPEUTIC TECHNIQUES IN COUNSELING

A. Techniques providing the student opportunity for free expression of emotional tensions

1. The student may be encouraged to give an unhurried and uninterrupted verbalization of his present feelings concerning his stated problem and other relevant material such as
   a. early experiences
   b. parent-child relationships
   c. tabooed behavior, attitudes or topics
   d. his attitudes toward himself, or of others toward him
   e. fears and worries
   f. various individuals in their relationship to his situation.

2. The student may be encouraged to write out additional autobiographical material between interviews. This may include connected written accounts of such things as dreams or reveries, or lists of various kinds such as
   a. wishes or goals
   b. points of superiority or inferiority in himself
   c. types of situations in which he feels adequate or inadequate
   d. individuals who add to or detract from his feeling of effectiveness.

3. The clinician may act as a source of temporary emotional security for the student during the period of emotional readjustment by
   a. accepting him uncritically as a worthwhile individual with unfulfilled possibilities which can be realized
   b. giving him complete attention during specified times
   c. reading carefully any written material submitted, and discussing it with him objectively
   d. making him understand that his confidences are respected
   e. being intellectually and emotionally consistent in behavior toward him throughout the contacts
   f. standing between him and certain immediate consequences of his ill-advised behavior
   g. acting as mediator between him and other individuals involved, such as parents, faculty or administrative officers
   h. assisting him in analyzing his conflicting obligations and loyalties.

B. Techniques providing the student the opportunity for securing information and for gaining better interpretation of relationships

1. Information may be furnished through books, lectures, and personal discussions on topics about which the student is confused

or deeply concerned such as sex, marriage, heredity, insanity, ethical standards, or religious viewpoints.

2. The student may be guided through personal discussion to clarify his interpretations of

   a. inter-personal relationships such as those between

     (1) student and student

     (2) student and faculty members

     (3) student and his family

     (4) men and women

   b. differences of viewpoints on such matters as race and religion as they may represent areas of confusion in his parental home or in his choice of friends or mate

   c. desirable attitudes to adopt in view of such situations as

     (1) parental expectation of unreasonably high grades

     (2) parental pressure for early or financially advantageous marriage

     (3) parental insistence on a vocational choice in a field in which the student is uninterested or incompetent

     (4) undue parental self-effacement or self-sacrifice

     (5) previously unverbalized resentment toward some member or members of his family because of early experiences such as punishment felt to be too severe or unmerited, unfair comparison between children, or lack of parental affection

     (6) parental disharmony or separation.

3. Realistic attitudes toward self-evaluation may be encouraged through such methods as

   a. pointing out to gifted or to unusually emotionally mature students the reason for their apparent difference from the majority of their fellows

   b. pointing out that the attitude of the clinician is one of tracing causal relationships, not one of praise or blame, and encouraging the student to adopt the same viewpoint

   c. interpretation of scores on "mental" and personality tests. Retesting in cases of wide discrepancy with observed behavior

   d. pointing out by means of concrete illustrations, from the student's own behavior, abilities or disabilities overlooked or incorrectly evaluated by him

   e. observation by the student of the clinician's unperturbed reaction to his recital of his "sins and shortcomings" and guilty feelings

   f. tracing with the student the developmental history of various types of his behavior in order to help him realize their essential modifiability.

C. Techniques involved in the planning of specific activities for the student between interview periods

1. The clinician can judge the student's adequacy more objectively if he can arrange to observe him first hand outside the consultation situation, rather than being entirely dependent on his self-reports which may be very misleading. The mistake of entering into a social relationship with the client must, however, be avoided. It is possible to use reports from disinterested persons in the student's environment as partial substitutes for observation, provided they can be secured without invading the confidential nature of the relationship, or making the student the object of scrutiny.

2. The student may be assisted in giving a more accurate picture of his own behavior to the clinician and to himself by the use of various recording charts and written lists. Some of these methods are

   a. keeping a time schedule for a stated period and then comparing his distribution of time with tabulated results of similar studies

   b. keeping a financial account and facing it objectively with the aid of the clinician

   c. keeping a chart for recording instances of behavior which the student desires to develop or to free himself from, for example a chart of ascendant or of submissive behavior

   d. listing a number of things for which he would feel insulted to be praised (like knowing the letters of the alphabet or washing his face), and comparing it with another list of things for which he finds himself demanding approval.

3. The clinician may find it necessary to assist the student or to ask the help of other responsible individuals in arranging modifications of his client's situation such as

   a. finding him a different room or roommate

   b. securing him employment, loans or outright gifts of money

   c. arranging a more reasonable scholastic program

   d. getting him into various social groups in which he may broaden his contacts

   e. assisting him with problems of personal appearance, posture and speech.

D. Techniques involving contacts with parents, faculty members or administrative officers with regard to the student's problems.

1. The clinician may need to present a somewhat generalized statement concerning a student's difficulties to faculty members or administrative officers in order that they may deal with him more adequately in the light of such knowledge. There are cases, how-

ever, in which it is inadvisable to call the student to the attention of any school official.

2. Contact with parents is frequently essential to the successful handling of a student's problems. In other cases it is definitely detrimental for the parent even to learn that his child is consulting a clinical psychologist. A single unfavorable report about the student's school adjustment, sent out as a routine matter by some college office, may undo months of work on the clinician's part. Often the clinician needs to be able to secure special handling of school situations pertaining to his client's welfare.

3. Contact with parents may take the form of interpreting the student and his difficulties to them, of getting their point of view about his situation, or of enlisting their co-operation in granting him needed freedom or encouragement. Sometimes it is necessary to assist parents in adjusting to problems of their own, as well as to reassure them about their children's development.

For those who may want general principles and conclusions stated in a form for application in practice, a summary of specific suggestions completes this discussion of the interview in counseling.

SUGGESTIONS FOR THE INTERVIEW IN COUNSELING

1. *Provide conditions conducive to good interviews.* The school atmosphere, the entire policy and educational philosophy of the administration, should favor the modern conception of educational personnel work, which emphasizes the individual. The curriculum must be flexible. The instructional methods and the use of grades and test data should encourage students to seek personal conferences. The best interview often results when a student casually drops in on the interviewer.

2. *Assemble and relate to the problem all the facts available.* Ideally a cumulative personnel record of the interviewee's educational history should be at hand. In any event, his scholarship record, attendance, test scores, statements of teachers, and similar pertinent data should be brought together and freshly canvassed, before the interview when possible.

3. *Meet the interviewee cordially.* The friendly spirit must be natural, not condescending or patronizing. The interviewer should find genuine interest in the subject, avoiding any traces of boredom or impatience.

4. *Be sincere.* Behave in a way that harmonizes with your own personality. Do not try to copy some other person's style of meeting and interviewing people, for the student will detect this and suspect insincerity. Your attention to the purpose of the interview and your real interest in the student will breed confidence.

5. *Begin the interview with whatever topic will be of most interest to the person interviewed.* Before the main issue is approached, a foundation of rapport may well be established by arousing pleasant associations.

6. *Approach the problem as soon as rapport is assured.* Ask the student what is on his mind. Secure from him a clear statement of the problem as he sees it. This formulation may need revision and restatement as the interview progresses.

7. *Avoid a patronizing attitude.* The student may be looking for a crutch or for someone to treat him as a child, and it is tempting to play the rôle of a patron, but it does not help the student to grow.

8. *Uncover the real difficulty.* Listen to the obvious problem but watch for clues pointing to the real problem often existing behind it.

9. *Encourage but do not urge.* One who finds it difficult to reveal personal facts should not be told, "Go on," but should be asked, "Is there anything else?"

10. *Isolate the central problem.* The key to a situation is often found by disregarding the constant factors common to many students, and attending to the variables which appear in this case. A student has an unusual number of absences from his classes. Other students cut classes occasionally, but you may find that this particular student is doing so because he is worrying about his inability to meet college expenses. You isolate the variable factor. Remember that "emotional pressure often works itself off not at all with reference to the cause of the pressure, but simply where resistance is weakest," or through channels of habit and convention.

11. *Ask questions to direct attention to salient facts.* Then let recognition of the facts shape in the student's mind the inevitable conclusions.

12. *Make the interview a joint undertaking.* To ensure co-operation, help the student to feel throughout that the interviewer is frank, that nothing is being concealed, that no thought or line of action is being forced on him or being suggested subtly.

13. *Do not embarrass the interviewee unnecessarily.* To make it

easy for the student to disclose essential facts even though they may be unpleasant, do not pry into matters not related to the problem at hand. While it is true that an understanding of many maladjustments depends on intimate personal data, this does not give the interviewer unlimited license. In so far as possible respect the individual's privacy.

14. *Face the facts professionally.* Do not betray surprise, shock, or emotional tension at disclosures. Sentimental sympathy and antipathy must both be absent. Unpleasant facts must not be blinked or rationalized by either student or interviewer, but looked at squarely and objectively.

15. *Observe closely the student's behavior.* As a natural manifestation of your interest while listening, you can give attention to the student's mannerisms and facial expression. You may find in this way that his behavior reveals with what aspects of the total situation his emotional tensions and complexes are associated.

16. *Avoid putting the student on the defensive.* In case of resistance, resulting particularly from a difference of opinion, yield as much as possible.

17. *Alleviate the shock of disillusionment.* The student may come with childish dreams, fixations, superstitions, outmoded mores, or just plain misinformation. These must be revealed for what they are, and thus eliminated. Again, however, the process is one of readjustment or growth, sometimes requiring time. Care must be taken not to induce an unnecessarily severe emotional shock or psychic trauma that is as serious as the original trouble. Some accepted principles and beliefs must be identified to provide orientation during the process of readjustment. Identifying the student's misinformation, error, or difficulty as similar to that of many other persons often helps to allay chagrin, shock, or new fears.

18. *Establish a reputation for being fair and for keeping confidences.* Personal information should be kept confidential without exception. A guidance or counseling service should be separate from an office that is looked upon as having a disciplinary function. Neither are intimate records to be turned over to prying researchers who do not know how to respect the confidential relation between client and professional counselor.

19. *Let the student formulate his conclusions or plan of action.* If the outcome of the interview is to be a program in accordance with which the interviewee will act, it should not be laid down by the

interviewer but should grow out of the student's own thinking. It must be his plan, not yours.

20. *Allow time for insights to mature and attitudes to change.* One seeking counsel usually does not think through directly to a new point of view or experience a sudden conversion in attitude. These changes are more like processes of growth.

21. *Present alternatives for his consideration.* Possible courses of action may be proposed without the implication that you are trying to impose your own views.

22. *Give advice sparingly if at all.* If your advice is asked, you may say that you would rather not advise; but you can review the relevant circumstances and encourage the student to formulate the conclusions as his own. Do not be a crutch for a limping mind. Strengthen the student by requiring him to accept the responsibility of choice.

23. *Give information as needed.* Be free to supply facts about educational or vocational opportunities and requirements, or about the student himself and the way others regard him, unless you feel that he would benefit by being required to search out such essential information for himself. In that event, suggestions may be offered as to sources of information.

24. *Make certain that all vital considerations relevant to a decision are brought forward.* In several types of interviewing and particularly in vocational counseling, a schedule of the many essential points to be reviewed is almost indispensable.

25. *Make other services available.* Refer to librarians, clinicians, and experts having information or professional experience that can contribute to the student's insight into his problem; but avoid shuttling him unnecessarily from office to office and person to person. Bring these contributions to a focus through one person or office.

26. *Achieve something definite.* Do not let the interview close until recognizable progress has been made and agreement reached on at least the next step. The interviewee should leave with the realization that he has the answer to some question, the solution to some element of his problem, a fresh glimpse of insight, a reassured morale.

27. *Make subsequent interviews easy.* Remember that more than one conference is often needed. Do not attempt too much in the first interview. At the close, make another appointment, or at least leave the way open so that further conference, if desired, can be easily initiated.

REFERENCES

1. BORDIN, E., *Psychological Counseling*. New York: Appleton-Century-Crofts, 1955.
2. CALLIS, R., POLMANTIER, P., and ROEBER, E., *A Casebook of Counseling*. New York: Appleton-Century-Crofts, 1955.
3. DARLEY, J., The structure of the systematic case study in individual diagnosis and counseling. *J. consult. Psychol.*, 1940, 4, 215-220.
4. DRESSEL, P., The evaluation of counseling. In Berdie, R. (Ed.) *Concepts and Programs of Counseling*. Minneapolis: University of Minnesota Press, 1951.
5. GUSTAD, J., The definition of counseling. In Berdie, R. (Ed.) *Roles and Relationships in Counseling*. Minneapolis: University of Minnesota Press, 1953.
6. HAHN, M. and MACLEAN, M., *Counseling Psychology*. (Second Edition) New York: McGraw-Hill, 1955.
7. KAHN, R. and CANNELL, C., *The Dynamics of Interviewing*. New York: Wiley, 1957.
8. PARSONS, F., *Choosing a Vocation*. Boston: Houghton Mifflin, 1909.
9. PEPINSKY, H. and PEPINSKY, P., *Counseling Theory and Practice*. New York: Ronald, 1954.
10. REUSCH, J. and KEES, W., *Non-Verbal Communication*. Berkeley: University of California Press, 1956.
11. ROGERS, C., *The Clinical Treatment of the Problem Child*. New York: Houghton Mifflin, 1939.
12. ROGERS, C., *Counseling and Psychotherapy*. New York: Houghton Mifflin, 1942.
13. ROGERS, C. *Client Centered Therapy*. New York: Houghton Mifflin, 1951.
14. ROGERS, C. and DYMOND, R., *Psychotherapy and Personality Change*. Chicago: University of Chicago Press, 1954.
15. SNYDER, W., *Casebook of Non-Directive Counseling*. New York: Houghton Mifflin, 1947.
16. STOGDILL, E., Techniques of Student Counseling. *J. consult. Psychol.*, 1940, 4, 176-180.
17. WILLIAMSON, E., *Counseling Adolescents*. New York: McGraw-Hill, 1950.
18. WILLIAMSON, E., Counseling and the Minnesota point of view. *Educ. psychol. Measmt.*, 1947, 7, 141-156.

13. The Clinical Interview

ANOTHER kind of interview which has as its major goal the alteration of attitudes and behavior is conducted in a clinical setting. We indicated in the previous chapter that it was virtually impossible to draw any firm and defensible line between the counseling and the clinical interview. Nevertheless, there are some differences worth noting, differences having to do mostly with the settings, the kinds of clients, and the kinds of problems. It is doubtful whether there are major differences in techniques employed.

First of all, with respect to differences in settings, the clinical interview, as its designation implies, is employed in clinics, hospitals, mental hygiene agencies, child guidance clinics, private psychotherapeutic practice, and other places where the problems presented and the clients dealt with indicate therapeutic treatment. It is also sometimes employed in counseling agencies, in industry, and in settings where the counseling interview is commoner.

The major characteristic of the clients seeking the clinical interview is their relatively greater emotional disturbance compared to the clients seen in counseling. This is not always so, and there is considerable overlap, but it holds as a general rule. Certainly, it is clearly so in the extreme cases of hospitalized patients who are suffering from severe neuroses and psychoses. In general, the clinical interview is more often concerned with disturbances of personality, less with such reality problems as the choice of an occupation or the development of proper study skills. The reader should not infer from the above distinctions that there are differences in difficulty or in the skills required on the part of the interviewer. Both the counseling and the clinical interviews make great demands on the interviewer, albeit of somewhat different kinds.

The clinical interview as employed in the mental hygiene or outpatient clinic is probably most representative of this form. We shall

therefore consider this example in discussing the clinical interview
in detail. Before we do, however, some brief background, some sketch
of the development of this interview form seems indicated.

Background of the Clinical Interview

Fundamentally, the clinical interview is employed to assist an individual to regain emotional composure or control, to overcome distressing or debilitating symptoms which have interfered with his or her
being able to lead a normal happy life. The clinical interview must be
viewed against the background of the treatment of mental disorders.
Oddly enough, the kind of attitude and approach to mental illness
which is embodied in the clinical interview is of comparatively recent
origin. Until the end of the last century, individuals afflicted with these
disorders were more likely to be savagely attacked than they were to
be helped. Any good textbook on abnormal psychology will give
the reader an account of this history.

Suffice it to say that the recognition that mental illness was in fact
an illness, that its victims deserved the best treatment available, and
that treatment should be something other than flogging or torture,
mesmerism or incantation, is a development of the nineteenth and
twentieth centuries. The individual most centrally responsible for
the development of the conceptions now generally accepted about
mental illness was Sigmund Freud. His basic theories have been modified many times, but virtually all clinical interviewers will, if they
trace the history of the ideas underlying their practice, sooner or later
arrive back at Freud's work.

To disagree with, to criticize Freud's work now is easy. Most
undergraduates can do a better job than Freud's contemporaries.
Much of what he said was subject to perfectly valid criticism, but the
fact remains that, without his profound insights and brilliant theo-
rizing, psychotherapy through the interview would probably not be
anywhere near its present state of development.

To appreciate the significance of this starting point, we must see
therapy as it was when Freud found it. As a post-doctoral student in
neurology, Freud became intrigued by the work of certain French
psychopathologists, especially that of Janet. Going to France to study,
Freud found the French involved with hypnosis as a major technique.
Janet, particularly in his work with hysterics, had found in hypnosis
a means for removing symptoms, for relieving his patients. Under
hypnosis, patients were often induced to give up their symptoms.

The troubling thing was that other, equally distressing symptoms tended to appear after the so-called cure had been affected by hypnosis.

The Contribution of Freud

Freud soon became disenchanted with hypnosis as a therapeutic technique, and he began searching for some other alternative. What he finally developed came out of his theories regarding personality, especially as these latter reflected his conception of the content and operation of the unconscious. While it is true that Freud was not the first to postulate the presence of the unconscious, he certainly did more with this concept than anyone else.

This recognition of the importance of the unconscious in human behavior had important consequences. For one thing, previously inexplicable behavior became, in theory at least, understandable. For another, it meant that direct, intellectualized approaches to personality had to be abandoned. The patient is himself unaware of the content of his unconscious. Therefore, it makes little sense to ask him direct questions about it, about why he does or feels as he does. Some other tactic had to be devised.

Hypnosis, it is true, seemed capable of getting at certain aspects of unconscious behavior. The frequent recurrence of symptoms which had been previously relieved by hypnosis led Freud to feel that it was not a sufficiently powerful method. He also felt, after considerable study of the matter, that what could be approached through hypnosis could also be approached in other ways.

Establishing a practice in Vienna, Freud undertook therapy with a number of neurotic patients. He also analyzed himself. Accounts of this self-analysis make fascinating reading. The recent biography by one of his pupils, the British analyst, Jones (4), is recommended for all who are interested in pursuing this topic.

Freud conceived of personality as operating at three levels: the id, the ego, and the superego. Freud conceived the id as being the primitive starting point, the source of what might loosely be called "mental energy." This energy was largely sexual in nature, not narrowly sexual but broadly so.

The id, needing some way of dealing with the outside world in order to satisfy its cravings, found an outlet or contact in the ego. The ego is the self, the developed personality, the more or less public image.

Finally, Freud described a controlling mechanism, the superego (although the ego had some controlling functions also). Roughly analogous to what is commonly called the conscience, this acts as a brake, as a restraint on the primitive, childlike id. Arising out of the child's interiorization of the values and norms of society as embodied in his parents, it completed Freud's tripartite conception of personality.

In his practice, Freud noticed that many of his patients seemed to be suffering from punishments inflicted on the ego by the superego, "angered" because the ego had given in to some unsocial demand of the id. Sometimes, these guilt reactions were conscious, as when the patient had committed some act of which he was consciously ashamed. More often, however, the problems were imbedded in the unconscious, pushed out of awareness by a repressive mechanism. From these unconscious feelings, a variety of painful symptoms developed.

We mentioned earlier some of these so-called mechanisms or dynamics of behavior which Freud postulated. Repression, the process of rendering some idea or memory unconscious, was the most important. Given repression, the other mechanisms followed.

From this brief over-view, it is apparent that Freud found himself confronted by personality problems whose roots were imbedded in the patients' unconscious. His problem, then, was to develop a technique for getting at these problems, for finding out where the troubles lay. He early assumed that sheer insight—the patient's ability to understand the roots of the trouble—would lead to cure. In some cases, it did. In other cases, however, it did not, and Freud had to extend his system to cover these contingencies.

The major exploratory techniques which Freud developed were free association and dream analysis. In the classical psychoanalytic session, the patient lies on a couch and is directed by the analyst to say whatever comes into his mind. In normal conversation, people try to make sense, to make what they say seem reasonable and logical. They also inhibit many (to them) unacceptable ideas and statements. Neither of these conditions—logic and reasonableness or inhibition of improper ideas—was felt to be true of the unconscious and the id. Therefore, free association, by suspending the usual rules of conversation, opened the way to the patient's unconscious processes. By listening attentively, often for many weeks or months on end, the analyst could form hypotheses about the sources of the patient's conflicts.

Dream analysis was another technique advocated by Freud. It was his feeling that dreams were a kind of high road to the unconscious. Dreams, he felt, were elaborate ways of expressing conflicts, usually in symbolic fashion. He spent a great deal of time in developing a lexicon of dream symbols. It is now felt that he sometimes went too far, forgetting that such symbols probably vary from culture to culture and from individual to individual. Nevertheless, his was a major attempt to provide a basis for interpreting dream content relative to unconscious processes.

Free association and the description of dreams make psycho-analysis seem like a one-way street with the patient doing all the talking. This is not the entire picture. The analyst might, it is true, make the patient continue free association for a considerable length of time without participating in the process other than to insist on the patient's free associating. In time, however, the analyst begins, typically, to take a more active role as his hypotheses about the patient's problems become clearer. This participation takes two common forms: interpretation and questioning.

Questioning needs little comment. The analyst may ask specific, factual questions, or he may ask for more information about feelings or the meanings of statements. Interpretation involves explaining the relationships among statements, feelings, and events. If, for instance, a patient presents a history of trouble with superiors and people in authority, the analyst might interpret this as a reflection of a buried conflict with the father.

There is one other aspect of Freud's method which is of particular importance. We mentioned earlier that insight was sometimes followed by remission of symptoms, that sometimes it was not. Freud saw that the relationship between the analyst and the patient was of prime importance. Both parties to the process had feelings, and he felt that these were important in determining the outcomes of therapy. Many times, early in analysis, the patient might develop unreasonably strong feelings of affection and even love for the analyst. These Freud called *positive transference*. The result of unconscious needs, these feelings led patients to assume childlike and highly dependent attitudes. Later on, many patients reversed themselves and developed equally strong feelings of antipathy toward the analyst, actively hating him, accusing him of being insensitive to their feelings, and of trying to do harm. These Freud saw also as products of unconscious processes, and he labelled them *negative transference*. In the process of analysis, both positive and negative transference feelings must be worked through and explored thoroughly. It was in dealing with these, the products of unconscious reactions to the other person in the interview, that Freud saw the major task of analysis.

Just as the patient has unconsciously motivated reactions to the analyst, so also does the analyst have such reactions to the patient. These reactions may also be either positive or negative, and Freud called them *countertransference*. While the analysts experience these reactions, their training, especially the analysis they themselves undergo, is supposed to help them in controlling these feelings.

Freud's work gave psychotherapy its major impetus. Psychoanalysis, as outlined by Freud and later by his pupils such as Rank, Jung, and Adler, has continued its development as one specialized kind of therapy employing the interview. Psychoanalysis is now commonly restricted to the treatment of certain kinds of neuroses, character disorders, and some psychoses. However, Freud's theories, embodied in interview methods of diverse kinds, may be seen today in the treatment of virtually all kinds of problems from simple maladjustment to major psychoses.

The contrasting theory of Rogers

The list of contributors to the theory and practice of clinical interviewing is long. We cannot here cover the many diverse developments in procedures which have occurred in the past half century. One other individual needs to be mentioned. That person is Carl Rogers.

We described, in the previous chapter, the position which Rogers holds with respect to the counseling interview. Seeing his work against the set of problems faced and dealt with by Freud and the analytic tradition will, however, indicate a major alternative conception about the clinical interview. Rogers himself (9) has provided a discussion of the theoretical and practical differences between his work and that of the analytic tradition.

Freud's theory is a developmental one in which the roots of problems must be sought in the individual's history. Rogers' theory, on the other hand, takes a phenomological point of view, one which insists that the individual's *present* feelings, his present perceptions are crucial. Where Freud is historical, Rogers is ahistorical. Where the

Freudian method is designed to provide the analyst with information on which to formulate questions and interpretations, the Rogerian method relies heavily on empathic responses to present feelings. Where the analyst's role is seen as helping the patient to achieve insight and understanding, the Rogerian therapist's is seen in addition, as providing a permissive climate in which the patient's innate growth potentials may be freed from blockage and allowed to correct the difficulties.

There are both theoretical and practical differences between these two major points of view. The major practical difference lies, as indicated, in the activities and role of the therapists. Those interested in exploring and mastering the details of the Rogerian approach are referred to Rogers' books (9) (10) (11) on the subject.

Typical Uses of the Interview

In the typical clinical situation, the patient may present any one of a wide variety of symptoms. The problem may vary from simple maladjustment and mild anxiety to outright psychosis. The patients may be young or old, men or women, self-referred or referred by other agencies, individuals, or courts. For treatment in an outpatient facility, the patient must be capable of carrying on to a minimally satisfactory degree between treatment sessions. If not, hospitalization is indicated. Treatment may be of any one of a number of kinds. In this, the interview plays a major role even if the treatment emphasizes the use of the tranquilizing drugs.

The Intake Interview

At the outset, the patient is usually seen by an intake worker. This person may be a psychiatrist, psychologist, nurse, or social worker. The purpose of this first interview is the development of some picture of the difficulty. Primarily, this will be a fact-finding interview, although attitudes are included. Some information may be given to the patient, especially about the facilities available, the costs, and any need for waiting for treatment to begin. Patient attitudes are also affected by this first interview even though it is not intended to be a therapeutic interview in the usual sense of the term. Increasingly, it is felt that one worker, the therapist, should make all of the contacts. The use of several interviewers during the early stages, however, is still somewhat more common.

The intake worker will normally begin the development of the case folder. He will ask for information on a variety of things such

as name and address, family status, occupation, work history, educational history, medical history, development and characteristics of
the symptoms, etc. Anyone who has ever been in a hospital for any
reason will be familiar with this procedure. In addition to the information collected by direct questions, the intake worker will also
record impressions based on observation of the patient. Ordinarily,
the patient will be encouraged to describe in his own words the problem which troubles him. How he does this as well as what he says are
of interest.

Preliminary or Diagnostic Interviews

Following the intake interview, the patient may be scheduled for
a preliminary interview with one of the staff therapists. Here, as in
the intake interview, the primary concern is with finding out about
the patient. In this preliminary interview, however, there is usually
less direct questioning and relatively more free discussion by the
patient of his troubles and their causes. The therapist listens carefully,
trying to see through the morass of conflicting statements, defenses,
and confusion in order to form some tentative impressions about the
dynamic picture of the patient. Frequently, he tries to arrive at a
tentative diagnosis. He also tries to estimate the severity of the problem so that, if the patient requires hospitalization, it can be recommended.

After the preliminary interview, diagnostic testing may be
requested. There is no standard time for testing. It may occur
almost anywhere in the process and even be done in several widely
separated sessions interspersed among other activities. The patient
will then be referred to a psychologist who will select and administer
a battery of tests. Usually included will be a Wechster Adult
Intelligence Scale (or, for a child, the Wechsler Intelligence Scale for
Children). He will also probably administer one or more tests of
personality. Commonly used are the Minnesota Multiphasic Personality Inventory, the Rorschach, the Thematic Apperception Test,
and the Bender Gestalt. If organic conditions are suspected, the
psychologist may administer such tests as the Hunt-Minnesota Test
for Organic Brain Damage. On the basis of the tests and of his impressions of the patient during the testing situation, the psychologist
will prepare his report. It should be remembered that most of the
tests employed are, in the last analysis, simply more or less
standardized interviews. Administering them adequately calls on many

of the same kinds of skills as in other kinds of interviews.

After the preliminary interview, there may also be a request for a social service report. A social worker will then visit the family, the employer, teachers, and others who know the patient, interviewing them and observing the situations in which the patient works and lives. These interviews are almost exclusively fact-finding in nature except that they should and often do have a secondary purpose of allaying the fears and apprehensions of family members, friends, and others concerned with the patient.

When the intake, preliminary interview, testing, and social service reports are assembled along with such other reports as physical examination, a staff conference is held to decide on the disposition of the case. Here, the entire staff meets, reviews the case, hears explanations and amplifications of the various reports, and discusses the case. Hopefully, a more accurate diagnosis can be decided upon and a recommendation for treatment made. Once this is accomplished, the patient is assigned to a therapist for treatment (unless the decision is made to refer him elsewhere for treatment not available in the clinic).

Supportive Interview

If psychotherapy is recommended, as it frequently is, it may be of several types. Sometimes, it will be decided to use supportive treatment. In this, the interviewer will see the patient regularly, talk with him, try to help him work through fairly immediate problems so that he can maintain himself in his community and job. This is commonly done when the problem appears to be of a temporary sort, one which will diminish with time but which troubles the patient at the moment. For example, a man overwhelmed by increased responsibilities of a new job might be given supportive therapy until he becomes adjusted to the situation. An otherwise healthy person shocked by the death of a family member or upset by a broken marriage might also be given supportive therapy. Essentially it does not change the personality of the patient, but it provides a crutch and encouragement until he can make his adjustment.

Sometimes, the recommended treatment calls for interviewing aimed at the development of insight combined with a prescribed set of opportunities to work out the problems in real life situations. Here, a social worker might be assigned to work with the therapist, the one concentrating on the patient's behavior in the office, the other helping him work through the problems outside the office. Or, a vocational counselor might also work with the patient, assisting him to achieve a better occupational adjustment which might, in turn, help the process of therapy along.

Psychotherapeutic interview

The other common approach calls for psychotherapeutic interviewing. This may be of any one of a number of types depending on the situation. However, the goal is to provide the patient with a situation, the interview, in which he can talk through his problems until he reaches a satisfactory solution. Insight may be developed, support may be provided, an opportunity to release disturbing feelings may be given to the patient.

It is difficult to describe any typical psychotherapeutic series because the client, the problem, and the interviewer vary so widely, and these variations affect the process. There is some evidence, however, that there is enough identity to make a general description useful. It must be kept in mind that each case will differ somewhat, perhaps a great deal.

The process of psychotherapeutic interviewing typically requires a longer time than does counseling. This is not because counseling is easier; it has to do, rather, with the ability of the patient or client to deal with the issues involved. In counseling, the client is usually more aware of these issues. More important, his problem solving abilities are not ordinarily immobilized by the pathology. He can be helped quite soon to see what the problem is and what must be done to solve it. Ordinarily, he can face this information without having to spend a great deal of time acquiring the necessary emotional tolerance and strength since he usually has these in normal amounts. In the clinical or therapeutic process, on the other hand, the patient must be first assisted in building up the strength he needs to be able to see the problem as it is. His problem solving abilities must be reinstated up to a level of minimum effectiveness.

There is also some difference due to the kinds of materials dealt with. While abilities, aptitudes, and interests are highly personal and emotionally involving aspects of personality, they are not usually as disturbing as are the painful sources of anxiety, of guilt reactions, or of conflicts which the clinical interview must break free from repression.

Another major reason for the length of the clinical interview process lies in the goals. When the patient comes for help, his personality is frequently so disorganized, so near to collapse that a very substantial rebuilding is required. Indeed, there is some feeling that the basic personality, from earliest childhood on, has been so deficient in adequate means for coping with problems that these deficiences themselves have militated against the individual's avoiding the development of neurotic symptoms. If this is so, then the rebuilding process is immense indeed. Most experienced interviewers who have dealt with neurotics have seen individuals who, apparently from childhood, have lacked the most elemental abilities to cope with problems. In some of these cases, psychotherapy has little hope of accomplishing much, because there must be something on which to build, some minimum core of potential to develop.

An example of this is a case with which one of the writers dealt several years ago. He was a young man of fairly substantial means whose parents had been divorced when he was a small child. He was reared almost in isolation from other children by a highly overprotective mother. Quite early in his life, he retreated into a phantasy world of his own, never learned how to deal with other people or his own feelings except in a most childlike and primitive way. Arriving at college, he was completely unable to cope with other students, and he was soon referred to the writer after a serious case of anxiety developed. Exhaustive study of this young man including interviews by one of the writers and by a psychiatrist failed to find any usable potential on which to build. Emotionally, he was a small child. He could not even face talking with adults in the interview situation, and he soon withdrew from school and fled home to his anxiously waiting and protective mother. The clinical interview is not, in other words, appropriate for every disturbed individual. There has been a considerable amount of research on the topic of likely response to therapy which has demonstrated this fairly clearly.

Steps in psychotherapeutic interviewing

The process in psychotherapy may involve one interview every week or two for a total of twenty or thirty interviews. At the other extreme, in some psychoanalytic sessions, it may involve five interviews a week for three, four or even five years, although brief analytic treatment is also common. Twenty to thirty interviews usually are considered to be very brief psychotherapy by psychoanalysts.

The first step in the clinical interview is the establishment of rapport. Because neurotics are usually so fearful and anxious, this phase may require a fairly long time, a substantial number of interviews. Because the material to be dealt with is so emotionally charged and so likely to be painful to the patient, it is essential that the rapport be of a very high order. While the analogy will not bear too much analysis, it is somewhat like surgery. Where minor surgery is contemplated, a local anesthetic may be sufficient; where it is long, where the insult to the body is great enough to produce serious shock, greater precautions must be taken.

In some cases, the interviewer must be on his guard against a premature development of rapport. Some neurotic persons, particularly those of hysterical nature, for example, often appear to work into the therapeutic process very quickly and well. The rapport formed, however, is brittle and superficial and can be broken easily when the process becomes stressful. In other cases, dependency is developed instead of real rapport, and this can hinder rather than help the therapy.

Establishing a sound working relationship is accomplished both by what is done and by what is not done. Perhaps the most important objective is to convey the feeling of permissiveness. The patient is helped to feel that he can talk about whatever is on his mind without fear of criticism or reprisal. Related to this is confidentiality. The patient must feel that what he says will not be discussed with unauthorized individuals. There needs, in addition, to be structuring. Patients find the therapeutic interview strange and sometimes frightening. In a warm, reassuring manner, he needs to be told what the process is about, and how he should proceed. Also, limits frequently need to be specified; for the interview is a professional relationship, not a social one, and time schedules must be held to. A too completely unstructured situation creates anxiety, frequently leads to behavior which cannot be tolerated and therefore must be stopped. This has deleterious effects on the relationship, and it is best to ensure that these things will not occur. For instance, children are often told that they may do what they like except hurt themselves or the therapist. Time is another limit. Many patients seek to express their feelings by such tactics as arriving late or staying past the end of the hour. This must not be permitted, or the therapist will lose necessary control of the process.

To be avoided are such things as criticism, direct or implied; any suggestion of breached confidence; overly hasty or deep probing; premature interpretation; toleration of infractions of rules or limits. In general, the interviewer must avoid doing things which will increase the anxiety and fears of the patient. Later on, when a sound working relationship has been established, he may need to arouse anxiety, but it is to be hoped that the relationship will by then be strong enough to support this tactic.

Usually, also, early interviews are made up of the patient's recital of his symptoms. Fairly soon, he may be encouraged to recall what to him are the significant facts of his life. Such self-study will be repeated, expanded, and modified many times during the course of treatment. Therapy might be described as like climbing a spiral staircase. The same scenes are seen again and again, each time from a slightly different perspective.

Sooner or later, transference reactions must be dealt with, worked through. The appearance of positive transference, which normally comes first, often misleads inexperienced interviewers. The patient seems in some ways so improved and so effusively grateful for the help he has received that there may be a temptation to conclude that he is well. He is usually not so by any means. In this phase, many patients will try to get the interviewer to accept gifts; sometimes, there will be overt or covert sexual advances, either heterosexual or homosexual, depending on the sex of the interviewer and patient and the nature of the problem. Needless to say, these must be resisted tactfully but firmly. Often, the patient will insist at this point that he is indeed well, that therapy should be terminated. Therapy should be continued until the patient not only feels well but also shows evidence of strength and success in handling his problems.

The appearance of the negative transference phase is usually threatening to the neophyte interviewer. To have a previously pleasant or perhaps diffident patient suddenly accuse the interviewer of being a heartless headshrinker, a snoopy pervert, or other equally unflattering and unsavory things can be a shock. Handling these reactions is doubly difficult because, in addition to their possibly raising counter-hostility in the interviewer and making it hard for him to remain objective, they usually create severe guilt reactions in the patient, sometimes so severe that the patient must, to avoid facing the interviewer again, break off treatment.

If the relationship is basically sound, the interviewer may suggest interpretations for this behavior. He must do this tactfully and gently, being ready to have these interpretations rejected and used as evidence of his lack of understanding. He may be well advised to remain largely silent, letting the patient vent his anger, realizing that this anger is the hurt child buried within the patient striking out against the only adult available and accessible. Therapists vary in their handling of transference. Some feel that it is essential to use this situation directly to further insight and cure. They employ fairly direct and penetrating interpretations. Others insist that the mere expression of such feelings by the patient is enough, that the interviewer's job is to encourage this expression without attempting to comment on it in any way.

There are many conceptions of what the process of therapy is about. Some, like Freud, base their theories on the cathartic, expressive function accompanied by interpretation and insight; others, like Rogers, feel that catharsis frees the individual from the shackles of maladaptive behavior so that his own natural adjustive tendencies can operate. Recent theorists, like Dollard and Miller (2), Mowrer (6), and Dollard, Auld, and White (1), have been making serious attempts to relate therapy to learning theory. The role of language has come under scrutiny since it is obvious that the therapeutic interview rests centrally on verbal interaction. Such analyses suggest that the therapeutic interview has its effects because words are close enough to deeds to permit the patient, in effect, to relive traumatic situations in the permissive, safe interview situation, and to work out, symbolically, better and more adaptive ways of dealing with problems.

To be more specific, this conception suggests that the patient, in talking about troublesome, disturbing situations in the past, actually relives them. In doing this in the protected interview situation, he learns that he can face the emotions engendered and deal with the threats posed by the situations. Thus, for instance, he can express his feelings of anger toward an overly severe father, doing symbolically what he could not do in fact as a child. Finding that he can express these feelings toward the father (perhaps substituting the interviewer for the father during transference), he comes to find that he can deal with his feelings about the father. Having cleared the air, he can then, again symbolically, talk about ways of dealing with other adults, especially authority figures.

Suggestions for the Clinical Interview

1. *Discover new approaches to a problem.* The problem as presented will seem to the person in trouble insoluble. That is why he is in trouble. A ready acceptance of the picture as he sees it would close the case. Try to see other people in each of the predicaments and see how they might solve them. All problems are essentially subjective.

2. *Begin at some point where the person feels a difficulty.* It may not be the root of the problem, but it is the only place at which help is really wanted. It will probably lead to the major problems.

3. *Evaluate each statement carefully, especially if it is emotionally charged.* Remember the large error in firsthand observation and the untrustworthiness of circumstantial evidence. What A tells you about B is as much or more information about A.

4. *Physical condition must be checked.* Take no chance on physical condition. Insist upon reliable medical examination and treatment. Do not take the client's word alone that it was provided.

5. *Mental status must be checked.* Secure adequate tests of intelligence and other relevant characteristics. Do not take merely your own impressions or those of friends or teachers.

6. *Everyone has limitations or blind spots.* Recognize this and always be ready to consult with physicians, psychiatrists, psychologists, and any other professionally qualified person who may contribute a new insight.

7. *Know other personalities affecting the client.* It is sometimes necessary to study persons other than the one immediately involved. A problem child means probably at least one and possibly two problem parents.

8. *Look for unrealistic patterns of behavior.* People in trouble usually exhibit unrealistic and unproductive reactions such as dependence, fear of new situations, avoidance of people, running away from situations, and making a mountain out of a molehill. Be on the lookout for these and for such dynamics as projection, rationalization, compensation, evasion, and regression. Help the client to understand his own realistic behavior.

9. *Maintain emotional objectivity and poise.* Patients will endeavor to arouse sympathy, to shock you, to hurt you with cutting phrases, to inflate your vanity, to get caresses, to make you pity and care for

them, to win rebukes, to provoke outbursts of your own ideas, or maneuver you into other forms of emotional behavior. Objectivity requires constantly being on guard.

10. *Deal with client fears.* Do not let the channels of exploration be determined by the emotional reactions of the client. Some things may be uncomfortable but are nevertheless relevant.

11. *Guard against stereotypes.* Watch out for stereotypes in your own thinking. When you find yourself getting a hunch in advance of careful investigation, a hunch which classifies a certain type of personal behavior, beware of it. Avoid pet theories and hunt for exceptions to them, particularly if you find yourself calling on them regularly. Remember that single experiences, even if vivid and compelling, do not often form the basis for sound generalization.

12. *Avoid the Jehovah complex.* Remember that you are not an infallible oracle. Remember especially that, if the client is to be helped, he must learn to understand himself and not just rely on your unsupported statements. The aim of the interview is for *him* to see, not for you to see.

13. *Guard against misunderstanding.* Even though you make every effort to keep your language simple and to the point, always be on the watch for signs that you have been misunderstood or misinterpreted. Often, these misinterpretations reflect the client's emotional state and provide the interviewer with valuable information.

14. *Help the client to develop self reliance.* Avoid the tendency to offer advice. Help the client to work through the problem and find his own solutions. Avoid either encouragement or especially discouragement as they may make the client dependent on your evaluations of his ideas and actions. Do not give the client help to do things which he can do for himself.

15. *Encourage the client to try new modes of adjustment.* When a client has developed new insights and ways of acting on them, encourage him to try them out, to evaluate their effects on himself and on others. Do not be satisfied with the client's developing just a verbal adjustment; include improved behavior in the goals of treatment.

16. *Work for realistic goals.* Remember that, even after successful treatment, the client, his family and friends, and his life situation will probably be very much as they were before treatment. There may have been substantial improvements, especially in his ways of dealing

with problems, but neither he nor others should expect that everything will be completely changed. Help the client to set goals which can be attained, even if they are limited. Reaching a sub-goal is often a powerful reward, encouraging the client to go on to more advanced goals.

17. *Be humble.* The interviewer must be humble. The balance of normality and abnormality, of satisfaction and distress in life might be none the worse if we were to go to a South Sea island and sun ourselves for the rest of our days.

REFERENCES

1. DOLLARD, J., AULD, F., and WHITE, A., *Steps in Psychotherapy.* New York: Macmillan, 1953.
2. DOLLARD, J. and MILLER, N., *Personality and Psychotherapy.* New York: McGraw-Hill, 1950.
3. INGHAM, H. and LOVE, L., *The Process of Psychotherapy.* New York: McGraw-Hill, 1954.
4. JONES, E., *The Life and Work of Sigmund Freud.* New York: Basic Books, 1953.
5. LAW, S., *Therapy Through the Interview.* New York: McGraw-Hill, 1948.
6. MOWRER, O., (Ed.), *Psychotherapy.* New York: Ronald Press, 1953.
7. PENNINGTON, L. and BERG, I., *An Introduction to Clinical Psychology.* New York: Ronald Press, 1954. Second edition.
8. RICHARDS, T., *Modern Clinical Psychology.* New York: McGraw-Hill, 1948.
9. ROGERS, C., *Counseling and Psychotherapy.* New York: Houghton Mifflin, 1942.
10. ROGERS. *The Clinical Treatment of the Problem Child.* New York: Houghton Mifflin, 1939.
11. ROGERS, C., *Client Centered Therapy.* New York: Houghton Mifflin, 1951.
12. ROGERS, C. and DYMOND, R., *Psychotherapy and Personality Change.* Chicago: University of Chicago Press, 1954.
13. SHAFFER, G., and LAZARUS, R., *Fundamental Concepts in Clinical Psychology.* New York: McGraw-Hill, 1952.

Part V

Conclusions

14. Conclusions about Interviewing

In THIS book about interviewing, we have attempted to do two things. First, we have examined the principles which seem to us to underlie all interviewing regardless of the setting or the specific goals. Second, we have considered the interview in a variety of the ways in which it is actually used such as in industry, in opinion polling, in counseling, and in legal practice. It is time now to try to summarize the main themes, to set forth those generalizations which seem to characterize the interview as a process.

The first and, we believe, most important point to be remembered is this: *the interview must be seen as a process of interaction between persons.* It is essential, if one is to understand the interview, to consider both the interviewer and the interviewee *in interaction.* To consider either separately will lead to an incomplete and biased conceptualization, because it is in the interaction between the participants in the interview that its effects are produced.

This idea is not new. At the same time, it has not received the attention it seems to merit. The implications of this idea are far-reaching and important. They reach to the selection and training of interviewers, to methods of conducting the interview, and even to the possibility of selecting interviewees.

The purposes for which interviews are conducted vary. We said in the first chapter that there were three major purposes: obtaining information, giving information, and modifying behavior. These are usually not discrete; most interviews involve all three.

In the interview designed primarily to obtain information, it used to be thought that the interviewer had to resort to clever and subtle lines of questioning in order to accomplish his ends. Some people still believe that this is necessary. We do not. A recent example of the "tricky" approach may be seen in the work of the late Dr. Kinsey and his colleagues. They were, of course, dealing with materials likely to be buried beneath deep defenses. They utilized methods of questioning which, in effect, trapped the interviewee, subverted his defenses. Doubtless these methods succeeded in bringing out items of information which straightforward questions would have missed. Whether they missed more than they got and whether they got the most important facts must remain unanswered questions.

In defense of the "clever" approach, it is often said that, in many situations, the interviewee is motivated to conceal information or to distort what he chooses to report. The employment interview is a good example. Here, the interview is used, along with other devices, to determine whether the applicant shall be hired. The applicant knows—or should know—that this is the case. If there are facts which he feels will prevent him from being hired if the prospective employer knows them, will he not try to hide them? Will he not try to present the best possible picture of himself? Probably. If this is so, should not the interviewer resort to whatever devices he has at his command to penetrate the facade, to get at the real facts of the situation? The answer to this is complicated because it involves not only technical but ethical considerations.

Technically, it is likely that a highly skilled interviewer can, given the time and the inclination, penetrate the interviewee's defenses and get information which the latter intended to keep hidden. It is unlikely that the interviewer could successfully elicit *all* of the information that might be relevant. If, however, he found that the applicant for a position involving financial responsibility was heavily in debt to gamblers, he might not care about getting any other information. There are situations in which one item, if answered in the "wrong" way, is enough. Ordinarily, this is not true. The usual situation is that there are many considerations, that the plus and minus features must be weighed before a decision may be made. It is therefore important to obtain complete information.

If the interviewer and the interviewee can work together, can establish a good relationship, and can agree that they share a common goal, then a new light is cast on the interview. In the employment situation, this means that the interviewer and interviewee must come to see that the welfare of the applicant and the welfare of the company are *both* at stake. This makes of the employment interview a kind of counseling interview. Of course, all of the cards must be on the table, and the interviewer must not cynically mislead the applicant. If he does, the word will eventually get around.

Such an interview requires both more time and a better trained interviewer than are usually found. The increased attention being devoted to the selection and training of employment interviewers suggests that many companies feel that the added expenditure is worth while.

Another example of different approaches to fact finding may be seen in supervisor-employee relationships. Discipline is a common problem. Many supervisors feel that, when a rule infraction has taken place, their responsibility to the company requires that they find out who broke the rule, gather evidence, and either decide on punishment or pass the case on to someone higher who will act as judge and jury. In such a situation, the employee is, of course, motivated to cover his tracks, to prevent the discovery of his guilt. Sometimes, the supervisor, by subtle techniques or by bluster, can penetrate the deception and get at most of the facts. Many representatives of management are coming to realize, however, that this merely serves to stimulate rule violators to seek better ways of covering up. It also creates bad morale problems.

A great deal of work is now being devoted to training supervisors in how to deal with employees. Much of this involves training in interview techniques. As in the employment interview, however, the goal is seen as enabling supervisors to establish sound relationships with employees so that the roots of the trouble may be discovered, so that prevention of recurrences rather than punishment for past errors may be stressed.

We could go on with further examples of the shift in attitude toward the fact finding interview. The important point is this: in dealing with people, be they applicants, employees, students, or consumers, the establishment of a sound, cooperative relationship is likely to produce better results for all concerned. It requires more time, patience, and skill, but the results appear to justify them.

The interview which is concerned principally with giving information presents many of the same problems. Many people find it difficult to understand why simply telling someone something is not enough. One of the writers had an interesting experience which illustrates this nicely. Some years ago, a prominent counseling psychologist gave a talk on student counseling to a group which included counselors, personnel workers, and educators. He outlined a theory of counseling and related this to the solution of many student problems. Afterwards, the wife of a college president thanked him for a fine talk and then added, "But, Dr. ———, I still don't see why you can't just sit them down and give them some good, sound advice!" The old saw about leading horses to water and making them drink had escaped her completely.

Giving advice has an attraction which makes it almost irresistible. The quotation from Dressel cited earlier is to the point. Many would feel that, having given the advice or information, their responsibilities were discharged. That such advice is ignored in a large proportion of cases strikes them as irrelevant. Then why, one might ask, should one give advice or information? Simply to be able to say, at some later time, "I told you"? Such a legalistic view seems limited.

Information or advice ought to serve to alter behavior. The parent who tells his child that the stove is hot expects that the child will avoid touching it. The teacher who tells his students that the next quiz will cover certain points expects that they will study those points. The employer who tells his employees that helmets must be worn in certain plant areas expects that they will, in the interest of their own welfare, wear them. These expectations, reasonable as they appear, are often not fulfilled.

This being so, we must ask why people so often fail to act appropriately even when they have the information needed at hand. They may not believe what they have heard. Students are eternal optimists and are inclined to think that they can second-guess the professor's examinations. They may not understand. The child, for instance, may not have a meaningful conception of the meaning of the word "hot." They may not want to believe what they have heard. Perception is motivated, and we ignore such motivation at our peril.

Consider again the employment situation. In addition to obtaining information about the applicant, the interviewer usually tries to tell him about the job and the company. Working hours and conditions, rates of pay, benefits, union agreements, and other features are described. Too often, this information passes off as though it was not heard, and, often, indeed, it was not heard, because no motivated attention was given to it. In that this represents a waste of time for the interviewer and a source of difficulty for the employee and the company, management has begun to try new approaches to information giving. One technique is the improved interview.

The interview has the unique advantage that, in the relationship which a competent interviewer can establish, the information can be given in answer to the employee's questions. First, however, the employee must be made to feel that he has a stake in such matters and that he can ask questions without embarrassment. Moreover, his perceptions, which might otherwise serve to screen out certain information, may be recognized and dealt with. For example, the employee may feel, on the basis of earlier experience, that such benefits as an insurance plan are merely management tricks designed to mulct him of part of his pay. Knowing this, the interviewer can deal with such attitudes more effectively than any bulletin board or company paper.

The third purpose to which interviews are put has to do with changing behavior. The counseling and clinical interviews are perhaps the best examples, but others, such as the employment interview, also serve in the same way. Such a goal, changing behavior, puts the interview to its severest test. Behavior is the outward expression of the total personality as it seeks to deal with its environment. Changing behavior, then, may involve changing the environment; more often, it requires an alteration in the personality. This is no small order.

Of course, minor changes in behavior may be effected by relatively slight changes in personality. The worker who is persuaded that he should wear a safety helmet probably does not have to undergo psychotherapy to achieve this, although in a few cases, he may. When we speak of altering behavior, however, we ordinarily refer to more involved and complicated matters. An otherwise fine supervisor, for instance, may become incapacitated by anxiety and be unable to handle his job. A bright student may, because he has drifted into the wrong curriculum, get a string of low grades. These problems involve the total personality and must be dealt with as such.

Simply to clap the supervisor on the back, reassure him, even suggest that he take a two week vacation will probably do little or nothing toward alleviating the problem. It may intensify it. To discharge the student from school accomplishes nothing useful and certainly damages the student and may lose a potentially fine worker. Clearly, other approaches are indicated.

A number of techniques have been tried, but, to date, nothing has come along to supplant the interview as a means for influencing behavior. The reason seems to be that here, as in almost no other situation, the deepest levels of personality may be explored and conflicts dealt with. The student, for example, may have entered engineering because of parental pressure. He may be unable to see that he does not want to be there, that he resents the pressure. In the interview, he can express his feelings, consider what he is and what he wants to be. Once he is clear in his own mind, he is usually able to deal with parental pressure, the displeasure of deans, or whatever else is troubling him. The supervisor whose anxiety prevents him from dealing with his workers can, in the interview, be helped to see the origins of his feelings, to resolve his conflicts. Only then can he learn to handle his feelings.

In all that we have said about interviewing, we have stressed the importance of the relationship between the interviewer and the interviewee. The importance of this relationship cannot be overemphasized. It is in this relationship between two human beings that things happen. This is the strength of the interview; it is also its greatest danger.

We will not here summarize the literature on the interaction between persons. This is covered in the second chapter. Rather, we wish to underline, to stress the importance of these considerations. Not very much is known yet about the interaction between persons. We do know that it is important. We do know that the characteristics of the people in interaction determines whatever happens. Exactly how this interaction takes place, what cues are exchanged to carry ideas and feelings back and forth between the participants is not known.

While we hope that research will uncover these processes, we have enough information now on which to take certain actions. In the first place, we know that the interaction involves not only the higher mental processes but also, and probably more importantly, the affective, emotional aspects of personality. This being so, it is important that interviewers be selected and trained so that they can deal with both.

There is reason to believe, also, that even the best interviewers will, occasionally, encounter interviewees with whom they cannot deal. This suggests that care be taken to preselect interviewees so that they may be paired with interviewers with whom they can establish good working relationships. A great deal of work needs to be done before such selection can be done effectively.

It may be true that there are some people who will have difficulty in learning to become skilled interviewers, even with the best of training. Many more people than at present need to acquire at least a minimal level of skill in interviewing. If one considers the interview as a special kind of conversation with a purpose, most employers, supervisors, teachers, indeed, almost everyone at some time, needs to be able to deal with others in such a relationship. It may be true that comparatively few can become highly skilled interviewers; it is probably true that many, many more can acquire a fair degree of skill, enough to enable them to improve their relationships with others.

One other point should be stressed. Useful as the interview is, it should not be considered as the universal tool. Research has shown, for instance, that the reliability of the interview as a technique for obtaining factual materials is low. There are better ways of finding out factual information; these are frequently cheaper and more efficient, as well as being more effective. Much of the criticism of the interview rests on improper uses of the technique. Estimates of intelligence or aptitude, for instance, are much better derived from psychometric devices. The individual's perceptions of his abilities, however, can be obtained in the interview.

In general, then, the interview should only be used by persons trained to use it and in situations for which it is adapted. These situations are numerous, and they can all be identified if one keeps in mind that the interview is a unique method for permitting and encouraging the interaction between the participants. Where such interaction is important, the interview will be, in almost every instance, the chosen method.

Index